THE NEW
EGALITARIANISM

}{ policy network

About Policy Network

Policy Network is an international think-tank launched in December 2000 with the support of Tony Blair, Gerhard Schröder, Giuliano Amato and Göran Persson following the Progressive Governance Summits in New York, Florence and Berlin. In July 2003, Policy Network organized the London Progressive Governance Conference, which brought together twelve world leaders, and over 600 progressive politicians, thinkers and strategists. Hosted by Tony Blair, the conference was the largest ever international gathering of its kind.

A Progressive Network

Policy Network's objective is the promotion and cross fertilization of progressive policy ideas among centre-left modernizers. Acting as the secretariat to the Progressive Governance Network founded by Bill Clinton and Tony Blair, Policy Network facilitates dialogue between politicians, policy-makers and experts across Europe and from democratic countries around the world.

Our Common Challenge

Progressive governments and parties in Europe are increasingly facing similar problems and looking for modern social democratic responses. There are rising fears for security – combined with the contradictions of the traditional welfare state and employment policies, rapid change in science and technology, pressing global issues – all of which should be tackled in common, along with the need for fundamental democratic renewal.

Often, progressives have worked independently to resolve these problems. Today, there is a growing consensus on the need to engage with progressives from other countries, and to situate national responses within a broader international tide of progressive thinking, rooted in our social democratic values.

Chair: Peter Mandelson
Director: Matt Browne
Policy Network
Third Floor
11 Tufton Street
Westminster, London
SW1P 3QB
Tel: +44 (0) 20 7340 2200
www.policy-network.net

THE NEW EGALITARIANISM

Edited by

ANTHONY GIDDENS AND
PATRICK DIAMOND

polity

Individual chapters copyright © their authors; this collection © Anthony Giddens and Patrick Diamond 2005

First published in 2005 by Polity Press

Reprinted 2006

Polity Press
65 Bridge Street
Cambridge CB2 1UR, UK

Polity Press
350 Main Street
Malden, MA 02148, USA

ISBN: 0-7456-3430-3
ISBN: 0-7456-3431-1 (pb)

A catalogue record for this book is available from the British Library.

Typeset in 10.5 on 12 pt Sabon
by Servis Filmsetting Ltd, Manchester
Printed and bound in Great Britain by MPG Books Ltd, Bodmin, Cornwall

For further information on Polity, visit our website: www.polity.co.uk

Contents

About the contributors

Magdalena Andersson is State Secretary at the Finance Ministry in Sweden. Previously, she was head of the policy unit at the Prime Minister's office, where her primary responsibilities included industry, trade and growth policies, as well as energy policy and state-owned companies. Before that, Magdalena was an adviser to the Minister of Industry and Trade.

Robert D. Atkinson is Vice President and Director of the Technology and New Economy Project at the Progressive Policy Institute in Washington DC. He is also author of *The Past and Future of America's Economy: Long Waves of Innovation that Drive Cycles of Growth* (2005).

Ulrich Beck is a German sociologist of risk and the environment. Professor of Sociology at the University of Munich and the London School of Economics, he has written *Risk and Society* (1986), *Reinvention of Politics* (1993), *Power in the Global Age* (2005) and *The Cosmopolitan Perspective* (2005). He is also a regular contributor to *La Republica*, *El Pais* and *Die Zeit*.

Patrick Diamond is a Special Adviser in the British Prime Minister's Policy Unit.

Gøsta Esping-Andersen is a Professor and Dean at Universidad Pompeu Fabra, Barcelona. Previously Professor at the European University and Harvard University, he has worked extensively with international organizations and for the Portuguese and Belgian presidencies of the European Union.

Anthony Giddens is former Director of the London School of Economics and Political Science. He is currently Life Fellow of King's College, Cambridge, and a member of the House of Lords. Among many other books, he is the author of *The Third Way* (Polity, 1998).

David Goodhart is the founder and editor of the London-based current affairs monthly, *Prospect* magazine. Prior to that, he was a journalist at the *Financial Times*. He is also the author of books and pamphlets for the Fabian Society and the Institute for Public Policy Research.

Julian Le Grand is Richard Titmuss Professor of Social Policy at the London School of Economics. An economist by training, he has also published in the fields of philosophy, political science and social policy. His current research interests include human motivation and public policy, health systems and social exclusion.

Edward Miliband was appointed Chair of HM Treasury's Council of Economic Advisers in February 2004 to advise the Chancellor of the Exchequer, Gordon Brown, on long-term policy development. His appointment followed an eighteen-month sabbatical from the Treasury during which he was a Visiting Lecturer in the Department of Government at Harvard. Before that, as a special adviser to the Chancellor of the Exchequer after May 1997, he worked across a range of economic and social policy areas, including taxation, public spending, and labour market issues.

Anne Power is Professor of Social Policy at the London School of Economics and Deputy Director of the Centre for Analysis of Social Exclusion. She was awarded an MBE in 1983 for work in Brixton, and a CBE in June 2000 for services to regeneration and the promotion of resident participation. Anne Power was a member of the Urban Task Force and the government's Urban and Housing Sounding Boards, and in 2003 she chaired the Independent Commission on Housing in Birmingham. Currently she is leading a team from the London School of Economics on a new study to help produce a housing strategy for the London Thames Gateway, commissioned by the Thames Gateway London Partnership. Her books and publications include *Sustainable Communities and Sustainable Development: A Review of the Sustainable Communities Plan* (2004) and *East Enders* and *Boom or Abandonment*, both with Katharine Mumford (both 2003).

Saskia Sassen is the Ralph Lewis Professor of Sociology at the University of Chicago, and Centennial Visiting Professor at the London School of Economics. Her new book is *Denationalization:*

Territory, Authority and Rights in a Global Digital Age (2005). Her comments have appeared in the *Guardian*, the *New York Times* and *Le Monde Diplomatique*, among others, and her books have been translated into fifteen languages.

Robert Walker is Professor of Social Policy at Nottingham University and a Research Fellow at the Institute for Fiscal Studies, London. His policy concerns embrace social security and social assistance, welfare to work and labour market policies, policy evaluation and policy transfer. He is a Fellow of the Royal Society of Arts, a member of the Social Security Advisory Committee to the Social Security Select Committee of the House of Commons, the Joseph Rowntree Foundation Poverty and Disadvantage Committee and the Policy Council of the US Association for Policy Analysis and Management.

Richard Wilkinson is Professor of Social Epidemiology at the University of Nottingham and a visiting professor at the International Centre for Health and Society at University College London. His research interests include social determinants of health, health inequalities, income inequality and population health, and psychosocial influences on population health. His latest publications include *The Impact of Inequality* (2005), *Mind the Gap: Hierarchy, Health and Human Evolution* (2001), *Social Determinants of Health* (1999), and *Unhealthy Societies: The Afflictions of Inequality* (1996).

Acknowledgements

The chapters in this volume are the product of a series of meetings held under the aegis of Policy Network's working group on 'Community and Inequality', convened following the Progressive Governance summit and conference held in London in July 2003.

This group was chaired by the editors, and we would like to thank all those who attended – in particular Magdalena Andersson, Fillipo Andreatta, Luciano Astudillo, Frans Becker, Carlo Borzaga, Wouter Bos, René Cuperus, John Kay, Jens Erik Lund, Wolfgang Merkel, Anne Power, Robert Putnam, Gianluca Salvatori, Robertto Toniatti, Patrick Weil and Malcolm Wicks. In total, three meetings were held during the course of 2004, in London, Amsterdam and Trento, Italy. We wish to thank Rene Cuperus, Frans Becker, Wouter Bos and the Wiardi Beckman Stichting for their support and hospitality during the Amsterdam meeting, and Gianluca Salvatori and President Dellai for their warm welcome and assistance in Trento.

In the Policy Network offices, Branimira Radoslavova has worked tirelessly to organize these meetings, liaising with authors, editing early drafts and coordinating the production of this volume. Without her professionalism and dedication, the book would not have been possible. Thanks are also due to Olaf Cramme, Fran Sainsbury, François Lafond and Matt Browne for their whole-hearted support of the project.

Anthony Giddens and Patrick Diamond

Editors' introduction

The aims of this book are threefold. First, the volume offers an account of where we stand today in terms of levels of inequality in the industrialized countries. What do the facts show about the distribution of inequalities? What are the principal factors responsible for intensifying inequalities or lessening them?

Second, the book makes the case for a new egalitarianism, a case argued in detail in the editors' chapter below. In that chapter, we concentrate on Britain, but the ideas involved stretch much more widely. In the UK, Labour's own stated political objectives demand a greater focus than hitherto on a substantive economic egalitarianism. Tackling inequality, not only poverty, matters if New Labour is to promote a fairer and more open society.

Third, however, a renewed egalitarianism cannot simply adopt old nostrums of traditional social democracy. Revisionist social democracy starts from the reality of a structural transformation in the economy and society. It responds to intensifying global economic competition; the rise of a service and knowledge-based economy, where over 80 per cent of the labour force are employed in non-manufacturing jobs; and to the rise of a pervasive cultural individualism, itself linked to the decline of deference, and demands for choice and voice in public services and elsewhere. A commitment to egalitarianism today has to recognize these trends and work with them.

The opening chapter by Gøsta Esping-Andersen acknowledges that inequalities of income and wealth in the industrialized countries have been rising over the past thirty years. There are substantial variations between countries, nonetheless, indicating that the trends involved are not inexorable. Moreover, there is evidence that the rise in economic inequality may be beginning to tail off, or even go into reverse.

Even if we confine ourselves to economic inequality, there are many complex and partially contradictory trends at work. As Esping-Andersen points out, every welfare state manages to limit inequalities to some extent. There is a marked difference between pre-tax and post-tax inequalities in all countries, although it is most pronounced in the Scandinavian states and least effective in the US. Moreover, some structural trends act to mitigate economic inequality. The improving fortunes of women in the labour market, for instance, are one crucial factor.

As a result of the changes described, the balance of risks has shifted in modern societies, especially from the old to the young. Particularly vulnerable to deteriorating life circumstances are children and young adults. Unemployment and job insecurity are especially high among those aged 20–35. Among this group, on average, relative wages have declined steeply since the mid-1970s.

To use the rhetoric of egalitarianism is one thing. But how should the meaning of the term be pinned down, and what overall ideological emphases should drive our attempts to extend it? Ed Miliband analyses these issues in his contribution. His starting-point is a distinction between the necessity of markets in economic life and the acceptance of market outcomes. Post-1989, the left has accepted that economic prosperity depends on success in competitive markets. Market outcomes, however, do not always generate socially just outcomes, or even outcomes that are compatible with the long-term success of the market capitalist system. We should seek both to promote more opportunity – above all for those at the bottom of society – as well as to reduce inequalities of outcome. We should not regard economic success as inevitably a product of exploitation, as the old left sometimes did. Society needs its entrepreneurs. Yet success does not imply the disavowal of social and economic obligations towards the less fortunate. Countering inequality and promoting redistribution matter because unfettered market inequalities threaten both the solidarity of society and the self-respect of the least fortunate.

Robert Atkinson's chapter tackles the issue of inequalities driven by the rise of the knowledge economy. The transition to a service-based economy has generated new forms of economic dynamism, and has generally been associated with rising levels of employment. But it has also created some difficult countertrends that exacerbate inequalities of wages and incomes. The way forward, again, is not to try to reinstate older forms of industrial organization, but to accept the trends and work with them to contain their negative effects. There has been a steady increase in both 'lovely' and 'lousy' jobs. About two-thirds of new service jobs are well paid and otherwise rewarding, such as those in financial services. A third, however, are poorly paid, often repetitive and have few long-term career prospects. It is here that the problems lie, since those jobs cannot be wished away. Education and training are part of the answer but, as Atkinson suggests, no more than that. We need policies that allow those in low-paid jobs to raise their productivity, that upgrade the skill levels demanded in the jobs themselves, and provide real ladders of labour market progression.

For many years, poverty and inequality were thought of in a static way. It is only recently that research materials have become available permitting us to track what occurs to individuals over time. The availability of these materials has transformed both our understanding of the dynamics of inequality, and the policy options required to reduce inequalities. Robert Walker's chapter charts these developments in an original and insightful fashion. In modern societies, many more people experience spells of poverty than once was believed to be the case. For most, however, the experience of poverty is relatively transitory. Only a tiny minority of people are mired in poverty for long periods of time, although in some countries, including both Britain and the US, there is a pronounced 'carousel effect'. In other words, a substantial proportion of those who escape from poverty at any one moment are likely to fall back again. The policy implications of analysing inequality in a dynamic way are considerable. For instance, rather than concentrating only on the 'poor' at any one time, we might want to introduce policies that act to prevent those just above the poverty line from falling below it.

Anne Power focuses more specifically on urban poverty and inequality in the developed countries of Europe and America, examining urban neighbourhoods as the basic building blocks of cities. She assesses the historical patterns by which poverty and inequality became concentrated visibly in cities as a consequence of rapid industrialization in the mid-nineteenth century. Since that time, some cities have become dramatically polarized. She reminds us that even where income inequalities have been firmly contained by welfare states since the Second World War, as in the case of Scandinavia and the Netherlands, local neighbourhood areas characterized by concentrated deprivation have become more numerous and persistent over time. Neighbourhood polarization along sharp social and ethnic lines has become more acute, as fear of crime and violence has grown. The number of areas with transient, often unstable local populations has also risen, with poorer services and weaker informal social controls in evidence.

Power also reminds us that relatively few policy initiatives have succeeded in tackling deprivation and unequal conditions in very poor areas, or in containing the disorder and social damage they tend to produce. Not enough programmes seriously engage with the communities that are the subject of intervention. The desire of governments to transform neighbourhoods through large-scale targeted investment comes up against the problem of control and decision-making: how to design programmes that embrace poorer families in their daily lives.

Only by adopting a more custodial, regenerative approach to running cities, small area by small area, will the polarization of the least favoured areas be reversed. Those public interventions such as street cleaning, policing, lighting, public health, parks and the upgrading of social housing that originate precisely in the urban problems of the nineteenth century most need to be strengthened today. They are the critical elements of collective area-based provision.

In a globalizing age, as Ulrich Beck argues, inequalities can be neither analysed nor tackled at a purely national level. In this volume, we have not sought to address issues of inequalities across the world as a whole, or the divisions between the rich and poor nations. Beck's chapter, however, offers an incisive and original account of mechanisms of inequality in the most integrated transnational organization that exists today – the European Union. As he points out, we cannot assume that the same patterns of inequality that we identify on a national level exist on a pan-European scale. The way we currently address inequalities from within a national prism, Beck suggests, tends to diminish our perception of the inequalities that exist between societies in Europe, as well as obscure transnational divisions. Thus trade unions within the EU may demand 'equal pay for equal work'. But does this mean that wage-bargaining inequalities between European countries are therefore illegitimate too?

This is not just an abstract concern, Beck stresses. Why should low pay in Portugal and Greece not be raised to the German level, and what are the implications of such a policy? With the disappearance of Europe's frontiers, he concludes, the divisive character of European inequalities is not softened; on the contrary, it can be exacerbated. Much the same applies to the European regions. Within nations, there are normally many policy pressures to reduce regional inequalities, such as those between the affluent north in Italy and the poorer south. But regional differences on a European level are often regarded with insouciance, even though their explosive potential might be just as great.

As Saskia Sassen's analysis highlights, these regional and global transformations also require us to reconceptualize the notion of transnational classes. She questions the idea that 'global classes' are cosmopolitan, and out of the reach of national states. The new classes remain embedded in local environments, transforming existing class systems. For example, transnational immigrant communities are often also part of local disadvantaged neighbourhoods, working in local service occupations.

David Goodhart argues that the centre left now faces two critical 'progressive dilemmas'. The first concerns the potential conflict between solidarity and diversity in Western societies. The argument simply put is that the more distinct we become from one another, and the less we share a moral consensus or a sense of mutual belonging, the less content we are to support a generous welfare state.

The second dilemma concerns the nation-state. The left has historically battled for a universal notion of equal citizenship that is blind to wealth, status and, more recently, ethnicity. Yet citizenship stops at national borders, since we tend to favour our fellow citizens more than those of other countries. Citizenship is predicated on a notion of exclusivity. Goodhart explores the implications of the rights and duties of citizenship for tackling transnational inequalities in the future, such as development aid, human rights, and the maintenance of a fair asylum system. He argues that for the egalitarian project to flourish in industrialized societies, it is necessary to strengthen substantially the major dimensions of social integration, developing the collective sense of 'we' and 'us'.

In her chapter Magdalena Andersson explores the impact of gender on patterns of inequality, and analyses the costs imposed on societies by gender inequalities. Greater gender equality not only liberates women and strengthens their relative economic and political position in society; it can also liberate men from unfair or unequal economic and social expectations, and restore their role within the economy of caring work. Gender inequalities act to inhibit economic growth, since organizations will be most efficient if there is an optimum distribution of positions between men and women on the basis of merit. Equality complements productive efficiency rather than undermining it. Gender inequalities also tend to reduce female labour force participation, restricting labour supply in an age of growing demographic pressure.

Andersson argues that tackling gender inequalities requires a transformation of the social structure, not merely a rash of individual policy initiatives. Such an approach means encouraging a range of changes – the way that children are raised; decision-making structures within families; fiscal incentives such as family tax policies and the impact of the tax–benefit system; political institutions; and employment practice within the public and private sectors. She focuses particularly on family leave policies, arguing that a substantial proportion of family leave should be devoted to each parent. Parental leave must not become a reason for employers to avoid investing in younger women, and must compensate earners of high incomes for wage losses. Otherwise, the economic incentives that encourage fathers to take less parental leave will persist.

Richard Wilkinson's chapter considers another key dimension of inequality – inequalities of health. As Miliband emphasizes, inequality is not necessarily a 'bad' in and of itself. What matters is how it impinges on individuals' sense of self-worth and their capacity to live a full and rewarding life. Nowhere is this principle more important than in the field of individual health and well-being. In all industrial countries, Wilkinson shows, there are major inequalities between the life expectancy of the underprivileged and the more affluent. Other indices of health remain tightly bound to class differences. The evidence strongly suggests that these differences relate not to absolute but to relative inequalities. They will not be reduced by increasing levels of overall prosperity, only by diminishing inequalities of income and wealth. More equal societies tend to be characterized by higher levels of social trust and less social fragmentation than less egalitarian ones. Differences in health reflect these factors, and the psychosocial effects of low status and weaker self-respect tend to go along with them. These are the reasons why black American men, who have a median income four times higher than men in Costa Rica, have a life expectancy of nine years less.

Finally, Julian Le Grand reminds us that although politically freedom of choice has traditionally been the preserve of the right, the concept is gaining purchase on the left as a means of strengthening equality. Attempts to expand the scope of choice in health and social care in Britain, for instance, are being pioneered by the current Labour government. He quotes the Prime Minister, Tony Blair, who has argued that his government is 'recasting the 1945 welfare state' to base the service 'around the user, a personalized service with real choice'. Similarly, David Blunkett, when he was a senior cabinet minister, stated that 'many on the Centre Left argue that, whilst services should be responsive and user-friendly, the language and values of choice have no place in public provision. I reject that dichotomy. It would be foolish and politically suicidal, in my view, to reject the concept of choice, and the importance of tailoring services to individual needs.'

But there are many social democrats who reject the very idea of extending user choice in the welfare state. They do so primarily on grounds that are of direct relevance to the concerns of this book: its impact on equality. Thus Julian Le Grand points out that the Labour peer, and ex-deputy leader of the Labour Party, Roy Hattersley, has argued: 'Choice is an obsession of the suburban middle classes. But when some families choose, the rest accept what is left. And the rest are always the disadvantaged and dispossessed.'

Are these fears well founded? Will the 'new' public services, retaining public funding but providing choice for their users, worsen the plight of the poor? Or might extending choice actually reduce inequality in access to public services, and thereby help to create a more equitable and just society? These are the questions to which Julian Le Grand's chapter is addressed. He makes a persuasive case to the effect that, given the right contractual and regulatory framework, choice can further equality rather than threaten it.

1

Inequality of incomes and opportunities

Gøsta Esping-Andersen

The story of rising inequality has been repeated so often that it is now part of modern folklore. But the story is becoming a bit confusing. Until the mid-1990s, almost all research suggested that among OECD countries it was strictly a US and UK affair.[1] This appeared consistent with the institutional features that distinguish these countries from Europe. The more unregulated Anglo-Saxon countries allow wages to be set by markets and this may produce jobs but certainly not equality.[2] In Europe, inequalities will fail to surface because of strong welfare states and regulated labour markets.

But as I show below, the most recent figures indicate that the UK and the US may not be exceptions. The new tide of inequality may, accordingly, be of a more universal nature, a common structural feature of advanced economies. This would fit well with the claim of the doomsayers who believe that globalization will create a more unequal world wherever it penetrates. The data I shall present do show that more and more countries, including erstwhile bastions of equality such as Scandinavia, are experiencing rising income inequalities. But there are exceptions to the rule.

The doomsday scenario also lacks credibility because there are important countertendencies at work. For one, many welfare states manage successfully to stem the inegalitarian impulse that markets generate. For another, there is evidence that the rise in women's employment can constitute a counteracting force.

There are undoubtedly winners and losers in the process. There are many who believe in an imminent generational clash, arguing that older households do better and better at the expense of the 'young'. This is more false than true. Older households are now losing terrain in many countries. If by 'young' we mean the population aged 20–35 then it is more than evident that they are the most adversely affected. The real winners are mainly concentrated at the very top of the income distribution, not just because of wage polarization but also because they work far more hours. Women, too, are winners in the sense that they do far better than men across all skill levels.

If we care about equality we need to distinguish between here-and-now distributions, such as the level of poverty or inequality that obtains in any given year, and lifetime opportunities. Snapshots of inequality, like the poverty rate, can be very misleading since they lump together people at very different stages in their life course. A large proportion of the poor are students and youth who will eventually do very well. And for the majority, poverty and want are transitory. The key issue has to do with opportunities. To gain a real understanding of inequalities we therefore need to examine income mobility and persistency. Incomes over a lifetime may provide a far better picture of people's true opportunities. I therefore dedicate the final part of the chapter to what is happening to our opportunity structure. The core question here is whether rising inequalities of the here-and-now kind go hand in hand with more unequal opportunities across the life course and between generations.

One cannot automatically assume that a rise in income inequalities will also imply more inequality of opportunity. It all depends on how mobile citizens are. While the data on here-and-now distributions support the pessimistic view, the optimists are more likely to win the day in terms of the opportunity structure. On balance the evidence suggests that, in most countries, there has been no worsening of mobility opportunities and in a few they even appear to have become more equal.

Having promised to address all these questions, my chapter will easily tax the reader's patience. It will be loaded with data and must inevitably examine a very broad array of dimensions. I begin with the global picture of what is unfolding and then turn to trends in poverty for different social groups. Next I follow the 'welfare regime' perspective according to which households' total well-being is the composite of three pillars: work income, family welfare support (be it money transfers or in kind), and government redistribution. The task is to see how the three pillars combine to produce the outcomes we see. After that I move to opportunities and examine lifetime earnings inequality, the persistency of poverty, and intergenerational mobility.

The global view

Trends in wealth distribution

When we debate inequality we normally think of wages and incomes or, if we take a more dynamic view, of people's opportunities and life chances. Yet the truly massive inequalities are found in wealth ownership. To give an example, the Gini coefficient for asset ownership is everywhere about twice as large as for income inequality. US wealth concentration (with a Gini around 0.8) is greater than in Europe (where the Gini hovers between 0.6 and 0.7).[3] Its distribution is also far more skewed, with the top 10 per cent of households accounting for roughly half of all wealth and the top 1 per cent for anything between 15 and 35 per cent of the total, all depending on country. Cross-national differences in concentration mirror variations in income inequality (see below): far more concentration in the US than in Europe and exceptionally low concentration in Sweden.[4] Hence, the share of wealth possessed by the top 1 per cent of the population is 35 per cent in the US, roughly 25 per cent in Canada, Denmark and France, but only about 15 per cent in Sweden.

Trends over time are difficult to establish with any precision. There is no doubt there has been a historical decline in wealth concentration over the past century.[5] The question is whether this trend is being reversed or not. Those who argue the latter cite the impressive growth of pension assets, especially in the United States where funded pension plans cover a large proportion of workers. Those who argue the former cite the huge increases in returns to investment accompanied by wealth concentration.[6] Unfortunately, we know relatively little about what is really happening, mainly because data are limited and often unreliable. The Organisation for Economic Co-operation and Development (OECD) furnishes estimates of capital incomes, comparing the top three, bottom three, and four middle income deciles.[7] This, in other words, is not an indicator of wealth concentration *per se*. For what it is worth, trends in capital income do suggest a fairly strong polarizing scenario: in almost all countries, the bottom deciles are losing out while the top three are making substantial gains. Studies that more explicitly examine net wealth distribution conclude differently. For most countries (including the UK), the equalizing trend seems to persist into the 1990s. The only clear case of reversal is the United States, where the wealth share of the top 1 per cent jumped from 25 to 35 per cent from the mid-1970s to the mid-1990s.[8] The data on wealth do not support any theory of global convergence.

The resurgence in US wealth inequality is primarily due to redistribution from the very rich to the extremely rich, that is, a concentration that favours the top 1 or even top 0.5 per cent of the population.[9] This may be troublesome for many reasons, but it is unlikely to have any immediate effect on the welfare of most households. There is, however, some evidence that 'pension capitalism' does reduce wealth inequality. US data show that when private pension fund assets are included, the degree of concentration drops substantially (from a Gini of 0.8 to 0.5). This does not mean that asset ownership is becoming universal. Pension assets have eased concentration by increasing the 'wealth' of those below the 90th percentile by 3 percentage points.[10] The trickle-down effect of American pension funds is, in any case, limited to households above the median of the income distribution – and in Europe, private pension assets are far more concentrated among the rich.

Trends in income distribution

Most advanced countries embarked on a long wave of income equalization that began in the middle of the twentieth century and peaked in the late 1970s. In part, this was because the top deciles started to lose ground as progressive taxation began to take hold. And in part it was related to the improved position of the less skilled because of booming labour markets and more welfare state redistribution after the Second World War. Using American data, Smeeding shows that between 1947 and 1973, real income in the bottom fifth grew by 3 per cent annually, compared to 2.5 per cent in the top quintile.[11]

Many believe that we are now experiencing a U-turn. The top has recovered many of its erstwhile losses while the bottom is falling behind.[12] The U-turn is especially pronounced in the United States and Britain. In the US, real incomes of the top quintile grew by 2.3 per cent annually, while the bottom fifth experienced stagnation (a 0.3 per cent growth per year). But a significant reversal is under way in many other nations, too, including historical bastions of equality such as Sweden.

Most comparative studies end in the early 1990s. There are several reasons why we may want to update the estimates. For one, the 1990s were a period of sustained economic expansion and falling unemployment. Data for the early 1990s will invite overly gloomy conclusions because they coincide with a cyclical bust. It is nevertheless still possible that inequalities continued to rise even in the booming 1990s. European labour markets have been deregulated, the returns to skills

Table 1.1 Changes in household income distribution over the 1980s and 1990s, all households and working age households

	Working age		All
	% change of Gini: market income	% change of Gini: disposable income	% change of Gini: disposable income
Belgium (1985/96)	+ 2	+ 5	+10
France (1984/94)	− 1	− 2	0
Germany (West) (1984/94)	+25	+33	+ 7
Italy (1986/95)	+17	+15	+13
Netherlands (1987/94)	− 5	− 2	− 5
Denmark (1987/97)	+12	+ 4	+ 1
Finland (1987/95)	+29	+16	+ 4
Norway (1986/95)	+23	+ 4	+ 7
Sweden (1987/95)	+25	+ 1	+12
UK (1986/95)	+ 9	+14	+28
USA (1986/95)	+11	+10	+24

Inequality measures based on working age (25–55) household Gini coefficients for early 1980s and mid-1990s (the larger the number the greater the move towards inequality). Modified OECD equivalence scale used (1 for head, 0.5 for other adults, 0.3 for children). Calculations from Luxembourg Income Study (LIS) data.

have been rising, and continued growth of lone parent and other vulnerable households all point towards more inequality.

Table 1.1 presents a synthetic profile of income distribution over the past decades, distinguishing between inequalities in market income (income before taxes and benefits) and in post-redistribution disposable income. We compare trends in Gini coefficients for working age and for all households. We can now stretch the data to the mid-1990s and, for some countries, to 2000. As is evident, most nations experienced worsening inequalities in market incomes – France and the Netherlands being the sole exceptions. Countries that have been very egalitarian, such as the Nordic ones, seem to have fared worse (relatively speaking) than traditionally unequal ones, the US being a prime example. But here we must consider the point of departure: added inequalities will loom much larger in the former than in the latter. There are also indications that inequalities have begun to taper off in the UK and the US in recent years.

To real families it is disposable income that matters. Again, there is a trend towards more inequality, albeit less dramatic – and in many cases this was somewhat reversed in the latter part of the 1990s.[13] As one would expect, taxation and redistribution help diminish market inequalities, in particular in the strong welfare states of Scandinavia. We do, however, also note that the welfare state appears 'pro-cyclical' in some countries, notably in Germany, the UK, and even in Sweden in the late 1990s. That some welfare states seem to ride with the tide of inequality may be interpreted in two ways. One, welfare programme roll-backs have made the welfare state less effective in combating inequality; two, the inegalitarian tide simply overpowers the existing social safety net.

The new inequalities are not assigned at random. Indeed, contemporary debate is mainly about the winners and losers. As table 1.1 suggests, in some countries inequality has grown more within working age households than in the society as a whole and this implies that elderly households have fared relatively better. In others, especially Sweden, the UK and the US, inequality has risen more among the elderly. There are three interpretations of the changing shape of distribution: the top is pushing ahead of the rest, those at the bottom are being left further and further behind, or the twain go together.[14]

Earlier research traced trends up to 1990–5 and concluded, again, that if there is any polarization it is limited to the US and Britain – but in different ways. The US combines relative decline at the bottom with spectacular gains at the top.[15] In Britain it is mainly the top that has left the rest behind.[16] To examine if trends through the 1990s are producing more income polarization, I computed the (disposable) income ratios between households in the top and bottom deciles (P90/P10). The ratio has increased in all countries, even the ones that until the early 1990s seemed able to resist. Still, in the majority of cases the increase was modest. Consistent with earlier findings, the UK and the US stood out as polarizing, but one could add Italy to this group. Here, the rise was not dramatic but the level in 2000 was comparable to the British. The rapid rise in inequality in Sweden was also striking.

These data do not tell us who, specifically, have lost or won. This can be gauged by examining how the extremes fare relative to the middle, fifth decile. The data (not shown) suggest that in Italy, Sweden, the UK and the US the bottom is losing out but it is mainly the top that is pulling ahead. In most other countries the main effect comes from a deterioration at the bottom. The situation changes when we examine *market* incomes. In this case we see almost perfect convergence across countries (Germany being the sole exception), with substantial gains to the top two deciles and losses to the bottom.[17]

The second popular interpretation envisages a looming 'generational clash', because the 'old' prosper while the 'young' fall behind.[18] Table 1.1 above did suggest that the rise in inequalities often hit working age households more than the old. But in Belgium, Sweden, the UK and the US it would appear that the old have fared relatively worse. Moreover, the differences between 'young' and 'old' in Denmark, France, Norway and the Netherlands are not sufficiently large to warrant big words.

Still, if we differentiate more carefully by age the generational abyss scenario does gain some credence. Among households headed by young adults (aged less than thirty), the deterioration in disposable income *relative to older households* has been substantial in almost all OECD countries:[19] a relative decline of the order of 10–15 per cent in France, the Nordic countries and the US, and of 5–6 per cent in Italy and the Netherlands.[20] But this does not settle the question because, as we shall see below, the aged have begun to lose terrain in the latter half of the 1990s. The OECD has shown that the old have benefited from two simultaneous processes.[21] One, their relative disposable income continued to improve during the 1980s and into the 1990s; on the other hand, the beneficiaries were mainly within the lowest quintiles. In other words, the overall trend that seems to favour retirees over the 'young' is mainly due to more equality *among* retirees, coupled to the sinking fortunes of young families. All this, however, changed in the late 1990s.

Trends in poverty and deprivation

Summary measures, like the Gini, are not well suited if we are concerned with conditions at the bottom. One approach is to concentrate on the lower tail of the income distribution, that is, on poverty. The new practice within the European Union is to define poverty as less than 60 per cent of median income.[22] I choose here to follow traditional practice and measure poverty as less than 50 per cent of the median. This implies that we focus more explicitly on genuinely low income households.

A focus on poverty suggests that there may be some age polarization under way – but in a different form than usually portrayed. In an earlier study I show that the child-elderly poverty ratio increased from the 1980s to the mid-1990s in just about all countries. To exemplify, it jumped from 1.2 to 2.3 in the UK, from 1.1 to 1.5 in the US, and from 0.3 to 1.0 in Sweden.[23] Now that we can trace poverty up to the year 2000, we detect important changes. In some countries, old age poverty continues to fall – spectacularly so in France; in some there is a small increase, and in two (Norway and the UK) a substantial jump. With the exception of Scandinavia, families with children fare poorly just about everywhere, even in countries with high poverty rates to begin with (like the UK and the US).

One would expect that at least *some* part of the long-run trend may be of a cyclical nature. In fact, when we focus on the prosperous latter half of the 1990s (data not shown), overall poverty declined in Italy and the UK (by around 1 percentage point) and marginally in three other countries. Yet it also rose in three countries, in Germany substantially so (by almost 1 percentage point). Turning to child poverty, here the cyclical effect appears even more pronounced – not surprisingly since parents will be of working age. Now, poverty rates drop sharply in Germany (−3.8 points), in Italy (−2.4) and in the UK (a whopping −4.4 percentage points). And, quite surprisingly, in some countries the late 1990s were rather unkind to the elderly. Their poverty rates rose by 2.5 percentage points in Denmark, by 4–5 points in Sweden and the US, and by a full 6 points in Spain. Pension reforms in the late 1980s and 1990s may have cancelled some of the gains that especially retirees on low incomes made earlier.[24]

We can capture polarization better by focusing on extreme poverty (less than 33 per cent of median income). The share of child families at this low level is everywhere more modest: below 1 per cent in Scandinavia, France and Germany, about 4 per cent in the UK and 5 per cent in Italy and Spain. Some countries, especially Italy and the UK, suffered a rise in extreme poverty during the 1980s and early 1990s, followed by a decline in the late 1990s.[25] An alternative measure, following Rainwater and Smeeding,[26] compares the two tail ends, the extreme poor (less than 33 per cent of median) and the very rich (more than 300 per cent of median). Their data suggest a fairly clear pattern: in countries where there are many extremely poor households, there are also far more very rich ones than elsewhere. Hence, the United States combines 9 per cent extremely poor with 2.4 per cent extremely rich (the UK 5 per cent with 1.9 per cent, respectively) while Scandinavia, unsurprisingly, boasts few at any of the two tail ends (less than 1 per cent in either).

We cannot assume that low incomes automatically imply misery. It is, for example, known that year-to-year income variation is uncorrelated with year-to-year consumption levels.[27] Our poverty data refer to one year only and this may overstate genuine hardship if most poverty is short-lived. Citizens can offset temporary income shortfalls with non-cash consumption, savings, or familial support. For example, unemployed young adults in southern Europe will normally have no cash income at all and yet their poverty risk is modest because they remain in the parental home. Similarly, lone mothers in Italy and Spain have surprisingly low poverty rates, in part because they bundle up with kin.[28]

Inequalities and employment

Most agree that the new inequalities are driven by labour market change.[29] First, the returns to skills are rising and the less skilled are faring poorly indeed. Secondly, rising job precariousness and high unemployment are important contributing factors. Changes in the skills premium play a major role in some countries, but in others the main effect comes from changes in employment rates. Both will directly influence earnings distributions, but the effects may be compounded at the household level due to the prevalence of marital homogamy, that is, the selection of partners with similar levels of education.

Trends in earnings dispersion

The rise in wage differentials has, unsurprisingly, provoked intense debate. There is broad unanimity that changing returns to skills lie at the heart of the story.[30] Nevertheless, cross-national evidence suggests that other factors may be at play. For one, women have gained relative to men – especially in the United States.[31] Secondly, the trend is far more dramatic in the UK and US than elsewhere, and this suggests that the returns to skill may interact with nation-specific factors, such as minimum wage floors, unionization, and bargaining centralization.[32]

It is also possible that the low skilled in Europe have suffered less wage erosion due to more investments in productivity-enhancing technology. Yet another explanation has to do with the supply of skills. Acemoglu argues that the growth of highly skilled workers in Europe has been unusually strong in past decades, and this implies that their relative wages will have risen slower.[33] Finally, the relative earnings of young workers have eroded at all skill levels.[34] Since unemployment erodes skills and experience, and since European unemployment is concentrated among young workers, the youth wage penalty is to be expected. Juhn et al. show that young American workers have experienced a 70 per cent wage decline compared to mature workers.[35] Similar – if less dramatic – trends have been identified across the OECD.[36]

The rise in differentials does not appear to follow any clear logic. It has been dramatic in the US, the UK, the Netherlands and Sweden, and noticeable in Germany and Italy. On the other hand, differentials are stable or even declining in Norway, Finland and France. The jump in Sweden must, of course, be judged in the light of initially very compressed wages. The upsurge in wage inequalities during the 1990s is, in many respects, rather surprising when we remember that this was an era of job growth and declining unemployment. However, when we examine trends in the 90th/50th and 50th/10th deciles, we find part of the answer. Most of the inegalitarian trend is due to the very top decile distancing itself from the rest and far less to the bottom decile being left behind. Still, we note that the bottom has lost significant ground in precisely those countries where the top has enjoyed the sharpest gains.

The overall greater stability in the position of the bottom earners is consistent with data on low wage employment (defined as less than two-thirds the median wage). Since the early 1980s it has grown quite slowly, by about 2 percentage points, in all but one country surveyed by the OECD.[37] In 2001, a quarter of American workers and 20 per cent of British workers were low wage, compared to 13 in Germany and 15 in the Netherlands.

Trends in job precariousness and joblessness

Unemployment and precarious jobs are very concentrated among young and unskilled workers and the skills and youth effect on rising inequality will, accordingly, easily be compounded. Despite superior levels of educational attainment, youth fares poorly in contemporary labour markets. In a major survey published in 1998, the OECD showed that there was a clear deterioration from the 1980s to the mid-1990s. To exemplify, *involuntary* temporary employment was especially frequent among young workers: dominant in Finland, Portugal and Spain (50–70 per cent), moderate in the UK (26 per cent), and lower in the rest of Europe (15–20 per cent). These are large numbers however they are interpreted.

Unemployment was also substantially higher among young workers (and especially young women) in almost all countries and, worse, unemployment durations could be very long. There was also a strong 'carousel effect', that is, of intermittent employment with several spells of unemployment.[38] The experience of unemployment is especially severe for less educated youth.[39] To exemplify, French youth with less than secondary education are four times more likely to be unemployed compared to those with some tertiary schooling; in the US, the ratio approaches eight times.[40]

Still, the link between youth unemployment, exclusion and income poverty is not straightforward. The welfare support system makes a major difference here. Youth unemployment is far greater in southern Europe but, as noted, most avoid hardship by remaining with their parents. If we define exclusion as the joint experience of unemployment and no family support, youth in Denmark and the Netherlands fare much worse than in Italy and Spain (15–17 per cent in the former, compared to 2–3 per cent in the latter). This also means that income poverty among 'excluded' youth is far more prevalent in strong welfare states, like the Danish, than in weak welfare states, like the Spanish.[41] Here is one example of how families may still function as an antidote to market forces.

One trend that fuels fears is the seeming gap between work-rich and work-poor households. Unemployment tends to 'come in couples', concentrating welfare problems within workless households.[42] At the same time, we see the growth of dual-career, income-rich couples. However, it would be very difficult to argue that we are witnessing any serious polarization here. Data show that we are seeing a rise in workless households, but that in most countries it is insignificant. The real story is, rather, that the conventional single-earner household is giving way to two-income couples, on one side, and to single-adult households, on the other side. To illustrate, for fifteen OECD countries, the one-earner family has declined by 6 percentage points while the two-earner unit has grown by 4 points.[43] Workless households may not be growing, but there are reasons to be concerned simply because their income position is weak indeed.

From individual to household inequalities

It would be logical to expect that wage inequalities translate directly into household earnings inequality. Kenworthy shows a strong cross-national correlation between dispersion of wage levels and inequality in household earnings.[44] This does not really answer the question. It is very possible that the correlation *within countries* is far weaker and that differences in individual wages are not automatically echoed in interhousehold comparisons of earnings. First, being in a precarious job, being unemployed or suffering low pay may not imply that a person suffers hardship – if, that is, the person is only a supplementary earner. Secondly, household income inequalities are very much affected by the prevalence of non-active spouses. Hence, if many spouses have zero earnings, individual and household earnings correlations will end up being very modest. Thirdly, inequalities are also related to work intensity, as measured by hours or weeks worked per year. And, fourthly, inequalities in welfare at household level will depend on how many mouths need to be fed. If fertility is much higher in low income families, the net welfare distribution will end up more unequal.

All in all, the link between individual and household inequality is ambiguous at best. We have two strong leads to go by. We know that marital selection is the norm and is intensifying, and this should widen the gap between high and low wage couples and between work-rich and work-poor households.[45] Burtless shows that a substantial part of rising household inequalities can be ascribed to marital selection, not only because the strong marry the strong, but also because total labour supply (annual hours worked) has been increasing more among highly educated couples.[46] More inequality will also ensue if there is a rise in vulnerable single person or single parent units because, in both instances, the total potential household labour supply is naturally limited. To illustrate, the two-earner couple may potentially supply eighty or maybe even a hundred hours a week; the single-earner, half of that; and the lone mother, realistically far less.

But we should also expect that a rise in wives' employment should diminish interhousehold inequalities, simply because non-active women are mainly concentrated in low educated households.[47] In other words, the two leads may potentially point in exactly opposite directions.

There is evidence that supports a polarization view. There is a noticeable concentration of no-work households with very low incomes and high poverty rates. The share of all couples of working age (aged 20–55) with *no* employed adult varies between 6–8 per cent (Denmark, Germany, Sweden, and the US) and 13–15 per cent (Netherlands and the UK). No-work households may not be growing much, but they appear rather resistant to economic cycles – although we see a marginal decline in the latter part of the 1990s, especially in the UK. Work-rich households, that is, with two-plus employed adults, have been growing steadily as a consequence of rising activity rates among married women. The latter do very well. Two-earner couples with children are almost immune to poverty.[48]

It is, in other words, evident that the conventional male breadwinner family runs a considerable risk of poverty, and if the family is headed by a low skilled male, this risk is unlikely to abate in the future – especially in the US, with its large share of low income males. The relative income position of one-earner families has been deteriorating quite significantly in many countries, especially in the UK, where there has been a relative loss of 7 per cent over the decade.[49] Lone mothers are a second, related, high risk household that is also likely to persist. A substantial share of no-work households are, in fact, constituted by single mothers – especially in the UK, where employment among single mothers is exceptionally low. Lone parents usually represent 10–15 per cent of all families with children (Spain is the lowest with 5 per cent, the US the highest with 20 per cent). Even where, as in the Nordic countries, most single mothers do work, their labour supply, and hence earnings, are more limited. Accordingly, poverty remains widespread even among working solo mothers, albeit, once again, far less acute than if they do not work.

All this points to two concomitant processes. On the one side, demographic change and wage erosion among young and less skilled men will provoke a growth of vulnerable households. On the other side, this can be offset by an augmented female labour supply. Rainwater and Smeeding argue that even if wives' earnings are modest, they can nonetheless have a substantial poverty reduction effect.[50] As the OECD has also shown, low pay is rarely associated with household poverty because low wage workers tend to be secondary earners.[51] This may all be true, but a household's total labour supply *does* matter. Smeeding illustrates the dramatic difference in poverty rates between households that supply fewer or more than 1,000 hours a year, both in one- and two-earner families.[52]

Additional earnings will, by definition, always help to reduce poverty, but they may not have much of an effect on interhousehold inequality if those additional earnings are far greater in rich than in poor households. In fact, the data suggest that total hours worked have risen more sharply in higher educated households. Smeeding depicts a fairly similar picture for North America and Europe.[53] Couples in the top quintile work roughly two to three times as many hours a year as do the lowest, and about 20–30 per cent more hours than the middle quintile. In other words, marital selection manifests itself also in couples' intensity of work, and this alone will result in a rising income gap.

The main variation in families' total labour supply has to do with wives' activity rates. In the old days, female inactivity in the labour market was mainly concentrated in the upper classes, while working-class women were compelled to work. This all changed in the postwar decades when, both at the same time, working-class women became housewives and educated women began to pursue careers. This shift will have produced a widening household income gap, with single-earner working-class families at one end, and highly educated couples with dual incomes at the other. Moving the clock forward to present-day society, we see that employment rates among less educated women are everywhere relatively lower than those among more educated women, but in some countries (especially North America and Scandinavia) the gap has narrowed. And the gap is diminishing in most other countries as female participation gradually becomes the norm.

It is this recent wave of female incorporation that will be decisive for inequalities. The more that less educated women (or women in couples with low income men) are employed, the more we should expect equalization in the distribution of household incomes. The effect of converting zero earnings to some earnings can be large. This means that society will reap a non-trivial 'equality bonus' from any additional increase in female employment. One way to examine this is to disaggregate trends in total household income dispersion (for couple households) into the relative contributions of husbands and wives.[54]

Data from the European Community Household Panel show some interesting statistics for couple households. The correlation between husbands' and wives' earnings is low, but systematically positive – suggesting marital homogamy effects. A negative correlation for Germany tells us that there the wives of high income men work very little. When we look to see whether women's employment contributes to equalizing household income distribution or not, we find that in Denmark, Sweden and the US spouses' earnings do help in this regard. While the equalization effect is much lower in Italy and the UK, there has been change over time, indicating a decline in house-hold-level inequality in Britain – the opposite being true for Germany and Spain.

These findings would appear puzzling. We know that the decade produced substantial job growth and that women's activity rates rose. This should, all told, generate equalization if the basic argument holds. The answer has to do with the composition of the labour supply. If most of the increase in wives' employment occurs at the top, that is, among educated, high income women, we would in fact expect more inequality simply because the top households will distance themselves even further from the bottom. For women's earnings to create more equality we would require that most of the employment growth occurs at the bottom. This is evidently the situation in Denmark, Sweden, and the US, all of which were, incidentally, countries with very high levels of female employment to begin with. Denmark and Sweden are, in this context, telling examples because unemployment among less skilled women was fairly high in the early 1990s but not in 2001. There are also indications that the US may be undoing some of the equalizing effects that were previously harvested. Cancian and Reed argue that there has recently been a disproportionate growth in labour supply among wives with high income husbands, and additionally rising returns to education have helped widen inequalities.[55] Germany and

Spain represent the situation in which the rise in female employment was overly concentrated 'at the top'. When, accordingly, we take into consideration the composition of women's labour supply the puzzle evaporates.

One important lesson emerges here, namely that the cyclical effect can be quite substantial. The employment of less educated women is often very sensitive to the business cycle and this will produce fluctuations in household inequalities, exacerbating inequalities during recessions that then abate when the pendulum turns.

How are women faring?

The literature on gender tends to highlight the inequalities, discrimination and segregation that women suffer. No one denies that these still exist, but the risk is that we miss out on the substantial levelling that is unfolding. We have just seen that there are good reasons to rethink the standard association between women and inequality. The story does not stop here. Women are making important wage gains relative to men and both horizontal and vertical occupational segregation seems to be lessening. Indeed, as Goldin argues, the transformation of women's work is little short of revolutionary.[56]

One of the most surprising findings in recent US data is that women are doing far better than men across all skill levels. The erosion of wages at the bottom is far heavier among low skilled males, and professional women have made important earnings gains relative to similar men.[57]

This is not an isolated phenomenon. Blau and Kahn show that from the 1970s to the 1990s the female–male wage ratio also rose in Australia, Austria, France, Germany, Norway and Sweden, and sharply so in the UK.[58] Italy is a rare case of no change. The OECD shows that the gender gap in pay continues to diminish everywhere.[59] All this is not to say, of course, that gender pay inequalities are disappearing. Women are still much more likely to be low paid and the wage penalty to motherhood remains – although, again, it appears to be abating because women have fewer children and shorter interruptions.[60]

As, therefore, the gender wage gap closes in tandem with rising labour supply, women's relative importance for the household and the national economy increases. Women's share of total household income is approaching parity in Denmark (42 per cent) but remains modest in low participation countries like the Netherlands (26 per cent) or Spain (27 per cent). Viewed dynamically we see almost everywhere a seminal rise in women's relative contribution over the 1990s, in France, Netherlands and Spain by a full 5 percentage points. In only two countries has their share been stagnant (Germany and the UK).[61]

These trends may, theoretically, go hand in hand with heightened job segregation, either because mothers select themselves into 'mother friendly' jobs, as in the public services, or because employers shun women at childbearing ages. It is notable that most studies show substantially higher job segregation in the Nordic countries than elsewhere.[62] Anker's data show that just about 50 per cent of Nordic women are in female dominated jobs, compared to only 33 per cent in North America.[63] This would suggest that segregation may increase as women's (or, at least, mothers') employment levels rise. But the relationship is not straightforward. In fact, the growth of female employment correlates with a broader decline in segregation. As Dolado et al. conclude, there are too many nation-idiosyncratic factors involved to be certain.[64] The Nordic case may be unique, especially because wage differences are minimal. The general decline in levels of segregation over time does, in any case, appear related more to an increased integration of men and women in similar jobs than to changes in the job structure.[65] The OECD suggests that job segregation is far less among younger than older cohorts.[66]

We must distinguish between horizontal and vertical segregation. The discussion above is related to the horizontal dimension. When, instead, we examine vertical segregation, that is, the occupational pyramid, there are even clearer signs of desegregation. Women are doing quite well, both in absolute and in relative terms, with regard to moving into privileged positions, such as higher level management and the professions. In the OECD as a whole, women now account for 30 per cent in senior level managerial positions, and are virtually at parity in the professions. Here there also exist notable differences between nations. In senior level management, women's underrepresentation is far greater in Denmark, Norway and Sweden than in Britain or Ireland. Goldin shows a massive entry of US women into conventionally male studies and professions since the 1960s.[67] We should, nevertheless, not forget that women remain very overrepresented in traditionally female occupations, such as clerical work and the health and teaching professions.[68]

The overall strengthening of women's attachment to career, combined with rising education levels, account for a large part of their job and pay gains. Women not only have fewer children, but they also interrupt employment far less when they have children, thus diminishing the 'experience gap' with males. OECD studies show that the career penalty of having children (in terms of increased supervisory responsibilities) is modest in most countries – with the exception of Belgium, the Netherlands and Britain.[69]

All in all, it would seem that a perspective focused on women generates conclusions that diverge markedly from what standard inequality measures tell us. Still, we do know that overall income and wage distribution is becoming more unequal. The contribution of women helps to lessen but not to arrest the broader inegalitarian thrust. Put differently, we cannot put our faith in households to correct the trend, and this implies that the welfare state remains crucial.

The role of the welfare state

Considering ongoing measures to contain costs, one might expect that part of the rising inequalities can be traced to welfare state cutbacks or to less progressive taxation. There are indications that some welfare states (essentially the Nordic ones) have intensified their redistributive effort in response to rising inequalities (in particular those due to rising unemployment), while others have not (Belgium, France and the US). And there is a third group, including Germany and the UK, where the welfare state seems to weaken redistribution in concert with the rise in inequalities. This may have changed, however, during the 1990s.[70] On one side we find the Netherlands where family benefits declined sharply.[71] On the other side, both Germany and Britain stepped up their redistribution efforts in the late 1990s, in Germany notably through the introduction of generous family allowances in 1996, in Britain through an array of anti-poverty measures.

The standard approach is to disaggregate welfare state redistribution into transfer and taxation effects. Gottschalk and Smeeding review the evidence and suggest that a number of welfare states may have become less effective in holding up the incomes of bottom decile households.[72] Taxation has become somewhat more regressive and there is a parallel decline in transfers towards low incomes. But the trend is very nation specific and, in any case, nowhere especially strong. In Scandinavia, less progressive taxation has been offset by substantially more redistributive spending, while this was not true for Germany, the UK or the US. In any case, social transfers are of far greater importance for the economic situation of low income households than is the incidence of taxation.

Pulling together the evidence, the basic story seems to be that, for most countries, *changes* in poverty or in overall inequality (as examined earlier) during the past decades are, at most, only very marginally attributable to shifts in government redistribution efforts.

The dynamics of inequality

We have so far examined snapshots of distributions for select years. This can easily misrepresent real inequalities. First, poverty or hardship may be for many a sporadic experience that leaves no trace in later life. Secondly, a snapshot of, say, poverty levels amounts to comparing apples and oranges since we are lumping together people at very different stages in their life and career cycles.

For reasons like this we need to focus more specifically on life course dynamics. First, we need to estimate lifetime inequality. Secondly, we need to know to what extent low incomes, wages or poverty are transitory or persistent. If very few remain trapped for longer periods in hardship, even a rise in the incidence of poverty or low wages may not pose any serious welfare problem. If there is widespread (and growing) persistency, we would need to worry. One major problem we confront is that it is virtually impossible to trace trends in poverty persistence, simply because we do not have data going back far enough. Thirdly, and possibly of the most importance, we need to examine dynamics in terms of the intergenerational transmission of inequality.

Lifetime income inequalities

Estimating true lifetime incomes is very difficult since it requires data for the same people over decades. A few countries have data that permit fairly robust estimations. Studies of inequalities using lifetime incomes invariably show that our snapshot measures vastly exaggerate 'true' inequality. It has, for example, been found that despite more unequal wage distributions, US lifetime inequality is actually lower than in Italy.[73] This suggests that there may be more earnings mobility in the US. Similarly, a comparison between the US and France shows that the 60 per cent greater wage inequality in the US declines to only 15 per cent when we compare lifetime data.[74] Indeed, it should be obvious that lifetime incomes come far closer to what a normal citizen would consider meaningful in terms of his or her life chances, opportunities and welfare.

Using the lifetime approach, we can study inequalities in different ways. Most simply, we can compute lifetime Ginis (or decile ratios). Alternatively, we can map out the incidence and intensity of, say, poverty across people's lives. Recent studies on Denmark and Sweden tell pretty much the same story.[75] Lifetime based Gini coefficients of income inequality are dramatically lower than are one-year based Ginis. In the Danish case, the one-year based Gini for *market* incomes is 0.456 whereas the life cycle Gini is almost half, 0.259.[76] Similarly, the Gini for *disposable* income drops from 0.239 to 0.124.[77] The Scandinavian findings are pretty consistent with those for other countries.[78]

Comparing the top and bottom income deciles in Denmark yields similar results. The top–bottom income ratio for 1999 was 5:1, but drops to 2:1 when we compare lifetime incomes.[79] In other words, not only may we be exaggerating inequalities, but we may be *hugely* over-estimating income polarization.

The Danish study is interesting because it also estimates the proportion of people's total working lives spent in poverty. Following this approach we see that conventional research vastly *underestimates* poverty because a huge majority of Danes (93 per cent) have experienced some poverty at some point in time – usually in youth and during studies. Poverty, in other words, is a universal experience. Yet for most this hardly came to define or shape their lives. Almost 80 per cent of Danes experienced poverty for less than 10 per cent of their adult life. Another 18 per cent suffered a bit more, being in poverty between 10 and 20 per cent of their life. Only 1 per cent of Danes have experienced what we might define as a life seriously marred by poverty, that is by spending 30 per cent or more of their years in poverty.[80]

In sum, examining lifetime incomes introduces an important corrective to the conventional picture of inequality. Ironically, we now find both less and far more 'inequality', but what it all really means is that a huge share of the inequality we record via snapshots is transitory and, presumably, of little importance for true well-being. What is far more difficult to answer is whether inequalities of lifetime income are growing in tandem with here-and-now inequalities. A number of US studies have attempted to provide answers by disaggregating the longer-run trend into period-specific trends.[81] The picture that emerges is that, yes, inequalities in lifetime income parallel the trends in cross-sectional inequality, the main reason being that increasing returns to skills have distanced the top from the rest also on a lifetime basis. It remains an open question whether a similar pattern obtains for European economies.

The persistence of poverty

We have seen a recent accumulation of research on poverty and low wage dynamics, usually tracing exits out of poverty over periods of three to five years. As with lifetime incomes, it is very difficult to know whether persistency is on the rise, because we simply lack data back in time. The study of dynamics involves either simple tabulations of, say, years spent in poverty, or estimates of survival functions.

Most research concurs that the lion's share of poverty (or low wages) is transitory in nature.[82] Most spells last only one or two years and the proportion of people who remain trapped for long periods is everywhere quite small. There are, however, two caveats to this. One, there is a noticeable 'carousel effect' because of recurrent spells: many who leave poverty return later on. Two, there exist, if not dramatic, then at least non-trivial differences in persistency across countries. These differences appear strongly related to a country's overall inequality, so that the most unequal exhibit more persistency. The OECD's estimates of poverty durations over a three-year period (1993–5) bring this out clearly.[83] The percentages who remain poor in all three years range from 2 per cent in Denmark to almost 15 per cent in the US, with generally much greater persistency in countries with high poverty rates to begin with, such as Italy and Spain.

Three years are too few for an adequate assessment of the carousel effect. Studies with a longer time frame suggest that were we also to include returnees, the percentage of persistent poor would more or less double.[84] In any case, the country differences remain pretty much intact because there is more recurrent poverty where persistency is high.

Estimates of poverty persistence can be very influenced by population composition. If the poor in year one included a large share of young people, one would expect far higher mobility rates than if they included a disproportionate number of the aged. Perhaps the best and most meaningful way to get around this problem is to focus on families with children. Parents would normally be beyond the age of transition from school to work and, more to the point, the implications of persistent poverty in families with children are far more serious from a welfare point of view. In table 1.2, I present persistence estimates for poverty in families with children, utilizing all the eight panel years of the European Community Household Panel (ECHP). I estimate the probability of remaining in poverty for one, two, or three-plus years among families that *began* a poverty spell in 1994 or 1995.[85]

Table 1.2 The persistency of income poverty in families with children (Kaplan-Mayer survival functions)

	Year one	Year two	Three-plus years
Denmark	0.410	0.282	0.026
France	0.590	0.418	0.128
Germany	0.490	0.303	0.091
Italy	0.635	0.411	0.161
Spain	0.597	0.369	0.120
UK	0.494	0.287	0.110
US	0.814	0.704	0.576

Wilcoxson test for equality $Pr > Chi2 = 0.0001$ ($Chi2 = 26.53$). The higher the number the greater the likelihood of continuing to be poor.
Income poverty is <50 per cent of median, and moving out of poverty is >60 per cent of median.
Source: Data from European Community Household Panel, waves 1994–2001, and for the US, the Panel Study of Income Dynamics, 1993–7.

The coefficients tell us the likelihood of continuing to be poor one, two, or more years after having fallen into poverty. In order to minimize short-range movements out of poverty (that is, just crossing the 50 per cent line), I have stipulated that exit must imply *moving above 60 per cent of the median*. These figures are consistent with mainstream findings, namely that persistency is positively related to the level of inequality that obtains in any given country. As the OECD study shows as well (*Employment Outlook*, 2001), there is far less persistency in Denmark (almost 60 per cent of the poor have exited within one year, a little more than 70 per cent after two years, and the likelihood of remaining trapped in many years of continuous poverty is below 3 per cent). Again consistent with the OECD's figures, Italy, Spain, France and especially the United States display substantially more persistency, in particular with regard to long-term entrapment.

Whelan et al.'s study is of particular interest because it compares persistency rates of income poverty and of deprivation on a broader basic measure.[86] It concludes that the two mirror each other, displaying almost identical rates of transitory or persistent poverty. Yet if one estimates persistency in terms of those who are *both* income poor and deprived, the end result is far less long-term entrapment and far more transitional hardship. Again, this suggests that in very many cases a spell of low income will not automatically result in any drastic curtailment of consumption and living standards.

Research on *low wage* persistency comes to very similar conclusions. In a comprehensive comparison, the OECD examined mobility among full-time low wage workers over five years, 1986–91. There was everywhere a sizeable share of low paid workers who simply exited employment. Among those who remained, the share who continued to be low paid (receiving less than 65 per cent of median) five years later ranged from 6 per cent in Denmark to 34 per cent in the UK and the US. Sweden and Germany lay closer to Denmark, with 11 and 15 per cent respectively, and Italy and France fell in between with, respectively, 19 and 23 per cent. Data on mobility out of low pay are pretty much a mirror image of low wage persistency. If we stipulate that mobility must be longer in range, that is, jumping to 95+ per cent of the median, the rates range from 24–5 per cent in Denmark and Sweden to only 10 per cent in the US (but 18 per cent in the UK).

All the data indicate that the mobile are far more likely to be men and, especially, young. In other words, low wage workers include a sizeable transient component of youth and probably intermittently employed women. And then they include a hard core whose size evidently varies substantially across nations: small in the Nordic countries and quite large in the UK and the US

The estimates presented above refer only to workers who remain employed throughout the entire period, but some will have left the labour market. In the US, the latter account for 29 per cent after the first year and 38 per cent of those remaining after the second year – in other words, there is a sizeable group of the low paid that simply ceases to work. Nonetheless, here again we encounter the familiar picture of lower mobility in the more unequal societies. Still, the degree of persistency in France and Germany is surprisingly high.

I suggested earlier that low wages are generally not associated with being in poverty since so many workers with meagre wages are secondary earners in the household. There is nonetheless a non-trivial share for whom low pay coincides with poverty, in the United States particularly. The OECD has examined the degree to which low wage workers are also persistently poor and, once again, we revisit the familiar pattern: unusually strong persistency in the US (25 per cent remain poor over five years compared to 10 per cent in the UK and 7–8 per cent in the Netherlands and Germany).[87]

The concern with persistent poverty and low income is directly connected to the more general preoccupation with mounting social exclusion and the possible emergence of a 'two-thirds' society. In one sense, our findings would indicate that such pessimistic scenarios may be unwarranted, certainly for Scandinavia but probably also for Europe more generally. The lion's share of hardship is transitory, and lengthy durations are limited to a very small clientele. For some countries, particularly the United States, there seems to be some support for a pessimistic view of the kind that Wilson has depicted.[88] This country does quite stand out as a kind of two-thirds or, better perhaps, four-fifths society in which the bottom is comparably less mobile, and generally quite distanced from mainstream society. Britain, in some but not other respects, shares similar characteristics, at least when measured against a Nordic yardstick.

But all this does not really answer the question of whether we are *heading towards more* exclusion. Alas, this is an almost impossible question to answer because we are unable to trace longer run trends. One indirect way to approach the issue would be to take as a base the systematic correlation between persistency and levels of poverty and inequality. Since persistency is so much more accentuated in inegalitarian economies, and since we generally witness rising inequalities across the advanced economies, we might accordingly assume a shift towards greater persistency, or, if you wish, a convergence with the United States.

Among the few empirical attempts available, no clear answer emerges. Duncan and Rodgers survey persistence in US families with children over several decades and conclude that pre-transfer poverty persistence has increased.[89] But when we adjust for transfers and food stamps, the pattern becomes stable instead. If we compare poverty persistency during the 1980s with the 1990s for all US households, we find a small decrease. The likelihood of remaining poor three-plus years declines from 0.63 to 0.58. Analogous results were found for low wage persistency. In this case, the likelihood of remaining low paid three-plus years drops from 0.56 to 0.42. Fritzell and Henz's survey of trends in Swedish poverty persistence over two decades suggests that, if anything, it has possibly abated.[90] Hills traces low wage persistency in the UK, and his findings indicate an intensification of persistency.[91] The long-term data we have is too scarce to answer the question.

It would, I believe, be hazardous to assume that an increase in inequalities will automatically also produce more persistency. It is evident from all the data that the new inequalities are heavily centred in the young adult population. Since this is a highly mobile group, a rise in overall inequality will not necessarily translate into hardening persistency of poverty or low pay.

Nevertheless, the striking correlation between degree of inequality and degree of persistency seen across nations should be taken seriously and needs to be accounted for far better than is yet the case. This is particularly so because, as we shall see in the next and final section, patterns of *intergenerational* mobility and inequality conform almost perfectly to the cross-national differences we have, so far, identified: unequal societies also harbour less mobility across the life course and between generations; vice versa for the most egalitarian societies.

The intergenerational reproduction of unequal opportunities

Postwar egalitarians were convinced that educational reform would eventually create a world of equal opportunities for all. This was a logical assumption. For one, it was evident that human capital was becoming the key to people's careers, incomes and life chances. Hence, equalizing human capital would trickle down to all dimensions of distribution. For another, research consistently suggested that the key mechanism that linked parental status to their children's destinies lay in families' investment in their education. Now, many decades later, there is mounting evidence that educational reform has not seriously diminished the importance of social origins for life chances.

We have seen that the rewards to human capital are increasing.[92] Which skills are central is rather less clear. The lack of adequate formal education is problematic and, as a rule of thumb, those with less than secondary level credentials suffer wage erosion and far greater unemployment. Yet different human capital dimensions are gaining in importance, especially less identifiable traits such as social skills, cultural capital and, especially, cognitive skills. A person's ability to understand, interpret and productively utilize information is a *sine qua non* in knowledge economies, where technologies and skill requirements are apt to change rapidly. A brave new world of lifelong learning assumes, likewise, that people are able to learn and relearn quickly and effectively. And, to the extent that formal credentials remain crucial, again, we know that children's cognitive skills are one precondition for successful schooling. As so much evaluation research has concluded, remedial programmes later on in life are quite ineffectual unless a person possesses adequate cognitive skills to begin with. These are developed very early in a child's life, in large part *before* school age.

Life chances are therefore powerfully determined by what happens in children's life prior to their first encounter with the school system. It is this that explains why a century of educational reform has failed to diminish the impact of social inheritance; why parents' social status continues unabated in dictating children's educational attainment, income and occupational destination.

For both welfare and efficiency reasons this impact must be weakened. For citizens, a strong cognitive base is a precondition for educational attainment, subsequent earnings potential, and career chances. For society, it is vital that future generations will be resourceful and productive. They will be numerically few and are destined to support huge dependent populations. We can ill afford a future working population in which maybe 20 or 30 per cent are functionally illiterate and/or have failed to attain even secondary level education.

The question, then, is how to combat social inheritance. The traditional strategy, focused on education systems, pursued four objectives in particular: avoiding early tracking, sponsoring comprehensive schools, minimizing private schools, and affirmative action for underprivileged children. The first two are, in practice, part and parcel of the same problematic, namely to reduce social differences by keeping kids together in school as long as possible.[93] The third, it is well known, is doubly important, in part to ensure adequate funding for, and broad involvement in, high quality public education, and in part to avoid segregation by class, race or ethnicity. The fourth dimension is probably the single best documented, certainly in the case of the Head Start programme in the US. Head Start evaluations systematically report substantial gains in terms of school attendance and performance.[94]

The bad news, as far as educational reform is concerned, is that the real mechanisms of social inheritance lie mostly elsewhere. The prevailing view is that school and neighbourhood effects are decidedly less important than are factors related to the family milieu.[95]

What precisely are the attributes of families that help perpetuate inherited life chances? Contemporary research converges around two principal causal mechanisms, 'money' and 'culture'. The 'money' argument focuses on parents' ability to invest in their children. A large literature demonstrates that the income of offspring is strongly correlated with that of their parents. One surprising finding is that the social origins effect is far stronger in countries like the UK and the US than in Canada, Scandinavia or Germany.[96] The parent–child income correlation is, in fact, twice as high in the US as in Scandinavia.

Social inheritance, in brief, appears stronger in inegalitarian societies. This view also gains support from Harding et al., who show that the parent–child income correlation in the US rose in tandem with the rise in income inequality from the 1970s.[97]

Other literature shows that economic insecurity has harmful effects on children's educational attainment, subsequent earnings capacity and, perhaps most alarmingly, on the probability that – once adults – they will also become poor parents.[98] Long spells of poverty are especially damaging and it is therefore of vital importance that society provides ladders out of poverty.

All this suggests that a frontal attack on poverty in families with children would be an effective tool in the pursuit of more equal opportunities. This is also what emerges from international comparisons of intergenerational mobility. The two most authoritative such studies, namely Erikson and Goldthorpe's *Constant Flux* (1992)[99] and Shavit and Blossfeld's *Persistent Inequality* (1993), come to a similar conclusion – namely that there has been no real decline in social inheritance over the past half-century, be it in terms of occupational or of educational attainment. Yet both studies identify Sweden as an exception to the rule and hypothesize that this may be one of the salutary effects of its unusually egalitarian welfare state. As we have seen, in Sweden, as in neighbouring Denmark and Norway, child poverty is exceptionally low.

But 'money' is probably an insufficient explanation because there is mounting evidence that 'cultural' factors are also decisive, in particular for the cognitive and motivational development of children.[100] Analysing a microdata set of findings from the OECD's Programme for International Student Assessment (PISA), it is possible to compare the effect of parents' education, income and cultural level on their children's cognitive performance (at age fifteen) across countries. The 'culture' measure taps three features: the quantity of books in the home, the frequency of discussing cultural issues, and a highbrow item related to frequency of attending concerts, theatre, etc. It is important to note that 'culture' and 'money' are found to be weakly correlated.[101] When we assess the relative explanatory weight of each of the variables household wealth does not come out as an important factor, whereas parents' socioeconomic status does. But the influence of economic conditions easily pales in comparison with families' 'cultural capital', clearly the single most powerful explanatory variable – outperforming the socioeconomic variable by a factor of 1.5 to 2 in most countries. This is tantamount to saying that a strategy based exclusively on income redistribution may be necessary, but that it is not sufficient. An effective policy would also have to attack inequalities in parents' cultural transmission to children. Indeed, this is hardly a novel argument. Plato proposed that gifted children of uncultured parents be removed from the family.

We know that cognitive abilities are crucial to a child's educational performance and, later, to successful activation or lifelong education. To furnish one example, the probability of making the transition into upper secondary education typically doubles or triples for those who score high on cognitive tests, even when controlling for such factors as immigrant status or parental education.

The key lies in identifying those factors that may reduce the influence of unequal cultural and cognitive resources in the family of origin. This is no easy task, but one very suggestive clue comes from international comparisons of the impact of social origins on children's educational achievement across cohorts. The important information lies in comparisons over time: has a country been able to reduce the parental inheritance effect? The data demonstrates that in the US, Germany and basically also in the UK, there has been no real decline in the parent–child correlations across postwar generations. In contrast, all three Nordic countries exhibit substantial reductions, Denmark in particular. Indeed, the impact of the father's education on his child's secondary school attainment has disappeared altogether in the youngest Danish cohort! What previous research identified as Swedish exceptionalism is now, in reality, a common Scandinavian feature.[102]

How do we explain this? No doubt, the very child-centred nature of redistribution in the Nordic welfare states is crucial. But there is a second – and not rival – explanation, namely that these same countries – Denmark as the vanguard, Norway as the laggard – have now for decades furnished near-universal day care for pre-school children. With female employment becoming universal, children from economically and/or culturally weaker homes have come to benefit from pedagogical standards and cognitive impulses that are basically the same as for children from privileged backgrounds.

In a sense, the Nordic welfare states have unwittingly heeded Plato's advice. Hence, irrespective of origins, children arrive at the first day in school much more homogeneously prepared. And it is this which experts stress as important: the single most important phase of cognitive development occurs *before* school age. Children with lesser cognitive resources are likely to gradually fall behind in their educational progress because schools are ill equipped to remedy initial handicaps, and may indeed exacerbate them.[103]

In conclusion, international differences in intergenerational mobility opportunities are very likely to be linked to combined efforts within individual welfare states to minimize poverty in childhood and to equalize cognitive stimulus among pre-school age children. Indeed, a policy that promotes universal and high quality day care is a double winner. It equalizes life chances and it supports mothers' employment – which, as we have seen, yields an important equality dividend.

One major preoccupation attached to the rise of mothers' employment is that this will have adverse effects on the quality of children's development. In other words, the income dividend of mothers' work may be offset by a loss of stimulus for their children that, then, will harm their future. Existing research on this question fails to produce straightforward answers. Overview studies, such as those by Duncan and Brooks-Gunn and Haveman and Wolfe,[104] suggest that maternal employment is generally positive, or at least neutral, but that harmful effects occur when employment is combined with stress or fatigue. Ermisch and Francesconi, using British data, come to more pessimistic results and conclude that mothers' full-time employment is decidedly negative for children's learning.[105] The effect of part-time work is less clear. The interpretation of their findings is made difficult by the fact that negative effects of fathers' employment are also evident. From my own analyses of the PISA data, there is partial support for Ermisch and Francesconi's results. Mothers' full-time employment tends to be a negative factor for the cognitive performance of *boys*, but far less for that for girls, and part-time work has no adverse effects at all.[106]

The impact of parental employment is important to sort out. In the first place, it undoubtedly depends on *when* it occurs in the child's development. Negative effects are arguably concentrated in the youngest ages, as Ermisch and Francesconi insist.[107] Additionally, harmful effects are probably related to the nature of mothers' jobs more than employment *per se*. Second, we should probably expect *a priori* that the impact of mothers' employment will vary across nations – producing more problematic effects where non-family care of children is of low or uneven quality, and less problematic where care is of high quality. Returning to my analyses of the PISA data, there are clear national discrepancies: in the Nordic countries, mothers' employment, either on a part- or full-time basis, seems to have no effects whatsoever.

The one great question that we need to answer in the end is whether and how opportunity structures are connected to levels of income inequality. The data I have assembled suggest that there exists, cross-nationally at least, a connection between the two. There is more mobility, less ascription and a significantly greater levelling of opportunities in the Nordic countries that all stand out as also the most egalitarian in distributional terms. Vice versa, the old idea that inequalities are conducive to more mobility appears unpersuasive in the light of the systematically lower mobility rates, both within the life course and between generations, that we observe in the US and, less so, in the UK.

Such a correlation is arguably spurious unless we can point to the precise mechanisms that link distributions to opportunities. Some of these mechanisms do raise their head in our data overview. Returning to the 'money' and 'culture' debate, we know that parental investment in their children matters. The more unequal their resources are, the more unequal the investment, although this can be partially undone through government redistribution. This brings me to the second possible mechanism. Government redistribution tends to be far stronger in countries that are more egalitarian to begin with. Why this is so is not well understood. A tempting explanation has to do with the relative distance that separates the top incomes from the median: the greater the gap, the less the rich will be inclined to support redistribution in favour of the less fortunate.[108] Hence government spending may not automatically offset (rising) inequalities, in particular if the latter are caused by the rich pulling ahead of the rest – as has actually happened in many countries over the past decades.

A third mechanism is related to the huge asymmetries that we observe in intergenerational income mobility. By far the largest parent–child correlations are found among the very rich and the poorest quintiles.[109] As to the former, rich parents are probably able to save even their untalented offspring from downward mobility by, for example, endowing an Ivy League university with millions of dollars. As to the latter, we are here probably observing a mechanism similar to that depicted by Wilson with regard to the American ghetto poor:[110] the distance the poor must travel to be mobile in a very unequal society is comparably much longer than in a society without extremes. Or, being income poor in such a society is more likely to be combined with cumulative resource deprivation, making the task of substantial betterment all the harder. The distance effect is illustrated by the income gap between the poorest decile and the median. The poorest Swedish decile has an income about 60 per cent of the median; the poorest American, 39 per cent.

These links are of a speculative nature and the truth is that we really do not know. But if it is so that unequal distributions worsen the opportunity structure, then we have a strong case in favour of reversing the tide of inequality that is under way. If the causality is the other way, and it is strong social inheritance that produces unequal distributions, the case in favour of combating unequal opportunities is persuasive indeed because this would entail that the distributions are the outcome of injustice. We are, most likely, in a chicken-and-egg situation in which it is futile to isolate the single driving force. If so, the obvious remedy will be to attack the twain in tandem.

Conclusions

Since we are examining trends that continue to unfold, strong conclusions are unwarranted. There are indications that the very latest data disturb the prevailing view that the burst of new inequalities is an idiosynchratic Anglo-American affair. A number of European countries have, in the 1990s, begun to follow the American lead. But whether we are witnessing a truly global phenomenon is another matter, and our data cannot yet establish this. Here we should also recognize that inequalities seem to be stabilizing, or perhaps even abating, in Britain and the US. It is clear, nevertheless, that this will depend a lot on how welfare states react.

Much debate has focused on the brewing generational clash, citing the contrasting income developments of elderly and young households. Our data cast doubts on this scenario, essentially for two reasons. One, the long-term gains among the elderly appear now to have halted and are possibly even being reversed. We have identified a rather substantial rise in old age poverty in many countries during the 1990s. Two, it is clearly important to distinguish among the 'young'. The real drama centres on young adults in the age range of, say, 20–35. This is where most unemployment and job precariousness is concentrated and this is where relative wages and incomes have declined most sharply just about everywhere. Since this is also an age that coincides with family formation, the welfare implications can be severe, not only now, but also far into the future. And if there is declining income mobility among the more recent cohorts, as some US studies suggest, then their eroding position now is likely to be pervasive through their careers.

The welfare of young families was traditionally upheld by good wages and job security for the main breadwinner, but traditionally the timing of inheritance also helped smooth the income stream of young families (during Golden Age capitalism, parental longevity was ten years less than it is now, so that inheritance would occur when offspring were in their thirties). The new labour market is clearly unkind to young workers and their finances may be additionally weakened by the substantial delay in inheritance that follows from the leap in longevity. In fact, the new demography creates a huge asymmetry, since inheritance now occurs when children are at the peak of their earnings power.

Most accounts of the new inequalities tell a rather one-dimensional story – usually that everything is getting worse. It is certainly getting worse for families headed by young adults, but there exist countertendencies of considerable weight and importance. In part, these come from the welfare state, or rather from *some* welfare states, considering that their responses to heightened inequalities range from intensified redistribution to a relaxation of effort. Nonetheless, the main trend is that welfare states by and large have managed to stem much of the tide of inequality. And, in part, women's employment constitutes a potentially powerful counterbalance, in particular for low income households. There is no doubt that mothers' employment is key to minimizing child poverty, and it also seems clear that household income polarization can be countered by maximizing the employment of women married to low income males.

Social scientists who study gender inequalities usually highlight the big disadvantages that women face. Disadvantages obviously exist, but we also need to recognize that women's relative position is improving substantially and rapidly on just about all indicators. Here is additional ammunition, then, for the argument that women may be a key player in any search for a more egalitarian order.

We know very little about what is happening to the opportunity structure for the simple reason that we lack data. The evidence we have is certainly not strong enough to conclude that opportunities are becoming less (or more) unequal. Most intergenerational mobility research actually shows long-term stability. There are, however, important clues in the data that suggest that opportunities *can* be equalized. These clues come from Scandinavia, where we find far greater mobility out of low wages and poverty and where, even more importantly, we identify a distinct decline in the intergenerational transmission of opportunities.

The one great puzzle that probably no one can adequately unravel lies in the apparent association between unequal distributions and more unequal opportunities. The opportunity structure appears far more egalitarian in countries with more equal income distributions. But the mutual causality between the two is impossible to establish. If, as is possible, we are dealing with a chicken-and-egg problem, this may not matter from a *public policy* point of view because, in this case, a reduction of inequality on either of the two dimensions ought to have positive effects on the other.

2

Does inequality matter?

Edward Miliband

In what follows, I will begin with some historical background which attempts to explain why inequality fell off the political agenda in the 1980s and 1990s. Secondly, I will explain why inequality matters, drawing on recent work in political philosophy. Thirdly, I will try to explain what types of inequality we should be concerned with. Finally, I will conclude by attempting to summarize how progressive social democrats should approach the issue of inequality in the coming years.

I cast what follows not as a set of policy prescriptions – this chapter is not about changes in fiscal policy, corporate responsibility or the use of public policy – but more as an attempt to help provide a left framework in which to think about issues of inequality. The precondition of tackling inequality must be greater discussion about its causes and consequences.

As will be evident, I write from a British or sometimes Anglo-American perspective. I hope, nevertheless, there will be some useful insights in these thoughts for those from other industrialized countries. Certainly, as I indicate, I think that Britain has something to learn from the experience of other countries that have done better in constraining the growth of inequality.

Section 1: Inequality – a disappearing political issue?

In thinking about the historical evolution of debates about inequality, we can draw on T. H. Marshall's simple and broadly accurate framework about the nature of rights in our society.[1] The eighteenth century saw individuals granted civil rights (equality before the law), the nineteenth and early twentieth century brought political rights (equality of the franchise), and the early twentieth century onwards, increasing social rights (based on principles of equal access to education, health care, housing, etc.). Rough and ready this may be, but it provides two important insights: a sense that the material equality that we are talking about in discussions of equality and inequality is based on a background set of conditions, or at least assumptions, of political and legal equality; and also, that it is very much a twentieth-century notion, at least in execution.

The high water mark of material equality in the United Kingdom occurred during the 1960s and 1970s,[2] following years of low unemployment, progressive taxation and the expansion of the welfare state. What was as important as the static picture was the prevailing assumption of the day that advanced capitalism had a natural tendency towards greater equality, and most importantly, the perception that greater equality was now hard-wired throughout the society. As Anthony Crosland put it, the ethos of welfare capitalism was markedly different from what had gone before:

> No-one would argue that in the contemporary Welfare State the dominant ideology was one of self-help or aggressive individualism. And even within the business class itself . . . the worship of individualism has given way to a positive cult of team-work and group action. Nor does anyone now much believe in the over-riding rights of private property.[3]

The crises of the 1970s, the neoliberal turn of the 1980s, the events of 1989 and wider global trends have all undermined the society that Crosland perceived and the cause of those who would hope for a more egalitarian society. Four observations seem particularly relevant and inform what follows.

First, the economic crises of the 1970s laid the groundwork for the New Right's argument that too much equality could undermine incentives at the top and bottom and destroy the prospects for economic growth. How much one can attribute the failure of the British economy at that time to excessive equality is evidently contestable, but what is not in question is that the high tax rates of the time have become an emblem of the problem of overzealous egalitarianism.

Secondly, in a way that was particularly marked in Britain and the United States, the politicians of the New Right had the courage of their convictions in taking discretionary action which substantially increased inequality. This was accompanied by a change in the prevailing ethos of their societies such that market individualism did not simply undermine obvious institutions of collectivism such as trade unions, but also seemed to change norms of corporate and other behaviour which had, up to that point, tended to restrain the growth of inequality.[4]

Thirdly, the fall of Communist regimes, while potentially a liberation for European social democrats, had the effect of appearing to bolster the argument that to intervene in the market meant economic stagnation. It is worth pausing on this point, for the events of 1989 cast a long shadow which is insufficiently appreciated. The nightmare of political repression and failed central planning may be a long way from social democratic welfare capitalism but it is taken by some to serve as a warning against egalitarian idealism and excessive interference with the market, and is used as such by the right – with public institutions like the National Health Service equated with failed Soviet-style central planning.

Finally, the increasing globalization of the world economy, particularly the international market for skills and talents, has had a double effect: tending to increase inequality through greater rewards at the top, and at the same time, with the threat of the flight of the talented, making more difficult the notion of constraining inequality within one country. While the Scandinavians, for example, continue to prosper with a more egalitarian society, at the very least in terms of the nature of the debate, the impact of globalization is a real constraint.

In making these four observations I leave aside the balance of responsibility for rising inequality as between exogenous factors – such as the market for top talent – and discretionary action – cuts in tax rates and benefit levels etc. More important for my purposes than attributing responsibility is to portray the state of the current discourse on inequality. In the case of Britain, society has become more individualistic, egalitarian impulses have been seen to have serious dangers, and exogenous factors are driving inequality upwards while militating against tackling it. All of which leads one to ask whether inequality really should matter to progressives today, and if so which aspects of it?

Section 2: Does it matter?

An irony of the decline of inequality as a salient political issue is that it has coincided with an extraordinary renaissance of writing about inequality in the field of political theory. Beginning with John Rawls's *A Theory of Justice* in 1971, the discipline is awash with thinking about different aspects of the issue.[5]

Before proceeding to some of these debates, it is worth spelling out the basis of the progressive, egalitarian impulse. As Amartya Sen has pointed out, the conventional wisdom in political debate is that the left favours equality and the right does not. But in fact the picture is more complex than that. As Sen puts it, 'Ethical plausibility is hard to achieve unless everyone is given equal consideration in some space that is important in the particular theory. . . . It is difficult to see how an ethical theory can have general social plausibility without extending equal consideration to all at *some* level.'[6]

This is significant because it suggests that a contemporary political ideology cannot have moral legitimacy unless in the background it has a commitment to the equal worth of every individual. It is, at some level, a sign of the prevalence of egalitarian intuitions in modern society that all theories must have a commitment to equality in some dimension. Of course, this does not necessarily imply a commitment to material equality. The equality favoured by right-wing libertarians, for example, would involve equal protection for property rights and private behaviour, not, in, any sense, equal material outcomes.

What has distinguished the left historically is its belief, in some form, in a greater commitment to material equality than the right. But the question is why? To reach a satisfactory position regarding the sort of equality we should believe in, if any, we need to understand the ethical and moral underpinnings of this belief. I want to start by examining how we might justify the egalitarian claim that we should worry about the level of inequality of outcome. Later I will examine qualifications of this position which imply a weaker egalitarian claim, but for the purposes of exposing the full set of egalitarian arguments I want to start with the stronger version.

There are two sets of arguments which support a claim that we should worry about unequal outcomes. The first is a set of *procedural* arguments regarding how a particular set of material arrangements has been arrived at. The second is a set of *consequential* arguments about the effects of these unequal outcomes.

The procedural arguments are important because they call into question the notion that everything we earn, or fail to earn, in the marketplace is what we 'deserve'. If we really believed that success or failure in the marketplace was entirely down to our own efforts, it would be harder to make the case that inequality is a problem. Or at least, while it might be possible to say that inequality is problematic, it would be more difficult to justify redistribution. Indeed, it is only on the basis of the idea that market rewards are entirely 'deserved' that the right can credibly run the argument that any redistribution of market outcomes is 'theft' or 'expropriation'.

Of course, effort and hard work play an important role in deter-mining whether people succeed or not. But other factors which are evi-dently not within our control[7] also play a part. In fact there are good reasons for thinking that while ideas of economic efficiency should mean we value the role of markets, our intuitions about desert should make us sceptical that market outcomes are inevitably fair outcomes. There are at least three reasons for thinking this, reasons I call the arguments from unfair beginnings, arbitrary circumstance and public goods.

First, market-determined outcomes in our societies are not based on a fair starting-point. Accidents of brute luck – of birth, circumstance or even talent – play a defining role in the fates that befall people in the marketplace. If you believe that every citizen deserves a fair shot in life, then an interplay in the market based on these arbitrary begin-nings cannot be considered to produce a just outcome. And no serious analyst of the evidence on who succeeds and who fails in our societies can possibly argue with this. Of course, some people succeed despite humble beginnings, but to take one salient fact: those from poorer backgrounds are at least four times less likely to end up in the highest income range than those who are the children of rich parents.[8] It is, of course, not because the children of poor parents are less able, to para-phrase Neil Kinnock,[9] but because they do not benefit from the same starting-point in terms of material and other advantages.

The second procedural argument – that from arbitrary circum-stance – suggests that while it would be foolish to deny that effort does play a significant role in affecting people's market outcomes, it would equally be naive to suggest that there isn't some amount of arbitrari-ness involved in who succeeds and who fails in the marketplace. Michael Walzer cites the example of the author who publishes a book in lean economic times, which sells badly, and then years later, when it is reissued, in more propitious times, it sells very much better.[10] The writer has not become more deserving. He has just gone from being unlucky to lucky. Even more fundamentally, two people might make the same effort, work as hard as each other, but one may succeed and one may fail because of an infinite number of exogenous events: for example, the quality of management running their firm or changes in tastes and fashions. To take a vivid example, the worker at Enron who loses their job and perhaps their pension is no less deserving than the worker at a company run according to the rules and with greater success. Market outcomes have inevitably arbitrary effects which may bear no relation to individual 'desert'.

A third argument, to add to those from unjust beginnings and from arbitrary circumstance is what we might call the argument from public goods. Even having ensured equal starting-points and taken account of arbitrary circumstance, there are reasons for thinking that people's success is not simply due to their own private efforts. Nobody has put it better than Bill Gates Sr, who has written:

> Success is a product of having been born in this country, a place where educa-
> tion and research are subsidized, where there is an orderly market, where the
> private sector reaps enormous benefits from public investment. For someone
> to assert that he or she has grown wealthy in America without the benefit of
> substantial public investment is pure hubris.[11]

A public good is an institution or attribute of society from which nobody can be excluded. Clean air is a public good, so are stable property rights where they make market exchange possible, or good non-tolled roads and national defence. Beyond these public goods are many other forms of public investment on which our society relies, such as free education and health care. For Gates, this serves to establish the idea that private success is built on public institutions – and that hence the individual owes something back to society.

Now, even in the United States and Britain where inequality is among the highest in the industrialized world, our tax and benefit systems redistribute resources so that the inequality of final incomes is significantly lower than original inequality in the marketplace. Implicitly at least, therefore, there is an acceptance, reflected in the institutions of the welfare state, that unadjusted market rewards are not an accurate reflection of desert.

Having established these procedural arguments which might lead us to question certain patterns of inequality, there is a second set of arguments which don't address *how* the inequality arose, but the consequences of it. These provide us with better tools for analysing actually existing societies and working out whether the level of inequality within them matters. I want to cite three different types of argument in this category: what one might call the arguments from relative position, fraternity and spheres of justice.

First, relative position. The left must acknowledge that there is something superficially odd about arguments for equality. Take the United States, the most unequal of the rich democracies. It is fair to say that the standard of living of poor Americans today compares favourably with the average of a hundred years ago. So what are egalitarians complaining about?

This is where self-respect comes in – everything we know suggests people define their own self-worth in life relative to the community and the wealth of the community. So it's not much reassurance to the person struggling on welfare that they may be better off than the average of a hundred years ago, because what they see around them is the wealth of today.

Part of this is psychological. People compare themselves to their fellow citizens. But part of it is not just psychological: it is real. A society is shaped and defined around the position of the majority, and for those left out the effects can be corrosive. For example, if you don't have a car today in America, your ability to lead a full life is restricted since shops and entertainment will often require access to private transport. So poverty and position cannot be treated as absolute concepts but have an important relative component.

The second argument is about fraternity or community. It is increasingly clear in the modern age, for example in the literature on happiness,[12] that higher consumption on its own does not provide fulfilment; a sense of citizenship and community is also important.

And there are strong reasons for thinking it simply isn't possible to have a sense of community when vast inequalities of wealth and income mean that citizens are increasingly segregated in housing, schooling, etc. As Michael Sandel has written, 'The new inequality does not simply prevent the poor from sharing in the fruits of consumption and choosing their ends for themselves; it also leads rich and poor to live increasingly separate ways of life [corrupting the idea of citizenship].'[13]

This matters not simply because we might value a sense of community intrinsically, for its own sake as the above argument implies, but because of the instrumental value of community. As Albert Hirschman argues in *Exit, Voice and Loyalty*,[14] those who are the first to opt out of public institutions are likely to be those who are the most sensitive to quality, as well as being those who can afford to, and hence opting out is likely to lead to a decline in the quality of the institutions. This is quite apart from the effects on taxpayer support for collective institutions, and peer group effects in, for example, schools.

Furthermore, the undermining of community has other effects: as people display less and less concern for others because they have feelings either of great envy or great distance from them, the threat to social order and harmony would seem to increase. It is not simply a coincidence that the US is both the most unequal and most crime-ridden society among advanced democracies. If we want to build societies where there is genuine solidarity and fraternity, it is much harder to do so when there are vast inequalities.

Thirdly, I want to mention the argument against economic inequality which is based on a concern about what it does to other spheres of life – this is essentially Michael Walzer's argument in his book

Spheres of Justice. Within certain limits, Walzer doesn't mind inequalities in people's ability to pay for goods in the marketplace; what he worries about is these market inequalities spilling over to other areas of life where we want other criteria, or 'social meanings', to determine outcomes. For example, in the contest for political office, where we think competence and political argument not money should matter, or in health care, where medical need not resources should be what counts.

While it is possible to see how regulation can mitigate the 'dominance' that Walzer fears in the case of, for example, the contest for political office, we can see how greater inequality could lead, in the above cases, to greater dangers of spillover effects from the economic sphere. Greater inequalities will intensify the use of resources to gain political outcomes and probably make more likely different standards of public service provision depending on income.

So these three arguments point to some of the reasons why we might worry about the consequences of large inequalities for our society. But are these arguments too quick to see the wealthy as a burden to the society, rather than as innovators, entrepreneurs and creators? If there was less inequality in our society, wouldn't we be less prosperous overall, as individual effort and initiative was dulled and stifled?

Importantly, this argument points to the need to ensure proper incentives in our society. Equally it isn't credible to say that Britain couldn't prosper at lower levels of inequality than we have today. Indeed, as I have argued, there are good, self-interested, consequential reasons why it is in everyone's interest to have a less unequal society. To proceed further in this argument, however, I want to examine the question of what sort of equality we should favour.

Section 3: What sort of equality?

Having established some *prima facie* reasons for worrying about high levels of material inequality, I want to mount some philosophical challenges to this position which suggest that our aim should either be a weaker egalitarianism or that egalitarianism is not what we should worry about at all. In turn, I will examine the debate about equality of outcome versus equality of opportunity, the issue of whether it really is egalitarianism that we should care about, or rather the plight of the worst off, and thirdly, the question of 'desert' as it affects our concern for those at the bottom of the income distribution. Having discussed these challenges, I want to argue that a narrow focus on material inequality of outcome is too limited, and that a 'new egalitarianism' needs to be broader in a number of respects: notably that it needs to focus on services as well as wealth and incomes.

One feature of discussions on the left in Britain in the 1990s was an interest in whether equality of outcome or equality of opportunity was the most appropriate philosophical position for progressives.[15] To my knowledge, nobody actually advocated a position of strict equality of outcome; in fact, the argument is better explained as being a debate between those who thought *inequality* of opportunity was the most pervasive source of injustice in our society, and those who saw *inequality* of outcome as more important. Furthermore, the debate was partly about how government could better solve the problems of Conservative Britain: by giving people opportunities to gain a good education, to work and to improve their skills or by redistributing resources to the poor.

In fact, it is pretty clear that both are necessary. And moreover, opportunities and outcomes are inextricably intertwined. Most obviously, one generation's outcome is another generation's opportunity, since parental income deeply defines opportunity. That is perhaps one of the reasons why countries with less inequality of outcome show less of a difference in the performance of children from different social classes.[16] In addition, even intragenerationally, it is hard to argue that a huge difference in outcomes will not materially affect the opportunities that people have. The person with a significant private income who, for the sake of argument, needs to upgrade their skills will have much more opportunity to do so than the person with no income to fall back on.

The equal opportunity advocates are trying to get at something significant, however. They want to suggest that the answer to problems of inequality is not necessarily simply after-the-fact redistribution, but a redistribution of opportunities, through the chance of education for example, before market exchange. This is important – simply compensating people for poverty is not a complete answer to their problems, so tax and benefit redistribution on its own is not enough. Greater opportunities are important as ways in which people can dynamically escape poverty.

Yet, equally, a focus only on equality of opportunity cannot be enough for progressive social democrats in the early twenty-first century. Not simply because of the implications that a commitment to genuine equality of opportunity has for inequality of outcome, but also because of the consequential arguments set out above, which suggest that even if equality of opportunity were compatible with vastly unequal outcomes, we would have good reasons to worry about this pattern of outcomes in itself.

To put it another way, the left should not simply seek meritocracy, the equal opportunity to be unequal, preserving the same rewards but opening them to the talents. If we do that, we will have a more procedurally fair pattern of inequality, but many of the arbitrary features of inequality will not have been removed and, more importantly, the consequential problems of inequality such as lack of self-respect and atomization will not have been solved. Our vision of the good society is one that is both more open to opportunity, and has less inequality.

The second challenge to an emphasis on material equality suggests that what we really care about is not the gap between the poor and the rich, but simply the position of the poor. Known in political philosophy as sufficientarianism,[17] this position says that what really troubles us about our society is poverty not inequality, and that above a particular level which is 'enough' we should have no concern for distributive outcomes. As Richard Arneson, not himself a sufficientarian, puts it, 'Once we have brought someone to the good-enough level, what happens above that level is not a concern of justice. It might be that an acceptable quality of life requires ready access to a functioning car, but it does not matter from the standpoint of justice that I drive a Chevy and you drive a Ferrari.'[18]

What is attractive about sufficientarianism is that it gets at our intuitions about what is morally troubling about the societies we live in: the fact that some people are very badly off in what is generally a rich society. Clearly, defining 'what is enough' requires a benchmark of some kind. The argument from relative position suggests that this level will be defined relative to the society in which we live – for example, at an amount necessary for the full exercise of citizenship. But that implies, as with the British Labour government's child poverty target of 60 per cent of median income, a relative figure. Sufficientarianism, if it is to be plausible, looks as if it has a relative or egalitarian component.

The contribution of sufficientarianism is that it may offer us an ordering of priorities. We are most concerned about the plight of those who are badly off in our society, as sufficientarianism would suggest – the position of the poor relative to the median for example. That is not to suggest that we should stop caring about the overall gap between, say, the richest and poorest, but given economic and political constraints, it may be more urgent to help the poorest relative to the median.

The third potential challenge to a concern about inequality of outcome comes from a worry about the desert of those at the bottom of the income distribution. To put it starkly, those who are poor because they are irresponsible should not, the argument runs, be the object of our concern. Indeed, it would be to perpetuate a different form of inequality to make low-paid working people pay taxes to support those on 'rights without responsibilities' welfare.

This is not an overpowering objection to an egalitarianism which is concerned with outcomes. Egalitarians can be pluralist, in the sense that they do not pretend that egalitarianism is the only value they care about. A welfare system that demands appropriate responsibilities is perfectly compatible with egalitarianism. This obviously opens up a series of questions which need to be discussed about what responsibilities are and are not appropriate. There are strong progressive arguments which suggest that responsibilities need to show a proper balance between the demands of work and those of, for example, caring for children or others. What matters for the purposes of this discussion is that responsibilities are consistent with egalitarianism.

So a 'new egalitarianism' for the twenty-first century should in my view be concerned with outcomes as well as opportunities, can prioritize the position of the worst-off, and can demand appropriate responsibilities. But I also want to add that this new egalitarianism must go beyond a concern with material outcomes, measured in terms of income, in which the debate about inequality is conventionally conducted.

To put this in practical terms, research by the Institute of Fiscal Studies has shown that without the fiscal measures of the Labour government, the Gini coefficient which measures the level of inequality in the society would, instead of being at 34 per cent, have risen to 36 per cent.[19] It is, to my mind, a sign of success that the Labour government has at least prevented rising inequality.

But one needs only to visit a poor community to know that inequality is a much more complex, pervasive phenomenon than that measured by income alone. Indeed, if one thinks of Amartya Sen's 'capabilities' framework,[20] which puts egalitarianism in the context of giving people the real means to take control over their lives, both money and services count.

What does this imply about the tackling of inequality? Inequalities of wealth matter because the absence of an asset base appears to have an independent effect on the life chances of individuals. That is why the UK government has embarked on the Child Trust Fund, a payment to every child, higher for those from low income families, to provide them with a platform of savings from which to start adulthood. But beyond wealth, other factors matter also.

The government's drive to improve public services, particularly for the poorest communities is an essential part of the egalitarian programme. Investment in early years' services, now a central part of the government's agenda, in education and in other social institutions can help prevent the social problems of tomorrow and provide the opportunities that individuals need to prosper. Moreover, these public institutions serve another purpose not captured by narrower measures of inequality; they build social capital, and provide a focus for community life, in areas where atomization and alienation have bred frustration and discontent. A renewed commitment to equality must therefore be broad in its scope – covering not just income and wealth but the building of strong public services, public institutions and opportunities which can fundamentally make a difference to people's lives.

Section 4: Conclusion

So how should the left approach issues of inequality in the coming years? As I have argued, the government is doing much that will help to counter inequality – from its drive to help those in poverty in terms of income to its public service investments. A key to the future is to be clear about the position that progressive social democrats should take on the issue of inequality.

First, we applaud those who do well in the marketplace. But as our tax and benefit system recognizes, those who succeed owe obligations to others both because they have benefited from membership of society, as for example through public goods, and because all of us owe obligations to each other by virtue of our citizenship.

Secondly, inequality has damaging effects on our society and all of us who live within it. If we believe in solidarity, very great levels of inequality make it difficult to call ourselves or create a community. Moreover, the age of deference, in which inequality could coexist with community because 'everyone knew their place', has passed. To sew the bonds of community requires, over time, a less unequal society.

Thirdly, outcomes and opportunities both matter. The two are not in opposition, but are complementary. No sensible progressive today believes in strict equality of outcome, but it is much harder to achieve genuine equality of opportunity with very significant inequalities of outcome, particularly large amounts of poverty at the bottom of the income distribution.

Fourthly, inequality goes far beyond income and wealth and needs to be thought of holistically. It is about services and institutions and the broader fabric of people's lives. That is why the government is right to target all types of inequalities.

Is tackling inequality a majoritarian political project? This is a fundamental question for those seeking to build a political coalition. In my view it is, because the appeal to tackle inequality is not based simply on duty – the obligations we owe to each other – but on both self-interest and enlightened self-interest: the self-interest of those who suffer in different ways from inequality in their daily lives, and the enlightened self-interest of all those who would prefer a society less atomized, less divided, less competitive and more just.

Thirty years ago in *Socialism Now*, Tony Crosland wrote: 'A practising politician in . . . Britain . . . not cerebrating in the monastery cell but living day by day in the thick of things, is not required to answer the stern examiner's question: how much equality ultimately? He has plenty of harsh, specific and unmerited inequalities to combat in the next ten years; and a decade is my timespan not eternity.'[21]

Crosland was right in one sense and wrong in another. The 'blueprint' question – how much equality in the ideal society? – is unanswerable and futile for politicians. But he is wrong about timespan. The arguments practising politicians make today and the way they explain what they do will affect our society for decades to come in ways that should matter to us. When the 1945 government won the arguments about the new welfare state settlement, it locked in a certain type of society for decades to come. The New Labour government in Britain has shifted the argument about the importance of public investment and the need to fund it in a way which is changing the political landscape. Changing the terms in which we discuss inequality will also help to change our society, and secure a progressive legacy, in the decades to come.

3

Inequality in the new knowledge economy

Robert D. Atkinson

An imbalance between rich and poor is the oldest and most fatal ailment of all republics.

Plutarch

While the New Economy has brought renewed growth and dynamism, it has also brought a disturbing increase in economic inequality. Compared to the prior war mass production economy that provided a comparatively egalitarian labour market in which there was robust growth, widely shared, today the US, and a number of other advanced economies, enjoy growth, unevenly shared. Where tens of millions of poor and working families, even ones without much education, were propelled into the ranks of the middle class in the old economy, today we are creating relatively few middle class jobs. Where President John Kennedy could confidently proclaim, 'A rising tide lifts all boats', today a rising tide lifts the yachts much higher than the dinghies. Where a confident welfare state 'leaned into the wind' of the remaining income inequality with tax, spending and regulatory policies, today's conservative policies make existing inequalities worse.

Such growing income inequality has not been confined to the United States, although the US enjoys the dubious distinction of having the highest income inequality among developed nations. As that old economy exhausted itself in the 1980s and early 1990s, most OECD nations experienced a marked increase in income and wealth inequality as protections for workers at the bottom eroded in some nations, as technical change led to both an increased demand for higher skilled jobs and reduced demand for middle skilled jobs, and as robust competition in product and labour markets destroyed old egalitarian practices and expectations. On top of this, fiscal pressures and a growing mistrust of government led many nations to significantly trim the welfare state.

Within the United States, these trends, combined with a systematic set of plutocratic tax and spending policies from the Bush administration, have the potential to take America back to the kind of bifurcated society experienced before the New Deal. The stakes are not small. In his book *The Post-capitalist Society* business management guru Peter Drucker warned that 'there is a danger that the post-capitalist society will become a class society unless service workers attain both income and dignity.'[1] Indeed, the US economy is evolving in the direction in which there are two classes, a prosperous class of knowledge workers and a struggling class of service workers.

While there is considerable agreement among economists over what has happened, there is much less consensus over why inequality has worsened, whether it is a problem and what, if anything, governments should do to address it. Many on the right see growing inequities as actually a spur to growth. Many on the left blame the New Economy's dynamism and competition and pursue a Don Quixote-like effort to resurrect the old economy.

If we are to develop a third way on income inequality it will have to be based in the recognition that the New Economy has brought about fundamental new realities that can't be ignored or reversed. It will require new kinds of pro-competition, pro-innovation policies that foster both greater growth and egalitarianism. But it will also require embracing policies such as more progressive taxation, a higher minimum wage, better skills training efforts, and labour law rules that level the playing field for workers engaging in collective bargaining. In short, we need an agenda that takes both growth and progressiveness seriously.

The growth of income inequality

Before discussing this third way agenda, we need to first examine trends in income equality. While economists use a number of measures to assess changes in inequality, one common measure is to compare the changes in income for groups in different income deciles. For example, the 50–10 ratio compares the income of people in the 50th percentile of income to those in the 10th (the lowest). Likewise, the 90–10 compares the highest quintile to the lowest.

Within the United States the 50–10 gap began to grow significantly in the late 1970s and since the early 1990s has grown only slowly. In contrast, the 90–50 and 90–10 wage gaps have continued to grow since the late 1970s.[2] Because growth was slow and unevenly shared from 1979 to 1997, inflation-adjusted after-tax income declined for the lowest 20 per cent of households, increased just 5 per cent for the middle quintile, but skyrocketed more than 250 per cent for the top 1 per cent of earners.[3] One reason is that the earnings of the very wealthy (the top 0.01 per cent) went from fifty times more than the average worker's income in 1970 to 250 times by 1998. For example, the average compensation of the highest paid chief executives went from around $1.25 million in 1970 to almost $40 million in 1999. This 'winner-take-most' phenomenon has meant that the share of wage and salary income going to the top 10 per cent, 5 per cent and 1 per cent of taxpayers has not been higher since before the Great Depression.[4] As a result, for at least half the population, twenty years of economic growth have produced few gains, in part because over one-third of the total increase in US GDP over this period went to the richest 1 per cent of wage earners. Those lucky enough to be in the small elite group, whether they are chief executives, entertainers, sports figures, attorneys or doctors, have been able to increasingly live 'lifestyles of the rich and famous'. In fact, were the top 5 per cent of earners getting today the same share of national income as they did in 1978 and the economy were the same size, the average worker in America would enjoy earnings of $6,100 more per year.

Growing income inequality is not confined to the United States; most OECD nations have seen increases.[5] Smeeding found that between the mid-1980s and mid-1990s inequality grew significantly in seven of eleven OECD nations.[6] Canada, Finland, Germany, Great Britain, the Netherlands, and Sweden all saw incomes get more unequal.[7] For example, in the United Kingdom the richest 20 per cent earned four times as much in 1977 as the poorest 20 per cent, but seven times as much by 1991.[8] The richest 0.1 per cent of earners did even better, seeing their share of income increasing from around 1 per cent in 1978 to 3.5 per cent in 1998. However, not all nations have seen increases. For example, income shares have remained relatively constant in France.

Not only has the distribution of incomes gone out of kilter, but so has the distribution of jobs, as the share of those with middle income wages has shrunk. Wright and Dwyer found that during the 1990s there was 'strong growth in the top tier of the employment structure, moderately strong at the bottom, and extremely weak growth in the middle'.[9] Of the 15 million full-time jobs added between 1992 and

2000 almost one-third were in the top quintile, only 6 per cent in the middle, and 20 per cent in the lowest. This contrasted significantly with job growth in the 1960s, where the fewest jobs were created in the lowest wage quintile and the most in the highest. However, starting in the 1980s the 'U' shaped pattern of job growth began to replace the prior 'stair-step' pattern, and it became more pronounced after 1992. As a result, during the 1990s the job pattern was one of polarized growth, albeit weighted towards better jobs.

Unfortunately, this pattern has gotten even worse in the 2000s. While the economy lost over 825,000 jobs from 2000 to 2003, 540,300 jobs in the lowest-wage quintile were added, while 451,400 jobs in the middle quintile and 560,800 jobs in the fourth wage quintile were lost. The top two quintiles also lost jobs, 358,000, but considerably fewer.

Great Britain has experienced similar trends. Goos and Manning found that between 1975 and 2000 there was an increase in what they call 'lousy and lovely jobs': the lovely, best paid jobs, mainly in finance and business service sectors, and the lousy, worst paid jobs in occupations such as waiters, porters, shelf-fillers and checkout operators. Together with a decline in the middle-level clerical and skilled manual jobs in manufacturing, both Great Britain and the United States have seen a rising polarization in the quality of jobs and increasing wage inequality.[10]

Apologists for the current structural trends argue that they are simply temporary results of an economic slowdown in the United States. Yet the US Bureau of Labor Statistics forecasts that these trends are likely to continue. Between 2002 and 2012, BLS projects that jobs in the highest two wage quintiles and the lowest wage quintile will grow the fastest, with jobs in the third and fourth quintiles – the working and middle classes – growing much more slowly. Of the thirty-nine occupational categories where BLS predicts a loss of 5,000 or more jobs, only one, sewing machine operators, is in the lowest wage quintile. None is in the highest. In contrast, of the projected fifteen fastest growing occupations, six are in the lowest quintile and three are in the highest. For example, BLS predicts that in 2012 there will be 454,000 more fast food workers making $15,150 and 376,000 more operations managers making $83,590.

Why has income inequality increased?

Scholars have posited a wide range of factors for the increase in inequality. Indeed, there is considerable academic debate over the causes. Because of the complexity of the issue, while there is some consensus on the causes, there is also considerable disagreement as well as some uncertainty as to the complete causes.

Within the United States, some of the growth in the 50–10 ratio, and to a lesser extent the 90–10 ratio, appears to stem from the decline in the real value of the minimum wage, although it does not appear to account for the continued growth in the 90–50 earnings ratio since those making median income are well above the minimum wage. Autor et al. report that a simple regression of the 90–10 log hourly wage gap for the years 1973 to 2003 on the real minimum wage yields an R-squared of 0.71, a strong and positive relationship.[11] While the US Congress regularly raised the minimum wage to keep up with inflation, it reached its peak (in constant dollars) in 1979 and fell 37 per cent during the Reagan and Bush I administrations as the 50–10 and 90–10 ratios increased. In contrast, during the Clinton administration increases in the minimum wage helped it regain some of its lost value and the rise in the 50–10 and 90–10 ratios slowed considerably. This is not to say that other factors did not also play a role in the 1990s. Clearly, the strong labour market and low unemployment rate during the Clinton administration helped raise wages at the bottom of the labour market, just as the weak labour market of the Bush administration has suppressed wages at the bottom and middle of the labour market. Moreover, the higher productivity growth rates of the Clinton administration, particularly the second term, compared to the relatively weak rates of growth of the prior fifteen years made it easier for wages to increase across the board. As Frank Levy notes, 'the fast rate of average wage growth [in the 1950s and 1960s] was a safety net for change. By the time of the 1981 blue-collar recession, this safety net had disappeared.'[12]

The 50–10 and 90–10 gaps widened also because of the increasing wage gap between college educated and non-college educated workers. Since most low wage workers do not have a college degree, an increase in the college premium could contribute to increased income inequality. Starting in the 1980s there was a sharp slowdown in trend growth in college graduates, while the demand for college graduates continued to grow.[13] As a result, while the earnings premium for college graduates relative to high school graduates averaged around 25 per cent during the 1960s and 1970s, it rose steeply in the 1980s, reaching around 50 per cent for the first part of the 1990s and 70 per cent in 2000, and falling to 60 per cent in 2002.[14]

Yet, while the college premium thesis is appealing – it leads to a solution virtually everyone supports, more education – it alone cannot be the cause of the widening gap. If it were, then inequality among college-educated workers would not have increased. Yet from 1974 to 1988 the 90–10 split among college-educated workers grew and then stabilized, while the 90–50 wage gap continued its upward trend. As Auter et al. note, changes in education levels played some role in the growth of 50–10 and 90–10 inequality, but almost no role in the rise of 90–50 inequality.[15]

If the declining minimum wage and the growing college wage premium do not account for this growing gap between the top and the middle (the 90–50 gap), or the significant increase in earnings going to the top 10 per cent, what does account for it? Most economists have looked to explanations involving variables that can be quantified and put into econometric models. One factor they have looked to is the increased use of technology in the economy. This skill-biased technical change argument is intuitively appealing, suggesting that jobs are getting more skilled because of computers and information technology, and therefore demand for skilled workers is going up. However, while technical change appears to be creating higher skill requirements for jobs at the top, it is also leading to a hollowing out of routinized middle wage jobs and an increase in low skill jobs.

Two factors, trade and technology, have helped create a job market that looks like a 'U', with lots of high and low wage jobs and fewer in-between. While trade has lowered prices for consumers, at the same time it has not only put downward pressure on wages in some trade-impacted sectors, but also led to the elimination of some jobs, particularly lower middle and middle wage jobs. The Progressive Policy Institute (PPI) calculates that, since the end of 2000, increased imports and decreased exports have contributed to the loss of more than 830,000 manufacturing jobs, with approximately 70 per cent of these jobs in the second and third wage quintiles.[16] The growing trend of companies to move information-based service jobs to low wage nations such as India will only exacerbate this trend. Of the 3.4 million US jobs Forrester Research projects to be lost due to offshoring by 2015, PPI estimates that only 10,000 will be in the lowest wage quintile; almost two-thirds will be in the middle three quintiles.[17]

Technology plays an even bigger role than trade. Looking back over the last four decades, the growth of manufacturing in the 1960s and 1970s played an important role in the creation of middle wage jobs, while its decline in the 1980s and 1990s led to fewer middle wage jobs.[18] Since the end of 2000, higher productivity in manufacturing has been responsible for the loss of 1.1 million factory jobs, most of them paying middle wages. Job loss from automation is not confined to manufacturing. The rise of the digital economy is leading to a new wave of automation – dramatically reducing jobs in certain industries and occupations, particularly in the 34 million jobs that involve routine processing of information (such as insurance policy processing clerks) or human interactions (for instance, telephone operators). While the increase in service sector jobs in the 1980s helped create middle wage jobs to offset manufacturing jobs lost in that decade, in the 1990s growth in services was more polarized, with service jobs mostly created in high and low wage occupations as the IT revolution helped automate routinized middle wage jobs.[19] For example, this is one reason why the number of travel agent jobs declined by 6,580 in just three years, as more Americans booked their own trips. It's why the Bureau of Labor Statistics predicts that there will be 28,000 fewer telephone operators (average salary $29,340), 57,000 fewer secretaries ($26,390), and 93,000 fewer people in word processing jobs ($27,830) in 2012.

Trade and technology can be a plus since they reduce costs and raise incomes, but they play a role in the increasing polarization of jobs. This is because, as jobs involving routine processing of goods and information are eliminated, two broad occupational areas are expanding. One the one hand the new IT-driven global economy is creating higher wage managerial, professional and technical jobs. Managerial and professional jobs increased as a share of total employment from 22 per cent in 1979 to 28.4 per cent in 1995 and to 34.8 per cent in 2003.[20] In the 1990s, the growth of high tech accounted for over 50 per cent of the increase in jobs paying in the top wage quintile, and business services accounted for approximately another 22 per cent.[21] On the other hand, low wage service jobs in such fields as health care, child care, food preparation and the retail trade are expanding. For example, the occupations with the largest predicted numerical increases over the next decade are cashiers, janitors, retail salespersons and waiters/waitresses, all lower skill, lower wage occupations. In fact, of the ten occupations with the fastest projected wage growth between 2002 and 2012, three are in the top quartile when ranked in median earnings, none are in the second quartile, two are in the third, and five are in the lowest quartile.[22] These jobs are growing in part because they are hard to automate and because many are in non-traded sectors where lower skilled workers in developing nations cannot do the work.

As more people gain high wage and low wage jobs, income inequality can be expected to grow. Goos and Manning find that within the United Kingdom job polarization explains between 33 and 51 per cent of the increase in the log 50–10 differential between 1976 and 1995 and between 54 and 79 per cent of the increase in the 90–50 differential.[23] Similar rates could be expected for the United States.

But even if job polarization is taken into account, it still cannot explain all the changes in income inequality in the US, particularly changes within occupational categories; the fact that the very top-level earners have seen their incomes go up so much; and the fact that wages at the bottom have declined as demand for low wage labour has grown. With regard to the latter, standard neoclassical economic theory suggests that if demand expands, so should price (in this case, wages). There are several reasons why wages at the low end have not increased faster than at the top. First, rapid immigration into the United States, particularly of lower skilled Hispanics, coupled with the rise of global production systems employing wage workers in developing nations has meant that the effective supply of low wage labour has grown. Moreover, the low minimum wage combined with reduced unionization makes it easier for employers to create low wage jobs.

Non-market and institutional changes – changes that are hard to quantify and put into models – appear to have played important roles in explaining top level wage inequality. In the last two decades changing social norms have increasingly legitimized more unequal incomes. When Michael Douglas's character Gordon Gecko proclaimed in the 1980s movie *Wall Street* that 'Greed is good' he was reflecting a changed social ethos that much larger and growing distributions of income were now acceptable, even desirable.

While a new ethos may have legitimized higher income inequality, the erosion of old rules and constraints and the rise of intense competition have been the key driver enabling it. The new economy's intensely competitive markets drive companies to pay more at the top and less at the bottom. The global marketplace means that competitors now contest firms in more markets.[24] Twenty-five years of government deregulation has boosted competition in a host of industries. Ever increasing pressure from securities markets to raise shareholder value has meant that maximizing shareholder value has become the overriding goal of most companies. As Michael Useem observes, in the old economy, 'Managerial capitalism tolerated a host of company objectives besides shareholder value. Investor capitalism does not.'[25]

This heightened competition means that organizations reward workers differently. During the era of managerial capitalism workers were usually paid on the basis of seniority, not on performance or marginal productivity. Moreover, there was little market pressure on companies to force down wages at the bottom, and considerable social pressure not to do so. Most individuals worked their way up organizations and organizations would usually look to within for top management talent, abiding by informal anti-raiding norms.[26]

Indeed, as late as the 1970s it was unusual for mid and upper level executives who were seen as 'company men' to 'jump ship' and go to work for a competitor. Moreover, higher levels of unionization and national, industry-wide bargaining patterns moderated wage differences between and within industries and occupations. Finally, high marginal taxes acted as a break on high salaries, since it was expensive for companies to reward top executives, because they would 'lose' most of it to the government. All these factors acted as brakes on too much inequality.

However, as the New Economy emerged, with its intensely competitive markets and self-interested ethos, companies increasingly sought to cut costs, including wages at the bottom, and the 'market' was willing to bear it. As competition increased, wages became increasingly based on the marginal productivity of workers, with more highly productive and valuable individuals getting higher raises and bonuses. Moreover, what were once internal labour markets became external ones, with companies willing to hunt for the best talent and bid up their compensation to get them.[27] Likewise, as the 'organization man' became replaced by the 'free-agent man', individuals have become much more willing and likely to leave organizations in search of the best deal.[28] Economists Robert Frank and Phillip Cook have termed this the 'winner-take-all' phenomenon. They argue that such winner-take-all (or more accurately 'winner-take-most') markets 'have permeated law, journalism, consulting, medicine, investment banking, corporate management, publishing, design, fashion, and even the hallowed halls of academe'.[29]

Recent trends in one industry – the symphony orchestra industry – illustrate these trends. In the last decade, symphony orchestras have been under considerable competitive pressures, with audiences shrinking, recording contracts drying up, and government and private donations dropping. Because competition has gotten so intense, orchestras have embarked on intense competitive efforts to attract the best top level talent of orchestra executives and conductors. Not surprisingly, their pay has skyrocketed. The head of the Boston Symphony made $349,923 in 2003, while the conductor of New York Philharmonic earned $2.28 million in 2003 for just fourteen weeks worth of work, plus their annual tour. Star performers are increasingly sought in order to attract a shrinking audience, and because of this are able to command a significant premium. (Yo-Yo Ma, for example is said to pull down $65,000 to $70,000 per performance.) At the same time, since overall revenues are stagnant, the wages for the average performer have also stagnated and in some cases declined. The annual salary of the average violist will often not even top what a virtuoso like Yo-Yo Ma might make in one night. Moreover, to make ends meet, some orchestras are implementing staff cutbacks and wage freezes, and increased use of part-time workers. While the orchestra industry represents only a small segment of the US economy, similar patterns can be seen in most US industries.

Is rising inequality a problem?

While most observers across the political spectrum agree that the distribution of income has become more unequal, they don't agree on whether this is a problem or whether anything should be done about it.

Many conservatives blithely ignore rising earnings inequality, in part because they claim that as people move through the labour market, most spend only short periods of time in low wage jobs. Conservative economists Cox and Alm argue that 'annual snapshots of the income distribution might deserve attention if we lived in a caste society, with a rigid class line determining who gets what share of the national income – but we don't live in a caste society.'[30] They cite University of Michigan panel data showing movement. For example, only 5 per cent of individuals in the lowest income quintile in 1975 were there in 1991. However, there are two problems with their logic. First, a considerable portion of the movement of individuals from low wages to higher wages over the course of their lifetime occurs as students or workers in their first jobs gain higher wage work. Even chief executives started out making a lot less. Second, while there is some movement, it's not completely fluid. For example, of the individuals in the highest income quintile in 1975, fully 86 per cent were in the fourth or fifth highest quintile by 1991. This is not to say that there is not some movement of lower income persons into higher income quintiles, or that public policy should not encourage more movement. However, to blithely dismiss the problem of inequality as one that is really only about temporary stops at stages of life is to ignore the significance of the problem.

Conservatives also try to deflect concerns by claiming that while inequality might be unpleasant, it's inevitable. Cox and Alm argue: 'America isn't an egalitarian society. It wasn't designed to be.'[31] But it's absurd to argue as the right does that there are only two choices: a Communist society with perfectly equal distribution, and our capitalist society with whatever distribution happens to be in effect. Of course there are and should be inequalities – high wages reward the acquisition of high skills. The real question is whether they should be as extreme as they are today.

The right says large gaps in income fuel growth as they motivate people to work hard and take risks. They argue that 'in developed nations . . . economies have tended to do better when inequality is higher.'[32] Moreover, they warn that efforts to redistribute incomes may 'undermine economic growth and create an authoritarian government that opposes our freedoms' (such as the freedom to be taxed less).[33] Yet the link between higher levels of inequality and higher levels of economic growth is tenuous at best. If they were linked, why did the US economy grow faster in the 1950s and 1960s, when income inequality was lower, than in the 1980s and 1990s, when it was higher? Why did the economy grow in the 1990s after Bill Clinton restored the top marginal income tax rates back to their higher 1980s levels, lowering after-tax inequality?

Finally, even if inequality spurred growth, there might still be cause to question the high levels in the United States. While there is no doubt that strong economic growth is a precondition for progressive outcomes, it is not always enough. In this regard it's worth comparing Germany and the United States. During the last half of the 1980s and the first half of the 1990s, average incomes went up 15.5 per cent in the United States and just 10.4 per cent in Germany. But looking at median hourly income reveals a different story. US median hourly income actually went down 2 per cent while German median income went up 14.7 per cent. In other words, Germany saw less growth, but a significantly greater number of people benefited from it.

If the right celebrates the new inequity in an almost Panglossian way, many on the left reject the New Economy and its accompanying inequalities and instead try to resurrect the old postwar economy with its greater stability, more equal incomes and more egalitarian policies, even if it means sacrificing growth. The left's focus on stability and equity even at the expense of growth grows out of a long liberal tradition. Within the United States it is perhaps best articulated by the late John Rawls, a Harvard social philosopher. Rawls's influential 1971 book *A Theory of Justice* sought to establish bedrock principles that people could agree would lead to a just society. One of them was the principle of 'original position', where Rawls postulated that we should judge the ethical value of a particular economic arrangement based on no knowledge of our own individual economic or social position. In this position, Rawls argues, a reasonable, moral and self-interested person would support an economy that led to two people getting $1,000 more and that this outcome would be just. What if one person gets $1,000 more and the other only half, $500? Would this be just?

Rawls answers that it would be, since both parties benefited. What if one person gets $1,000 more and the other, nothing. To Rawls, this is an unjust outcome even though society as a whole is $1,000 better off and the allocation of that $1,000 is based on chance. Rawls's philosophy is a cornerstone of liberal democratic thinking and the source of their focus on distribution, for it sees income growth as bad if it leads to inequality.

Robert Reich reflected this philosophical position when he led a discussion with some college students when he was Secretary of Labor in the Clinton administration. He stated:

> I am concerned about the direction that the country is heading with regard to inequality. Let me ask you for a show of hands. Let's assume that I could offer you a deal, and I want to know how many of you would accept [it] . . . 'You have a choice either between the current economy, with all the good news and all the problems it has . . . or I will offer you a deal in which the top fifth of income earners get a 25 percent raise and the bottom fifth get a 10 percent raise.' Now the net result is more inequality than we have today, but everybody is better off . . . How many like that deal? Put up your hands. Have the courage of your convictions. Hands high in the air. This is a learning experiment here. OK. There are twenty-eight. How many of you do not like that deal? That's interesting. Sixty-three.[34]

Sixty-four, if Reich's vote is counted. In other words, even though low income Americans are better off today than they were in 1970, this is not an acceptable outcome because upper income Americans are even richer. Clearly Rawls's first choice, both groups getting the same amount, is the best. However, to reject an economy where everyone gains but where those at the bottom gain less is to lose sight of the fact that the progressive goal should be to raise incomes of the less advantaged. Again, this is not to suggest that the current unequal distribution of incomes and wealth is fair or even necessary – it is not. However, being ambivalent about growth is not the answer.

What should we do?

Many conservatives will say that if we intervene to make society more egalitarian we will only reward laziness and penalize hard work. Many liberals will say that equality is more important than growth, and thereby call for measures, such as trade and other job protections, that would slow growth. In contrast to conservatives, third way centrists believe that high levels of income inequality are a burden on economic growth. We believe, to paraphrase John Kennedy, that a rising tide is needed to lift all boats, but unless everyone has solid boats a rising tide may lift yachts the highest. In contrast to liberals, we believe that a robust growth agenda that supports high levels of market competition is a core component of an agenda to reduce income inequality.

When confronted with a labour market that has become more unequal, the default position of many across the political spectrum is to favour policies to help low wage workers improve. The right attributes income inequality to a lack of motivation and work ethic and suggests that improvements in character would solve the problem. The left argues that institutionalized racism and sexism keeps low wage workers down. All sides agree that more education and skills are the principal tonic for inequality. For example, when recently asked by members of the US Congress what the federal government should do about rising levels of inequality, Federal Reserve Bank Chairman Alan Greenspan counselled more skills, arguing that 'we have not been able to keep up the average skill level of our workforce to match the required increases of increasing technology.'[35] While there is no doubt that increased education is important, particularly in helping people who are now in the middle class move to the growing number of higher wage, higher skill jobs, more education will do little to affect the growing 'U' shaped distribution of the labour market. If the labour market keeps up its bifurcating path into more low and high wage jobs, unless we take other steps, simply providing more education and training for workers will not stop lower paying jobs from growing faster than middle paying ones. While it's true that more education can help an individual move from being a cashier to an accountant, for example, more education will not create relatively more accountant jobs and relatively fewer cashier jobs. In this case, social outcomes are quite different from individual ones.

This is not to say that efforts to boost education and training will not play a role in reducing income inequality or helping individuals move out of poverty, but by itself, it is likely to fall short. To make significant changes we need to adopt two kinds of policies. First, we need policies that work to shift the occupational structure of the economy so that there are relatively more higher skilled jobs and relatively fewer lower skilled jobs. Second, we need to put in place policies that help low wage jobs become more productive and help low wage workers earn more, including more after-tax income.

The first step means embracing what PPI has referred to as a robust growth economics agenda. Growth is important because the historical record suggests that while a rising tide is not always enough to lift all boats, without it, it's hard to lift all boats. This means putting in place an innovation agenda that not only boosts the rate of growth, but shifts the supply of jobs more towards the higher end. Only by building on its strengths in innovation will America be able to maintain its advantage and move into higher value-added work. To do this steps should be taken such as expanding public funds for research, boosting the R&D tax credit, and developing a national IT strategy to accelerate the transformation to a digital economy.[36] It also means policies to ensure robust competition, including global competition, fiscal discipline to keep interest rates low, and a monetary policy that tilts towards keeping unemployment low.

Expanding the number of higher wage, knowledge based jobs and running the economy at full capacity so that labour demand is high will help, but more needs to be done. Policies need to encourage the transformation of routine, lower skilled work into higher skill, more fulfilling work. We need to take Drucker's advice when he argued that 'to make service work productive is the first social priority of the post-capitalist society, in addition to being an economic priority.'[37]

There are two steps governments should take. First, policies should encourage companies to automate low wage jobs. To take one example, if government transportation departments created stronger incentives to use electronic EZ pass systems, most low wage toll-taking jobs would be eliminated within a few years, allowing the workforce to be reduced through attrition or transfer to other transportation jobs. There are a host of other opportunities to automate low-end work. For example, more robust deployment of radio frequency identification devices (RFID) and e-commerce would help automate retail trade jobs. Some have argued that if technological innovation enables a larger share of lower skill jobs to be automated, this will only reduce the demand for low skill workers, reducing their wages as well.[38] However, it is important to note that if more low wage jobs were automated, the occupational mix of the economy would shift towards more skilled and more highly paid jobs, raising incomes for workers. If coupled with better training programmes for workers, this shift would lead to increased economic welfare for workers currently in lower skill, low wage jobs.

One problem holding back automation of low-end jobs is that, because the pay for them is so low, especially within the United States, companies have little economic incentive to substitute capital for labour. This is one reason, as discussed below, why modest increases in the minimum wage make sense. Some might argue that raising the minimum wage would boost unemployment, and they point to Europe as a case in point. However, this confuses microeconomic forces with macro. Overall job creation in an economy is more related to macro-economic policies that affect an economy's demand for products and services. A significant reason for high levels of unemployment in Europe is the fact that unemployment insurance policies are so generous (in amount and tenure) and as such shift considerable consumer demand from the employed to the unemployed. Because workers are consuming less (because of the high unemployment insurance taxes) and because unemployed workers are consuming without producing, many European national economies remain stuck in an equilibrium of high levels of unemployment. In sum, to the extent a higher minimum wage has any labour market effect it is to shift job creation to higher wage work.

Second, workforce policies should encourage companies to remake bad, unskilled, dead-end jobs that cannot be automated into good, skilled and enriched jobs. To do this, companies need to capitalize on what are called economies of depth (such as copier technicians being able to rely on their own expert knowledge and problem solving) and economies of coordination (such as flight attendants, gate agents, baggage handlers and pilots working together to prepare an aircraft for take-off).[39] In other words, companies that now employ workers in low skill work environments need to find ways to enrich these jobs by methods that rely on workers' own knowledge and skills. One way to spur more kinds of high performance work organization efforts like this is to target government training funds at firms and groups of firms that are explicitly seeking to put in place high road strategies. The Blair administration in the UK has taken the lead in this area through its Sector Skills Council Initiative.[40] In the United States, Congress could do this by creating a quasi-public National Skills Corporation to fund industry-based skills partnerships.[41]

At the end of the day, even with automation and work enrichment, there will be still be low wage jobs. This means that even though people are working they may be poor. As a result, we need to take steps to ensure that the folks working in low wage jobs then have the opportunity to do reasonably well economically. Ensuring that workers have a reasonable right to engage in collective bargaining would be one step. Unions are making significant efforts to organize lower wage workers, but current laws and regulations make it more difficult. Raising the minimum wage and then indexing it to inflation would help create a floor under incomes at the lower end of the labour market. Sustaining the earned income tax credit that was expanded under the Clinton administration and is under attack by the Bush administration would ensure that people on low incomes continue to receive important support.

Finally, we need to consider policies that address the fact that even in the face of a growing and more dynamic economy, many of the gains have gone to a small share of top earners. This 'winner-take-most' phenomenon is not likely to change any time soon, as it stems from changed institutional, market and cultural factors.

The right either ignores the issue or offers broad platitudes like 'boost the skills . . . of those workers on lower rungs of the skill ladder.'[42] Even worse, the Bush administration tax cuts for the highest earners is blowing a typhoon at the back of growing inequality. In contrast, many on the left would want to stem growing inequality by attempting to tackle its root causes, such as globalization, immigration, heightened competition and technological innovation. But any attempts to restore the structure of the old, more equitable economy would be to throw the baby out with the bathwater, limiting the key gains that the new economy produces.

There are at least two ways to address this problem without harming economic growth. First, increased shareholder activism might help curb runaway chief executive and top executive compensation, particularly compensation that is not tied closely to corporate performance. For example, many companies are now adopting stock option plans that tie options to the financial performance of the firm. Developing corporate governance reforms that encourage shareholders, particularly large institutional ones, to better tie executive pay to performance can help.

However, even if top executive pay was more closely tied to performance there would still be significant income inequality in the corporate and professional sector. As a result, we need to consider how tax policy can be used to lean into the wind of growing income inequality. In fact, more progressive taxes may be the best and most market-friendly solution to rising inequality. More progressive taxes do not attempt to change the dynamics of the economy, but they do address the results of an economy that in its working produces increased inequality.

As a result, the Bush tax cuts on the top marginal income tax rates, on dividends, capital gains and inheritances should be repealed. In addition, social security taxation should be made more progressive by raising the top cap on wage and salary income on which social security taxes are applied. There should also be a commitment that Americans' after-tax incomes will not grow any more unequal than they were in 2000 before the Bush tax cuts were instituted. This could be done by indexing income tax rates on the top earners to growth in income inequality. To ensure that after-tax inequality gets no worse than it was in 2000, top income tax rates would be increased to 2000 levels. After this, top tax rates would be increased if necessary, up to a fixed rate (such as 50 per cent), to keep after-tax income inequality from getting any worse, but rates on other Americans would be lowered an offsetting amount so that any changes are revenue neutral.[43] As long as the US economy keeps growing, high earners would continue to see their after-tax incomes grow, but at a growth rate no faster than that of all Americans.

Conclusion

George Orwell once stated, 'We of the sinking middle class may sink without further struggles into the working class.' Orwell was wrong then, but for many Americans it is possible that there will be downward pressure on the wages of many workers in the middle, as well as relatively fewer middle jobs. The consequences of an increasingly polarized labour market are not insignificant. For years people have spoken about the American dream of owning a home, doing better than your parents. But this was always more than just doing better, it was a dream about all Americans moving up. Indeed, Bill Clinton captured this when he stated, 'We need a new spirit of community, a sense that we are all in this together, or the American Dream will continue to wither.' If we don't address growing inequality, then indeed the American Dream will wither.

4

Opportunity and life chances: the dynamics of poverty, inequality and exclusion

Robert Walker

Time is not just one of the four dimensions in which life is lived; it shapes people's experiences and their very existence. It is also a lens through which society can be observed and problems clarified. However, it is not long ago that poverty was viewed almost exclusively in the present and conceptualized as static and largely unending. Today, having expanded the time frame over which poverty is observed, it is seen to be dynamic, with spells of poverty beginning and ending and poor people endlessly changing places with others who were once not so poor.

The empirical lessons stemming from this new way of looking at poverty include the realization that many more people experience a shortfall in income than was hitherto thought and the fact that most spells of poverty are comparatively short. Indeed poverty is as likely to be a brief one-off experience as it is to be sustained. Often, though, individuals suffer repeated spells of poverty and, less frequently, at least in post-industrial countries, poverty may be permanent. Arguably, therefore, there are many different kinds of poverty defined in terms of the number, frequency and duration of spells experienced.

Taking a wider time frame also directs attention to the triggers that cause poverty, the factors that bring spells of poverty to an end, and the short and long-term consequences of poverty that shape the life chances of the adults and children affected and impact on society as a whole. The principal implication for policy is that simply making benefit payments is an inadequate, essentially stop-gap, response to poverty.

Being able to view poverty dynamically results from technical advances, notably the generation of longitudinal data and the invention of sophisticated analytic techniques to exploit them. Examples of the former include the linkage of administrative records from one year to the next and the implementation of panel surveys in which the same people are repeatedly interviewed. But the salience of such data also reflects developments in theory that may themselves mirror the social realities of modern life. Of utmost importance is the phenomenon of individualization, that is prioritizing individuals' aspirations over those of the social groups to which they belong, the associated emphasis on achievement rather than status, and the belief that both are by-products of modernization.[1] Freed of traditional constraints of faith, tradition and class, the modern individual is not only able to decide and act on his or her own initiative but is obliged to do so. Each person is expected actively to engage on their own life project, setting personal goals and monitoring their performance. Rather than following in the steps of their forebears and relying on family and community supports, people are required to choose careers, acquire qualifications, change jobs, select partners, choose whether to have children, take out insurance, arrange pensions and, generally, to aspire to financial success.

But while individual agency is prioritized, individual progress is shaped by the interaction of individuals with new secondary institutions that create risk and opportunity in unequal measure; these include markets for goods and labour, the media, and welfare systems. Research that takes explicit account of time and dynamics is beginning to reveal how life outcomes are determined by the distribution of risks and opportunities, and by the institutions and the prior circumstances that serve to expose individuals to risk or protect them, and that equip people to cope and prosper or cause them to slip behind in the modern achievement orientated society.

In this chapter, poverty is not conceptualized as a tangible social phenomenon to be 'identified' by social scientists but, instead, is taken to be a politically unacceptable manifestation of inequality, the bottom end of resource distributions. Therefore trends in inequality are considered first before examining the various forms of poverty and their origins. Finally, certain of the short- and long-term consequences of poverty are investigated before drawing together the implications for policy.

Inequality

Space precludes reporting on all the myriad forms of inequality. Suffice it to consider trends in income distribution as illustrative of broader shifts in social resources. In Britain, inequality in disposable income, the money that households have to spend after payment of benefits and direct taxes, rose markedly in the decade or so to the late 1990s but has since stabilized and possibly begun to reverse.[2] This trend towards greater inequality was shared by around half of the countries in the OECD, with the increase in differentials generally being more marked among people of working age than among old age pensioners.[3] Young people aged between eighteen and twenty-five often lost ground and the position of lone parents and workless families frequently worsened relative to other groups. No country experienced an unambiguous reduction in inequality over this period.

Nevertheless it is important when focusing on inequality to recognize generally rising living standards where these occur. When this is done, it is apparent that real incomes increased across the entire income distribution in fourteen of the twenty OECD countries for which there are data, including Britain, Germany and the United States. Even so, in these three countries the proportionate increase in real incomes experienced by families in the lowest quintile was less than that enjoyed by the top quintile (whereas in Ireland and Denmark, for example, the opposite was true). Indeed, in Britain, in the 1990s, incomes became more equal for 80 per cent of the population, while those of the poorest tenth fell behind, and those of the richest 10 per cent, and of the top 1 per cent in particular, rose markedly. In 2002, the top 1 per cent of individuals received 8 per cent of all household income.[4]

In most OECD countries, increasing inequality can be explained by a combination of three factors: widening wage dispersion; increased worklessness and an associated polarization of employment between work-rich families with more than one worker and work-poor families in which no adult is in paid work.[5] There is, though, debate about the root causes of these processes and the role of globalization. In many countries increased inequality has been associated with deindustrialization, the decline of manufacturing industries relative to the service sector, and a shift in demand away from unskilled workers. Low-level service jobs have fixed or indeed lowered the wage floor, increasing the need for families to have two earners. Welfare retrenchment, however, has not generally been a major factor. Rather, the existence of tax and benefit policies, notably unemployment and family benefits, has meant that, in many countries, the growing inequality in market incomes has not been evident to the same degree in disposable incomes.[6] Indeed the positive redistributive effect of tax and benefit policies generally increased between the mid-1980s and the mid-1990s (the latest period for which comprehensive analysis is available). In Britain this was true of family and unemployment related benefits, although with a redistribution away from working age adults to children and the elderly, while the US and, to a lesser extent, Canada were unusual among OECD countries in that transfers among working age people became less progressive. Thus, during a period in which, according to some, the welfare state was in crisis, its achievements in curtailing growth in inequality were typically increasing.

Focusing on individual dynamics offers a further corrective to the idea of immutable increases in inequality. Although incomes in the lowest deciles fell behind those of other groups in many countries between the 1970s and the 1990s, it does not follow that individuals with low incomes in the first period also lost ground either compared to their contemporaries or relative to earlier or later cohorts. Take, for example, the US, which experienced a substantial increase in inequality between the early 1980s and late 1990s, and Germany, where increases in inequality were much less and declined over time.[7] In both countries, the disposable incomes of persons initially in the lowest decile actually rose faster than that of those who began the period with higher incomes, thus demonstrating the equalizing effects of economic growth (progressivity). However, over time people on downward income trajectories replaced them with even lower incomes. People changing places (re-ranking), which served to increase income inequality, and progressivity both occurred on a larger scale in Germany than in the US, but re-ranking in the US far outweighed progressivity, resulting in the significant increase in inequality reported above.

Unfortunately, similar analyses have yet to be undertaken for the UK. Nevertheless simulation studies of lifetime incomes reveal that the fact of people changing rank in the income distribution means that inequality in lifetime incomes is much less than that observed in any one year. However, further research is required to disentangle 'natural' career progression and the later falls in income associated with planned withdrawal from the labour market from undesirable and potentially avoidable downward mobility.

As far as poverty is concerned, therefore, the economic environment has been inauspicious, with widening income inequality in many countries and, in Britain, only a hint that the process is being reversed. If income growth has benefited some poor people, others initially better off have seen their fortunes substantially reversed.

Patterns of poverty

For convenience, poverty is initially defined relative to median income, adjusted to take account of differences in household composition.

Taking as a threshold 50 per cent of median income, it is evident that in the mid-1990s poverty rates varied markedly between OECD countries (from 4.9 per cent in Finland to 17.1 per cent in the US and 21.9 per cent in Mexico). More surprisingly, perhaps, while poverty before government transfers increased everywhere between the 1980s and the mid to late 1990s, many countries managed to hold post-transfer poverty rates constant and some to improve on them.[8] Britain over this period was conspicuous both in terms of the high level of poverty and the rate of its increase; only in Britain and the Netherlands did poverty rise among all demographic groups. However, between 1998 and 2001 poverty in Britain (defined as 60 per cent of median equivalized household income) fell more than in any other European country except Ireland (while the upward trend in the Netherlands continued).

However, simple head-count rates of poverty only hint at the diversity of poverty within and between countries. To take account, for example, of the poverty gap, the average amount by which the income of poor people falls short of the poverty level: in the mid-1990s this ranged from 12 per cent of the 50 per cent median income poverty standard in Ireland to 42 per cent in Sweden.[9] While the poverty rate may have been almost twice as high in Ireland as in Sweden, poor Swedes were financially more adrift from their non-poor compatriots than their Irish counterparts.

Consider, too, the ratio between the rate of poverty measured annually and the proportion of people who experience poverty at some point over a longer period. The higher this dynamic ratio, the greater the volume of transient poverty; the smaller the ratio, the more poverty is long term or permanent. The US poverty rate is not only comparatively very high, the low dynamic ratio suggests that it is also often long term; given that poverty in the US is also geographically concentrated in urban areas, certain suburbs and in the south, with long-term poverty being experienced predominately by people of colour, it is small wonder that the US was the first country to fear the growth of an underclass of poor people cut off economically and morally from the wider society. Likewise, in Britain, the risk of poverty and the chances of it being long term are comparatively high, but not to the same extent as in the US. Poverty is also comparatively long term in Finland, which has an exceptionally low poverty rate, in Germany and in Portugal. By contrast, spells of poverty in Spain, a high poverty country, Belgium and the Netherlands are relatively short and, as a corollary, the risk of poverty is more widely shared than in other countries.

Of course, it is an oversimplification to think solely in terms of short- and long-term poverty. Many individuals – indeed probably most of those who ever experience poverty – suffer repeated spells of variable frequency and duration. Moreover, there is growing evidence that the temporal pattern of spells shapes different forms of poverty, with different patterns of causation and differing consequences.[10] Rigg and Sefton reveal that over half (52 per cent) of Britons experienced poverty during the decade to 2000 but only 24 per cent of these (or 12 per cent of the population) were continuously poor.[11] Forty-seven per cent were poor more than once, of whom under half escaped poverty for just one year in ten. Eleven per cent of those who suffered poverty seem to have escaped from poverty long term but they were replaced by slightly more whose downward financial trajectory crossed the poverty threshold. Across Europe as a whole, 39 per cent of spells of poverty end within a year, 49 per cent in Belgium, 24 per cent in Portugal and 36 per cent in Britain, but at least a third of people experience a second spell of poverty within five years.[12]

Poverty, then, is very diverse even when defined simply as a shortfall in income.

Triggers and protectors

In Britain, most spells of poverty are triggered by labour market events such as lower wages, unemployment or ceasing work, but changes in household type and health status are also important and may occur simultaneously. (In the US, by contrast, change in the family is the most important immediate cause of poverty since employment is less of a protection against poverty).[13] The incidence of these risks is still closely associated with class and stage in the life cycle, notably less skilled employment, parenthood and retirement.[14]

However, the majority of households can sustain deleterious events without slipping into poverty: 52 per cent of Britons experiencing downward income trajectories during the 1990s succeeded in escaping poverty altogether.[15] Prior circumstances, accessible institutions, individual agency and the timing and nature of the potential triggers are all important in determining poverty outcomes.

In Britain, suffering a fall in benefit income and becoming a lone parent pose the greatest risk of triggering poverty but, even in these circumstances, 69 per cent and 65 per cent respectively of those affected do not experience poverty within the subsequent year.[16] (Because becoming a lone parent is comparatively rare, this trigger accounts for just 3 per cent of all new spells of poverty and 5 per cent of spells lasting for at least three years.) Whether the coincidence of events increases the risk of poverty is as yet unknown, although Jenkins and Rigg report multiple triggers of poverty and qualitative research documents cumulative events that in certain circumstances fuel trajectories from poverty to social exclusion (and vice versa).[17]

The precursors to different kinds of poverty are not identical and vary from country to country. The radar plots in figure 4.1 show the characteristics of people experiencing poverty in the mid-1990s compared to non-poor individuals (who if plotted would have scored 1 on each radial axial). The bigger the polygon, the more poor people differed from the non-poor; they, especially the long-term poor, differed markedly from the non-poor in the US but much less so in Italy. The more irregular the polygon, the more differentiated the risk of poverty. In the US, and to a lesser extent in Britain, lone parents are disproportionately at risk of poverty, in the US especially long-term poverty. This is not so in Italy and not to the same extent in Germany. Worklessness is a risk factor in Britain, Germany and Italy, but low wages in the US mean that employment offers protection there only against long-term poverty. High retirement pensions in Germany succeed in protecting the old better compared with Britain or the US, where those without social insurance are likely to suffer long-term poverty. In Italy, the elderly are actually marginally less at risk of long-term poverty than younger people, possibly because they reside with kin rather than alone.

Insufficient work has yet been done on the factors that protect people confronting a crisis from slipping into poverty. However, welfare provision is an important protector and differences are apparent across Europe. As already noted, cash benefits and transfers reduce the poverty rate but the anti-poverty effectiveness of social transfers varies markedly across countries, where Europe is concerned being lowest in Greece, Italy, Spain and Portugal and highest in Denmark and Sweden.[18] The risk of poverty associated with unemployment is reduced by over 75 per cent in Finland and Denmark and by up to 50 per cent in corporatist countries such as Germany, France and Belgium, whereas in Britain, Italy, Luxembourg and Greece the protection afforded by transfers was less than 10 per cent. Indeed, in the late 1990s an unemployed person in Britain faced a greater chance of being poor than in anywhere else in Europe. British children were similarly more at risk of poverty than most of their continental European peers, partly because family benefits reduced the chances of their being poor by only 20 per cent compared with 50 per cent in Luxembourg and 75 per cent in Denmark. (This pattern may have changed with policy developments in Britain since 1997.)

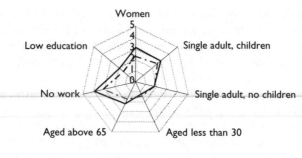

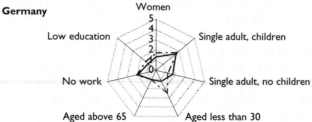

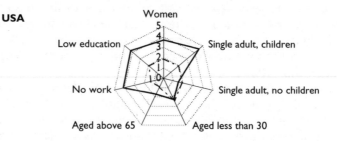

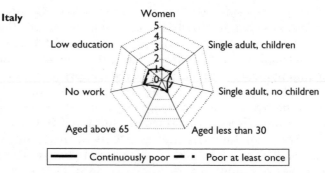

Continuously poor ▬ ▪ Poor at least once

Figure 4.1
Different shapes of poverty: poverty status over three years in the mid-1990s

Source: Based on data from OECD, 'When money is tight: poverty dynamics in OECD countries', *Employment Outlook* (OECD, June 2001), pp. 37–87.

Prior income level and asset holding are also likely to be important protectors and may, in turn, be associated with the stage in the life cycle. So, for example, comparative analysis across member states of the European Union has found that people aged 55–64 can weather life events better than other groups, presumably because of their accumulated assets.[19] Similarly, although a quarter of Britons who become parents or have an additional child suffer a sustained long-term decline in income, most are relatively well-off to start with so that only 30 per cent go on to experience poverty within the subsequent ten years.[20] But the role of individual agency cannot be neglected and may well increase in importance as people are encouraged to supplement state welfare provision. Many people clearly do engage in defensive saving, although the ability to predict rare events such as unemployment is low and studies suggest that, income aside, the key factor discriminating between those who save and those who do not is a predisposition to risk aversion.[21]

It follows that, because the ways in which individuals repeatedly interact with and respond to the social and economic structures that generate and mediate risk, the actual experience of poverty is even more unevenly distributed than the risk events that can precipitate it.

Short-term consequences of poverty

The first response to poverty for those who experience it may be one of disbelief, perhaps even shock. Of course, people are seldom, if ever, aware that their income has fallen below X per cent of median income. They are much more likely to be conscious of the trigger event: separation, the onset of unemployment, or the need to claim for social assistance benefit. Alternatively, they may gradually come to recognize that they can no longer make ends meet. Quite frequently there is denial and a continuance of spending levels, or the occasional failure to resist the temptation to splash out on some luxury.[22] Sometimes people simply do not have the skills to manage on a low budget. For many, the early result of poverty is indebtedness and, as would be expected, those with low incomes have higher arrears of household bills and credit repayments than other families. But much more important than low income as a predictor of arrears is a recent fall in income.[23] Once arrears are acquired, poor families are much less likely to pay them off.

Generally, people rapidly learn the art of financial survival, maximizing the probability of having sufficient resources when needed.

As already noted most spells of poverty are in fact short-lived, while the chances of escaping from poverty are noticeably higher for people of working age. For those who remain poor, circumstances make it imperative that they plan budgets meticulously, set priorities, make lists before collecting welfare benefits, tally up bills while in the store and shop frequently to avoid premature consumption. Experience and stability may make persistent poverty easier to cope with than the repeated dashing of hopes associated with recurrent spells.[24]

Inevitably poverty often means going without. The British evidence points to a hierarchy of priorities, with families with children sacrificing leisure activities and clothing before food and basic consumer durables. Even so, families with incomes in the lowest quintile in 2002 averaged food deprivation scores that were two and a half times the national average and sixteen times those of families in the top quintile.[25] Moreover, it is apparent from across most of Europe that the time spent in poverty increases the risk of material deprivation.[26] Taking a 'comprehensive' measure that includes enforced lack of consumer durables and reduced leisure and arrears, a year of poverty (below 70 per cent of median equivalized disposable income) increases the deprivation score by 49 percentage points, two years by 78 percentage points and three years by 118 percentage points. (Only in Denmark is this association between multiple deprivation and duration of poverty broken.) Moreover, Europeans poor in each of three years in the mid-1990s were 93 per cent more likely to be deprived of basics than other people and 79 per cent more likely to go short on desirables such as a car, telephone or microwave.[27]

However, poverty, even persistent poverty, does not always result in material deprivation. Taking the comprehensive European measure of deprivation discussed above and poverty measured as 70 per cent of equivalized disposable, no more than half of the people in any country who were poor for three years during the mid-1990s were also materially deprived: 47 per cent in Portugal, 42 per cent in Britain, 34 per cent in Germany and 11 per cent in Denmark.[28]

Care is needed in the interpretation of such findings. For example, taking a more severe poverty threshold (60 per cent of equivalized median income) and a more extensive assessment of deprivation suggests that as many as 67 per cent of Britons who were income poor in 2001 were also multiply deprived. Nevertheless, it is clear that low income families can avoid deprivation, although it is less obvious how. Some may be well prepared with financial, material and other assets to draw on: in Britain those who avoid indebtedness tend to be better educated, to have a job, to be in good health, to have fewer children and to own their home.[29] Some may be well embedded in networks of support, both informal and formal; the link between poverty and place is less strong than sometimes thought but there is evidence that some neighbourhoods can be enriching and others, perhaps more evidently in the US than in Europe, corrosive of individual life chances.[30] Yet others on low incomes may, through favourable circumstances, good judgement or luck, adopt coping strategies that are both successful and socially approved. Those who do not may be caught in an economic and social down-draught that leaves them at risk of social exclusion.[31]

Social exclusion

The term social exclusion is not used here simply to describe multiple deprivation, as it sometimes is. Poverty is inherently multidimensional both in its causes and in its consequences. It follows that the score of a person on each dimension of deprivation serves to locate them a multidimensional social space that describes the nature and manifestation of their poverty. It is also possible that each dimension has a dynamic of its own such that changes in a person's scores serve to map a trajectory though different kinds of poverty and, as a goal of progressive policy, into comparative prosperity.[32] It is only for reasons of space that the focus of this chapter is largely restricted to poverty defined in terms of low income.

Social exclusion is here defined as the state in which certain poor people feel obliged to live outside accepted social norms in order to cope with poverty and to survive financially. In this sense, social exclusion is a consequence of poverty, the destination – temporary or permanent – of trajectories that take people into a fourth world, beyond the moral margins of mainstream society, that comprises fraud, prostitution, crime, homelessness, self-harm and other behaviours and circumstances that most people prefer to shun. Defined in this way, the concept of social exclusion shares much of its original French meaning but avoids the judgemental component associated with Social Catholicism. It also gains in precision. The ambiguity associated with the term social exclusion was helpful in keeping the poverty debate alive in Europe during the 1980s and 1990s when the British and German governments refused to utter the 'p' word, but it has hindered analysis and policy formation.

The extent to which poor families engage in illicit coping strategies is not known with precision. That some do is indisputable. The need to support a family leads some people not to declare income to tax or welfare authorities, or to engage in other illegal means of raising income: theft, peddling drugs, prostitution and robbery.[33] People who are financially desperate may also be more vulnerable than most to swindles and fraud or to being drawn into criminal activity. In addition, a proportion will be further burdened by illiteracy, disability, mental illness and/or substance abuse and become trapped in a vicious cycle that demands ever greater coping expertise from people who are the least able to cope.[34] But most benefit recipients, when asked about fraud or abuse that they acknowledge, argue that they had no choice but to cross the moral line.[35] Many, though not all, are self-reflective and some quite anxious about the illegality of their action and also about its possible consequences.[36]

While many forms of criminality and dangerous and anti-social behaviours are statistically associated with poverty and deprivation (for example, youth crime,[37] prostitution,[38] drug use,[39] homelessness,[40] teenage pregnancy[41]), the pattern of causality is often complex and not well understood.[42] Within a choice set shaped by structural factors such as the labour market, neighbourhood, financial, legal and penal systems, people in ostensibly similar circumstances nevertheless respond differently to known triggers, including financial crises, relationship breakdown, opportunity and peer example, in ways that variously reflect family background, education, health status, risk aversion, moral precepts and a multitude of other attributes.

What is clearer is that there is asymmetry on the trajectory to and from social exclusion, with the return journey being altogether more difficult. Trading in drugs brings with it the risk of addiction and then the need to fight dependency. Criminality risks conviction and a criminal record that in turn reduces employment prospects and ratchets up the chance of reoffending.[43] Homelessness is a barrier to employment and even, in some circumstances, a barrier to securing housing.[44] With no choice but to live in the poorest neighbourhoods, the socially excluded are disproportionately likely to suffer as victims of crime and may have access only to negative social capital, social contacts that at best can offer no positive assistance and at worst, reinforce an anti-social lifestyle.[45] In a classic British qualitative study, Kempson et al. found that over a two-year period only eight low income families from an initial twenty-six who were engaging in illicit or socially unacceptable activity managed to 'reform', and that these were replaced by a further thirteen who could see no other way of making ends meet.[46]

Such asymmetry implies that without policy intervention the number of people suffering social inclusion inexorably increases. It also suggests that preventive strategies are likely to be more effective than remedial ones.

Longer-term consequences of poverty

There is mounting quantitative evidence that the effects of poverty are sustained, but less clarity about the processes involved. However, seems likely that these longer-term consequences are affected by the nature and timing of poverty.

The chances of being poor are increased by the experience of having been poor.[47] It is not simply that the prospect of escaping from poverty declines rapidly the longer a person is poor, something that is largely explained by people who are able to leave poverty quickly doing so and leaving behind those who cannot. (The chances of leaving poverty fall most dramatically in Belgium, from 49 per cent in the first year to 25 per cent in the third, and in Britain, from about 36 per cent to 18 per cent over the same period.)[48] Statistical (Markov) models indicate that the simple fact of having been poor significantly increases the probability of being poor, having taken account of factors associated with becoming poor in the first place.[49] Moreover, whereas the risk of becoming poor varies markedly according to a wide range of individual characteristics, the probability of remaining poor varies little between one person and the next. In Britain, it appears to be affected only by the presence of children, by being of Pakistani or Bangladeshi ethnic origin (which both increase the probability of remaining poor), and by having an education to A-level and living in a multi-family household (which reduce it). (This finding is, of course, consistent with the above discussion of asymmetry affecting social exclusion.)

It is not yet clear for how long the increased risk of further poverty persists or what processes are involved, but in Germany poverty has been shown to reduce employment prospects and to increase household dissolution, from which, more contentiously, researchers concluded that 'poverty experiences can be associated with processes of demoralization, depreciation of human capital and with incentive problems'.[50] Some processes of transmission are clearer than others. For example, state, private and occupational pension provision in which benefits are based on some combination of contribution record and past earnings simply reproduce low income acquired in (or out of) the labour market as poverty in old age. But the more subtle processes are not well understood, although there is speculation that the increased risk of poverty may be mediated through the interaction of different dimensions of poverty, including erosion of assets, lack of access to financial products (financial exclusion) and loss of human and social capital.[51]

There is much ignorance, too, about the apparent transmission of disadvantage from parent to child and the scarring effects of child poverty. The persistence of occupational hierarchies across generations has long been well documented,[52] while more recently it has come to be accepted that the effects of childhood poverty are pervasive.[53] Analysis of the British National Child Development Study (NCDS), for example, shows that children experiencing poverty in the 1970s were more likely to suffer psychological malaise in adulthood, to become parents early, to have multiple partners and to suffer low income and/or be unemployed at age 33.[54] Likewise, in the 1990s, young people from low income families left home earlier, achieved less educationally and were more likely to become unemployed than their more affluent peers.[55] US evidence points to the destructive effects of poverty in the first months and years of life and in early adolescence and suggests that long-term poverty has more negative consequences than transient spells.[56]

Cogent stories can be told to explain these patterns.[57] Poverty results in stress, anxiety, depression and feelings of isolation and powerlessness that may all work against successful parenting. Financial strain may erode relationships and the inability to make ends meet may create a sense of personal inadequacy. Conflicts may arise between parents and children, especially if, because of fluctuating income, parents are unable to respond consistently or to engender stable expectations in their offspring.[58] Both children and adults may be unable to participate constructively in the community because of lack of income.[59]

Nevertheless, stories they remain since neither theory nor data are yet strong enough to support them as explanations of the long-term effects of poverty.

Conclusion

While there is much yet to be discovered about the dynamics of inequality and poverty, policy agendas, internationally, are already beginning to respond to new insights. Most important is the shift from so-called passive policies, concerned with the payment of cash benefits, to active ones to support people's escape from poverty. But research findings point to scope for further radical reform and suggest possible strategies, albeit some that need to be supported by further research.

The findings indicate the differentiated nature of poverty, with short spells being far more numerous than long ones and many people experiencing repeated periods of financial hardship. Short spells of poverty may have few long-term consequences (although research is required to determine when this is not so), but it is important to prevent short spells from becoming long ones. To date, many active policies in Britain are triggered only when a person has claimed benefit for a comparatively lengthy period, by which time protective factors such as social and human capital may already have eroded. Indeed, long spells of poverty, though rare, are more common in Britain than elsewhere in Europe, certainly among lone parents but possibly among other groups also. Given evidence of material hardship and of an enhanced risk of social exclusion associated with long-term poverty, especially if geographically concentrated, a priority should be to reduce long-term poverty to at least European levels. Techniques used in the US and elsewhere to identify people vulnerable to long spells of poverty for pre-emptive assistance at the point of an initial benefit claim that are now being investigated in Britain may have a role to play in this.[60] Likewise, given the high probability of people experiencing repeated spells of poverty, it is rational to design active policies that not only help people escape poverty but also provide them with the knowledge, skills and support to remain free from poverty. In this regard, the employment retention and advancement demonstration projects being conducted in Britain (and the US) are important first steps.[61]

Arguably, different forms of poverty warrant different policy responses. To the extent that transient spells indicate temporary departures from otherwise comparatively prosperous life trajectories, incomes and opportunities might be boosted by access to additional bridging funding, perhaps linked to past or future income flows. Recurrent poverty might point to a tenuous attachment to the labour market or to a particular health condition and the need for training or other support to break the cycle of frustrated aspirations. Social exclusion is likely to require a package of measures both before and beyond attempts to increase labour market attachment. A sudden fall in income associated with a life event might necessitate yet other approaches depending on the likely prognosis and whether or not the event was potentially insurable.

Poverty prevention has long been preferred to poverty relief on grounds of social justice, but the research findings above emphasize the practical relevance of this prioritization. As Cappellari and Jenkins note,[62] because 'differences in the probabilities of being poor appear related more to differences in the lengths of time spent out of poverty rather than to differences in the lengths of time spent in poverty', greater leverage can be secured by preventing people ever becoming poor, or returning to poverty if they do, than by attempting to bring existing poverty to an early end. This entails reducing the incidence, and arguably the concentration, of poverty-inducing events and lowering the probability that such events will result in poverty. There is evident scope for this since market poverty in Britain, that existing prior to social transfers, is higher than anywhere in Europe except Ireland, while the proportional reduction achieved by government action is less than in all but the Mediterranean countries of Italy, Greece, Spain and Italy.

However, reducing risk and the consequences of risk is a challenging policy agenda. Evidence on the incidence of events and on the likelihood that they will result in poverty is vital to determining priorities and a preventive strategy, both to ensure that targeting is effective and because government may often be better equipped to influence the consequences of risk rather than the risk itself. Because blows dealt by the labour market are so common, a reduction from one in five to one in six in the number of households suffering poverty when their earnings fall could produce almost a 20 per cent reduction in the total number of poverty spells. On the other hand, although falls in benefit income are rare, two-thirds of single pensioners who are affected in this way suffer poverty, and so protecting benefit income could reduce episodes of poverty among this group by 8 per cent. Even more marked reductions could be achieved if falls in non-benefit, non-labour income could be curtailed since these account for 46 per cent of poverty spells among pensioner couples, 37 per cent among single pensioners and 19 per cent among lone parents (when they are comprised mostly of child support payments). Focusing preventive action on people at risk of long periods of poverty would yield disproportionate benefits in terms of enhanced social welfare and reduced public expenditure, hence the importance of policies to support children, disabled people and those with certain chronic health conditions.

It is not yet clear what a comprehensive risk reduction strategy would look like in terms of a detailed policy specification. Risk is an inherent part of modern life, often positive and sometimes an unavoidable counterpart to opportunity. But equally, dynamic analyses demonstrate that negative risks are very unevenly distributed and the outcome of risk in precipitating poverty even more so. In response, there is a need to extend and complement the first generation of active policies, typified by advisory and counselling services with their emphasis on individual responsibility and activity, to more strategic and collective action designed to lessen risks and their consequences. This is likely in Britain to require the continuation of policies to reduce market inequality and poverty such as enhancement of the minimum wage and tax credits. It could also involve the development of progressive social insurance to cover modern-day risks such as the need for career shifts and fundamental retraining, the loss of a second earner, the requirement to relocate in order to find employment, the costs of relationship breakdown and the outlay incurred to meet the care needs of a relative.

In the context of a flexible labour market characterized by unstable employment, such a strategy might require a shift of focus from individual employability to engage with the activities, responsibilities and needs of employers in the shaping of labour demand. For example, sector-wide skill development programmes might aim to create trajectories of career advancement for people employed on a sequence of short-term contracts. Providing small employers with access to peripatetic human resource management expertise, perhaps via subsidized insurance, could equip them better to manage personnel crises, to implement equal opportunity and diversity policies and to promote employee well-being more generally.

In sum, a comprehensive risk reduction agenda is likely to entail policies to influence the workings of institutions that create risk, continuing advice and support to individuals planning and pursuing their life projects, and novel forms of collective insurance to meet newly emergent risks.

5

Where are the poor?
The changing patterns of
inequality and the impact of
attempts to reduce it

Anne Power

Introduction: urban poverty is a global problem

This chapter focuses specifically on urban poverty and inequality in the developed countries of Europe and America, drawing on work by the author and other urban poverty researchers. In our other studies, we have taken urban neighbourhoods as the basic building blocks of cities, while recognizing that most urban functions are interconnected across wider areas, including whole cities.[1] Most urban residents of all classes attach great importance to their neighbourhood, its social and environmental conditions, its services and community conditions. They pay as much as they can afford to secure as good a neighbourhood as possible, because the inequalities in neighbourhood conditions are recognized as impacting heavily on people's opportunities and difficulties.[2] The chapter sets European and American urban problems within the context of world population pressures and the major threat of climate change, because these worldwide problems are creating new kinds of urban poverty and inequality in the West. The problem of urban inequality in developing countries today follows historic patterns of rural depletion and urban growth in the already urbanized countries, but at a scale that is unprecedented.

Throughout the history of human development, a majority of the world's population, and the poor among them, has been concentrated in the countryside.[3] Within the next few years, for the first time in human history, a majority will live in cities and towns, and concentrations of poverty within them will expand greatly.[4] This urban shift reflects the magnetism of cities as centres of growth, opportunity and prosperity, attracting the ambitious, the young and the energetic into their orbit. It also reflects the impoverishment of rural communities, resulting from overpopulation, agricultural consolidation and environmental damage.[5]

This urban transformation of the globe, with all its consequent pressures on urban inequalities, has accelerated over the last thirty years. Broadly, in 1960 the world population was 3 billion, of which 35 per cent (1 billion) was urban; by 2000 the world population had doubled to 6 billion, of which 50 per cent (3 billion) was urban; by 2030, the growth in world population will have slowed significantly but is projected to reach 8 billion, of which 60 per cent (5 billion) will be urban. Thus, while world population is expected to grow by 30 per cent, the urban population will increase by 70 per cent. Almost all new population growth worldwide, except in Africa, is expected to be urban.[6] Although most of this growth is in the developing world, there will be major impacts on cities all over the developed world, from Vancouver to Berlin to Sydney. Some of these are already acutely felt, in cities like London and Paris.[7]

Urban consequences of the industrial revolution

Since the industrial revolution, cities have grown in a very different way from earlier models of cities, where they were more integrated with the wider environment, more dense and compact, and therefore more internally integrated through limited but shared public space.[8] Extraction, energy demands, mass production, waste creation, contamination and sheer volume were the basis of the new urban wealth, taking what could be taken as cheaply and as fast as possible from the natural environment, and dumping what was not useful without regard for long-term impacts on people or place.[9] The resources the new industrialists drew from elsewhere, the methods they used, the machinery they required and the levels of rubbish, damage and pollution they created were unprecedented.[10] Carbon emissions began to rise seriously under the impact of industrial and urban growth around 1800 and have been on a strong upward trajectory ever since.[11]

The sheer density of the urban population, the size of the indus-trial workforce and the rising birthrate made newer industrial cities and their hinterland far more unmanageable than their urban pre-decessors.[12] A majority of new urban dwellers were poor, but the hope of betterment continued to attract more people to towns in their millions. Nonetheless, poverty became endemic in urban neighbourhoods, initially around new factories in Britain and later in Europe and America.[13] Britain became known as the workshop of the world.

In northern Europe, and particularly Britain, which urbanized on a large scale earlier than anywhere else, poverty and inequality became visibly concentrated in cities over 150 years ago. In the 1830s the death rate actually rose in urban areas, and social reformers and writers like Karl Marx, Friedrich Engels, Charles Dickens, Henry Mayhew and Lord Salisbury recorded the depths of human degrad-ation that became commonplace in urban slums.[14] Northern Europe became predominantly urban over much of the twentieth century, while southern Europe shifted from being mainly rural to over-whelmingly urban in a single generation following the Second World War.[15] Many parts of North America urbanized only in the twentieth century.[16] Thus the domination of urban over rural settlements and urban over rural inequalities in Western developed countries is a rela-tively recent product of our development, offering still visible lessons for the currently urbanizing world.[17]

The growth in wealth and opportunity offered by cities is premised on predatory methods: cheap food from the countryside and cheap raw materials from far-flung places. A vast new supply of resources – energy, land, people, materials and environmental capital (water, trees, space, etc.) – was required to fuel and support urban growth. Every aspect of urban life became quickly dependent on somewhere else: bricks, timber and slates for homes, warehouses and factories; coal, gas and oil for energy to drive industrial pro-duction; watercourses for cleansing, dumping waste and growing food; cheap labour for raw material production, mining and urban services.

Urban development became not only socially but also environ-mentally brutalizing, with poor rural migrants treated as labour fodder, and land, air, water and their products treated as free resources to be taken and used to create a new kind of wealth.[18] Eventually the poisoning of rivers, air pollution and land contamin-ation generated new solutions, but the environment of older indus-trialized cities today is largely a result of this damaging legacy.[19] Cities of the developing world adopt the same model today, with little learnt from two hundred years of urban damage in Europe and America.[20]

One consequence in more developed countries, with their older industrial infrastructure, is that many urban neighbourhoods have become unattractive to people with choice. This puts pressure on better areas and pushes up house prices as people scramble to escape problems. A process of rapid suburbanization developed in response to these pressures over the twentieth century in highly urbanized countries and sifted out more successful, more established households, leaving decayed urban neighbourhoods for new urban migrants, for poorer, lower paid indigenous households, and as a convenient refuge for social misfits and rejects.[21] New migrants arrived from the parts of the world where colonial and trade links had already extracted vast resources at relatively low costs, distorting rural economies in favour of the needs of far-away industrial cities – for food, raw materials, environmental goods and eventually people.[22]

The long-term costs of industrial urban growth and urban sprawl in relation to the obvious gains in wealth have long been undervalued.[23] Today, in the already developed countries, the burden is born by the urban areas and particularly disadvantaged neighbourhoods of concentrated poverty within them – poor, degraded, dislocated and depleted. The multicultural dynamism of successful global cities like London, New York and Paris rides on the back of a deepseated urban polarization, shunting low income, marginal households and newcomers into the least favourable areas, often outside the urban core.[24] Worldwide virtually every small community is now caught up in this urban-industrial production process, no matter how remote they are, how little they get out of it or how 'rural' they appear.[25]

Urban and rural poverty go hand in hand. Urban problems in the developed world parallel acute dislocations and pressures in the developing world. The amount of arable land per head of population is in absolute decline worldwide; loss of tree cover and expanding deserts are leading to acute falls in available water for agriculture in some regions, while causing increasing floods in others;[26] and overuse of energy in developed and rapidly developing nations is a major factor in climate change, causing an increase in natural disasters, particularly in less developed regions, and driving people into cities. These elements combine to increase the numbers of poor people migrating to urban areas. Cities throughout the world are becoming hosts to these 'huddled masses' as onward migration to richer countries becomes common.[27]

New kinds of poverty

The wealthy, industrialized 'old' and 'new' worlds of Europe and North America changed the nature of poverty around new forms of work, new patterns of housing and new mixtures of populations. While urbanization led to unprecedented wealth creation through mass production methods and machines, it also led to deep and lasting cleavages, concentrated in ever more distinct areas of 'multiple deprivation'.[28] Some cities have become more polarized than others, often driven by different welfare systems.[29] But all countries saw the problems of area inequality grow over the late twentieth century.[30] Even where inequalities were minimized by the welfare state, as in Scandinavia and Holland, areas of intense deprivation, distinct from the mainstream, developed and became persistent.[31] The brutal methods of industrialized production, the loss of family links through urban mobility and redevelopment, and the quick-in, quick-out approach to jobs changed social systems out of all recognition.[32]

A common response of northern European countries was to create publicly subsidized new housing areas, targeted at slum families. Originally these were pioneering experiments in model estates or even model towns, funded through philanthropic concern.[33] They were intended to lift their inhabitants out of poverty and slum conditions into thriving, socially progressive communities. Virtually every European country pioneered these new Utopian models of urban reform.[34] But the scale and intensity of urban problems, coupled with the terrible urban damage of major wars in the twentieth century, led to uniform, minimalist, mass produced, large-scale block styles of building flats to cope with appalling neighbourhood conditions. Low income 'social' housing areas over the second half of the twentieth century became distinct, separate, targeted at desperate families and often located far from the original urban centres. In the case of Britain, a major slum clearance programme to create space for 'the new Jerusalem' spanned fifty years, displacing millions of people and blighting run-down urban areas for two or even three generations while the slow process of rebuilding blighted inner cities into large public housing estates took place.[35]

One major consequence of these new forms of urban growth, building on older forms, is conspicuous rejection of these areas by people with money due to severe environmental and social degradation. This above all else fuels polarization within cities, and the suburbanization of urban populations in the more developed cities, reinforcing the expansion of unequal neighbourhood conditions. As a result, the sheer spread of modern cities determines the shape of polarization. A cycle of outer house building, drawing out the better-off, based on the garden city ideal, determines decay within. Sprawl building is now entrenched across the developed world.[36]

Unlike the natural environment that can 'remake itself' over time, the built environment requires constant human intervention to make it good. Resources have not been available on a scale that matches the scale of urban decay. Nor have upgrading programmes been continuous enough to maintain the ageing urban infrastructure. The resulting inequalities are starkly revealed in the English House Condition Survey, showing that residents in neighbourhoods with high proportions of people who are poor experience double the level of environmental disorder and damage compared with the average.[37] We now know that this creates fear and withdrawal, which in turn damages social cohesion, 'community spirit' and essential social supports, particularly for families with children, as we show below.[38]

International migration

The worldwide exodus from the land into urban areas grew steadily until it became a flood over the last three decades, changing the character of urban poverty. It coincided with the rapid mechanization of agriculture in parts of the developing world, the industrialization of many developing countries and the incremental deindustrialization of developed countries.[39] Thus ghettos grew rapidly in American cities after the Second World War; racially and ethnically distinct urban communities in Europe became common during the late twentieth century; and earlier mass industrial poverty in Europe and America became minority urban post-industrial poverty.[40]

Virtually every city in Western Europe, small and large, now has 'third world enclaves' within it, while cities in the developing world, almost without exception, have high cost, supermodern, industrially produced, luxury 'first world' enclaves. In other words, urban inequality is growing as a consequence both of historic urban industrial damage within urbanized countries, and of internal and international migration. The modern internationalized economy drives inequality of both income and area.

The people who have been left behind in the shift from a strong industrial economy to a post-industrial suburbanized society in the West jostle for the poorest urban spaces with former colonial citizens, former rural residents. The oldest, most decayed areas are the cheapest places to get a foothold on the ladder to progress. The cost of repair and improvement to older property far exceeds the capacity of low income households to invest. In any case they are mainly tenants. Landlords of low income households and public landlords have little capacity to maintain or upgrade property that will only bring them low rents anyway.[41]

Mass housing estates

The legacy in Europe of tackling urban slums through mass housing programmes is now infamous. At first the large new publicly subsidized estates – about 20 million homes in northern Europe over the first postwar generation – housed mixed communities of relatively well-paid industrial workers. But they were built as monofunctional dormitory areas for a mass workforce. Over time the large, dense, concrete blocks of flats became hard to manage, hard to maintain and difficult to live in for families with children. Thus public intervention to eradicate slums, through proactive housing policies all over Europe, created the very social ghettos it was trying to avoid. Governments subsidized owner-occupation alongside this increasingly unpopular housing form, to encourage those with resources to move to make room in cheaper, subsidized flats for those in greater need with less choice. An intense process of sifting was set in train.[42]

The pattern of mass-produced public housing made up 33 per cent of all housing in Britain by 1980; between 10 and 20 per cent in other northern European countries; up to 50 per cent in eastern Europe; but less than 1 per cent of all housing in the United States. The US was far more market oriented and its much more limited public housing policy followed an even more polarized pattern than in Europe, largely within inner city areas, where it quickly became seen as ghetto housing.[43] The US offers the most extreme examples in the developed world of concentrated area deprivation and inequality.[44]

The problems of intense overcrowding, unsanitary conditions and lack of welfare in the early phases of industrial urban growth were dramatically displaced in the late twentieth century by the new social problems that came together in the poorest urban neighbourhoods, particularly the mass housing estates. The disappearance of male industrial jobs, which had begun in the great depression of the 1930s but greatly accelerated after the end of the postwar boom, had huge repercussions, creating not just large-scale unemployment but a new social malaise: economic inactivity, male deskilling and the loss of the breadwinner role. The consequences for families were far-reaching.[45] The rapid growth in single-parent families partly arose out of these wider economic changes.[46] An ageing population in Europe led to significant growth in isolated elderly households and the in-migration of extremely poor people from developing countries. Such major demographic changes made the make-up of European cities, particularly the mass housing estates and poor, decayed inner city areas, very different from that of earlier eras.[47] Neighbourhood polarization along sharp social and ethnic lines became far more acute as the fear of crime and violence grew. Some neighbourhood problems intensified as a certain type of 'social unravelling' took place, particularly concentrated in the most disadvantaged areas.[48]

Neighbourhood change in twelve representative areas

Over the last seven years the Centre for Analysis of Social Exclusion at the London School of Economics has been tracking twelve of the poorest neighbourhoods in Britain to understand the drivers of polarization and identify changes for better or worse over time.[49] The high poverty areas are almost exclusively urban. The twelve areas represent different regions and different types of urban decline; two are in east London; two are in cities in the industrial Midlands; two are in the North West; two are in the North East; two are in Yorkshire; one is in South Wales; one is a coastal town. All are suffering acute decline but some are inner, some outer; some have mixed housing; some are almost exclusively commercial estates. Most are in depopulating former industrial regions and cities, but three are in growth areas.

The 284 most deprived areas we identified were mainly clustered together in large poverty concentrations. For example, half the city of Liverpool, a third of Manchester, and nearly half of Hackney, Tower Hamlets and Newham in east London were in giant 'poverty clusters'. The 'poverty clusters' are not dotted around but heavily concentrated in older industrial urban areas, with all the signs of decay, contamination, neglect and environmental damage that we identified earlier in the chapter. The areas house a shifting, often transient and ethnically mixed population. The high turnover reflects the desire for betterment. Poor environments and high crime and decay have made many people want to leave. Half the areas have fast growing concentrations of households belonging to ethnic minorities. The others are in regions of such steep decline that immigrants are not attracted, except through official dispersal programmes for refugees. Because of the extra demands a shifting population and the 'new poverty' have imposed, services are far poorer than average and informal social controls are weaker.[50]

All the areas have been the target of major interventions of one kind or another, in an attempt to address not just the deprivation and unequal conditions, but to contain the disorder and social damage they cause. The spillover effects of inequalities of condition are in fact far-reaching, affecting property values, investment decisions and confidence over far wider areas.[51] The attempts at regeneration had many positive and measurable impacts, but in almost no case did these interventions firmly reverse the unequal conditions. There is high resistance in more affluent, more secure areas to displacing problems and dispersing low income households into their neighbourhoods. This tendency reconcentrates problems continually in the least favoured areas. Most importantly, so far few policy initiatives have seriously engaged with the communities that are being targeted. Attempts to do this are fraught with problems of communication and conflicting perspectives on investment. Two New Labour initiatives, the New Deal for Communities and Sure Start, which both aim to actively engage the community within targeted low income areas, have in practice hit up against the problem of control and decision-making, even though they have generally positive impacts. There is a local desire for small, practical results that help poor families directly, contrasting with a government ambition to transform area conditions through generous levels of spending on large-scale targeted investment.

The special perspective of families

In order to understand at closer hand what is really happening 'under the skin' of these areas and what it is like for residents experiencing the problems directly, we are collecting evidence from four of the twelve areas, two in London, two in the North, by tracking 200 families, talking to them, mainly in their homes, about how neighbourhood conditions affect bringing up children. We are currently interviewing the same families for the sixth time over seven years. Families living in neighbourhoods and discussing their problems give us a particularly intense insight into the problems we have set out thus far. We illustrate our findings with words taken directly from our interviews, mostly mothers as they are invariably 'the most present parent'.

Almost half the families are from a minority background, a majority born abroad, mostly in former British colonies. The white families are a mixture of British, Irish and European, but they are mainly long-standing local residents. Half are lone parent families, with more lone parents among white and Afro-Caribbean than among other minority families. Around ten are refugees from Kurdistan, Kosovo, Brazil, Somalia, Kenya, Sri Lanka and other troubled corners of the globe. Over half the mothers work, a majority part-time. The women's jobs tend to be local and low paid, but most mothers say they like their job, in spite of the pressure it puts on them. They feel it helps their children, not only financially, but in offering a role model for their children's future. Most of the families rent from the council and quite a lot are overcrowded. About 40 per cent want to move out, but in one area in London 70 per cent do.

Looking at the nature and extent of area problems through the eyes of families with children inevitably weights what we learn in favour of women's experience. The mother is almost always our main interviewee. In five cases the father is the main carer. Mothers in most families spend more time on child care and home making, so they generally have stronger links into the local community, spend more time in the home and its surrounds, and have better informed views on local conditions. They use local services more than childless households – schools, doctors, local shops and buses are more critical to women with children than to more mobile households. They need open spaces more because they use the streets, outdoor play areas and parks more, anxious to let their children burn off their energy, grow and socialize. They participate more in community affairs because they are more present within the community where they live and need it more than people without children. Families with children are particularly sensitive to neighbourhood problems, because of their need for security and their vulnerability.

The areas affect families in many negative ways. Often a mother feels that the area is not good for children, does not feel safe and is out of control – at least to some degree.

> The most scary thing is that where I lived before I was in a village, where everyone knew one another. This place is so big here; I have no control over bad company and other things. (Helat)

It certainly doesn't feel family friendly.

> I'm afraid that they'll be hurt, beaten up. I'm worried about them in this area. (Julie)

Even though some mothers like many aspects of the area – friendly neighbours, caring schools and teachers, closeness to jobs and services – most worry for their children's future in the area a lot of the time.

> Now I'm a mother, I'm in the area . . . I feel sometimes there's no future for the children here . . . This is their world and I don't want this to be their world. (Fatima)

Services are often of poor quality, leading to lots of rubbish lying around, empty, boarded-up houses, too little provision for children out of school (particularly older children) and parks without maintenance, facilities or park-keepers.

> There are days when I get up and I feel more positive about the area. But there are days when there is rubbish all on the floor. Usually you see children walking along throwing fireworks and I am with my eight-year-old daughter. I want somewhere nice for my daughter to grow up. (Annie)

Crime and disorder dominate mothers' views of their neighbourhoods. A small number of spectacular crimes generate a huge level of anxiety in mothers.

> Somebody's child was stabbed and killed in East Ham. My son is fourteen, so when he goes out, I tell him not to get involved in fights because I don't want him to get stabbed. It's scary. (Naomi)

This fear applies particularly to drugs and drug related crime, which dominate mothers' fears for their children.

> Round here, they have a lot of crack houses. I don't want it being in my children's faces, so that they think that it's the norm. (Faye)

The high level of physical disorder gives a signal to all residents that no one cares, no one is in control and anything goes.

> The place is neglected, poor quality of everything. Everything here is just the lowest grade – very dirty. (Delilah)

> I think, oh my God it's like another country – scruffy, dirty, like somewhere in India. (Fatima)

In parks and playgrounds, the lack of supervision and poor environmental conditions deter mothers and encourage bullying, aggressive, negative behaviour.

It's not a nice park but we use it. It's got a broken climbing frame which is a death trap because it's got no rails . . . and not proper surfaces, and it's covered in glass . . . last time we went up there, kids were making petrol bombs and throwing them at us. It was two older lads (ten and eleven) getting a younger lad (six or seven) to throw them. . . . I take them because I want them to play with the kids round here. (Becky)

In sharp contrast with these pressing anxieties, the existence of community spirit is extremely important in mothers' eyes. Over 70 per cent feel it matters. Without it, mothers feel unsupported and unconnected with their neighbours. With it, their task as parents is made far easier; they feel more secure and they are happier for their children because there is more social contact and activity.

Community spirit matters because I live here in this atmosphere and environment and it affects me. (Fatima)

You see it if someone's got a problem, people rally round and try and sort it out. (Julie)

There's no community spirit now. People are too frightened to come out. (Linda)

Most mothers feel some kind of identification with their neighbours, local relatives, local schools, churches and other groups. Social contact is the main counter to the negative pressures of area problems. Organizing more activities and creating more attractive meeting places – parks are often cited – would help mothers and also their children.

All the activities are important because it's giving kids opportunities to experience things they might not otherwise experience. Plus they get more of a sense of belonging. (Becky)

Many mothers believe particularly strongly that provision for young people in their teens would greatly reduce neighbourhood problems. This is not something mothers or families can do unaided. As children grow they move away from the family into friendship groups and social activity outside the home. The absence of a positive focus for this peer gathering is a major cause of problems that requires separate examination.

I just see these teenagers looking for something to do then getting involved in mischief which could get out of hand sometimes. (Delilah)

One aspect of community and neighbourhood life that is particularly important to families is race relations. Community spirit was affected by it both positively and negatively. From the negative side long-standing families felt squeezed out and displaced by incoming minority families – particularly in access to housing and school places in more popular schools.

> I mean I'm not racialist, I'm really not, but . . . they've just piled loads of people in here, and pushed US out. . . . I just feel like people are just coming in from everywhere, walking in, and getting their houses, getting the school places, and getting all the help. (Lesley)

This feeling was expressed by black and Asian families as well as white, because of its impact on local community relations.

> There's more African people in the area, and there are more white people going away. I feel bad, because it's like we are chasing them and they don't want to live with us. (Josephine)

> As time goes on, they reduce and the number of black families tend to increase. . . . People keep coming and going, refugees, people from all walks of life . . . it's always new faces to know. (Delilah)

Some minority families experienced severe racial harassment:

> Eggs were thrown at her house, vomit and faeces were left on her doormat, and cigarette butts were put through her letterbox. Throughout all this their elderly neighbour, a white pensioner, proved to be their staunchest supporter. The council finally moved them to another area after the family's door and doormat had been doused in kerosene. (Interviewer)

Others felt more confident as their ethnic group became more dominant.

> My mum's half Indian so she feels at home here. There are a lot of Africans and white people. As an ethnic minority, I felt like an outsider for a long time, but now I feel more settled. (Oni)

Overwhelmingly families wanted to maintain good relations, supported the idea of mixing and thought living in a mixed community was good for their children because they saw the world going in that direction.

> I think it's mainly the older groups finding it hard to mix – for the younger ones it's not such an issue. (Caroline)

> I think most of the time it's OK . . . I think it's more positive because it makes you more flexible and understanding. (Joyce)

Whatever the different families' reactions to the problems they face, the daily struggle to survive local conditions and help their children grow up happy and well dominates all their thinking. Overall the views of the 200 families in our study reflect their strong sense of the unequal conditions they face.

> Why is this place so bad? Is it because it's the East End? West London is a different area completely . . . They have every corner – leisure centres, parks . . . Why can't we have half of what they've got? (Delilah)

Unequal neighbourhoods

Low incomes, poor education and other social problems such as crime exert a strong influence on people's lives, but their very concentration in specific areas reflects area conditions which drive the divisions between urban neighbourhoods. People facing greater obstacles end up in the places which those with choice reject, reinforcing those very handicaps: 'the double handicap of the weak'.[52] Long-run sifting processes have created such areas in cities all over the Western world. Worldwide urbanizing pressures fill the vacuum of low-value space within low income neighbourhoods in more developed cities with migrant workers, turning them into a microcosm of the world's intense demographic, environmental and urban pressures.

Declining neighbourhoods continue to decline under wider pressures to house the poorest, most insecure households. Problems of poverty, ethnic status and social dislocation all combine to make these areas difficult to live in and difficult to manage.[53] The least manageable areas attract the most deprived households. Therefore forms of neighbourhood management based within the actual areas facing such difficulties become a prerequisite of success. The British government is currently adopting this approach in some of its most troubled areas, but we still need mainstream and relatively modest funding for this innovative, hands-on, community-focused method of organizing basic services and enhancing security in poor neighbourhoods.[54]

Only by adopting a more custodial, more regenerative approach to running cities, small area by small area, along the lines of neighbourhood management, will the polarization of the least favoured areas be stemmed. The adherence to ideas of solidarity by diverse families in extreme conditions, in spite of the intense pressures poor neighbourhoods are under, would support continuing intervention by the wider community of cities and government to prevent the extremes of ghetto collapse witnessed in many US cities.[55] Many aspects of public intervention and management originating precisely in the urban problems of the nineteenth century, such as street cleaning and repair, policing, lighting, public health, public baths, parks, housing upgrading and universal education, are the very elements of collective, area-based provision most in need of strengthening today. Neighbourhoods are not just a microcosm of global conditions but are the nexus for addressing problems that seem out of control in this 'runaway world'.[56]

6

The new egalitarianism: economic inequality in the UK

Patrick Diamond and Anthony Giddens

In this chapter we set out the case for a new egalitarianism. Social democrats must revise not only their approach to, but also their conception of equality. It is generally accepted that inequalities of income and wealth have risen in the majority of developed societies since the early 1970s. We focus specifically on poverty and inequality in the UK, drawing on extensive research findings. We hope, however, that the relevance of our discussion extends well beyond Britain.

Countering inequality has been a persistent concern of the left for the last century. Over the past decade it has also emerged as a primary source of division between traditionalists and modernizers on the centre left of British politics. Many on the 'old' left see the modernizers as having abandoned an effective commitment to equality and social justice.

This criticism is not wholly justified, and rests on a series of simplifications. An emphasis on equality of opportunity, it should be made clear, still presumes redistribution of wealth and income. Without such redistribution, one generation's inequality of outcome is the next generation's inequality of opportunity.

Since 1997, as we discuss below, New Labour's policies have in fact made a significant contribution to reducing levels of poverty, especially child and pensioner poverty, and to containing the rise in income inequality. Yet there remain doubts as to whether existing policies are sufficiently far-reaching to have a major impact on long-term trends in economic inequality. 'Economic inequality, refers to inequality between individuals in respect of income, wealth and other factors that directly lead to differences in disposable material resources.'[1]

In the 1980s and early 1990s, under the impact of the Thatcher governments, Britain embraced an Anglo-American model of market capitalism that produced spiralling economic inequalities. Lack of competitiveness, plunging profits and widespread bankruptcies forced a radical restructuring of British industry, leading to three million unemployed and rising wage and income inequalities, reversing postwar trends towards greater equality. Inequality increased hugely in three main ways. First, pre-tax earnings became more unequal than at any time since records began. Second, average direct tax rates were sharply reduced at the top of the earnings distribution but not at the bottom. The UK appears as one of the most unequal of all industrial countries in terms of income distribution.[2]

Today, levels of overall economic inequality, and of persistent poverty and child poverty, remain uncomfortably high in comparison to the majority of European Union countries, and even more generically in comparison to the OECD states as a whole. The UK suffers from high levels of relative poverty, and the poor in Britain are substantially poorer than the worst-off in more equal industrialized societies.

In the opening chapter of this volume, Gøsta Esping-Andersen documents the rise in economic inequality from the 1980s to the late 1990s. A few further salient statistics might be in order. In 1979 the richest tenth of the population received 21 per cent of total disposable income. This figure rose throughout the 1980s and 1990s to reach 29 per cent by 2002–3. More than half this increase was accounted for by the top 1 per cent of income earners – most of it by the top 0.5 per cent. Two-fifths of the total real increase in personal incomes between 1979 and 1999 went to the top 10 per cent of earners. The rise in wealth inequality was even more marked.

The changes at the bottom were equally clear-cut. In 1980 the poorest tenth of the population received roughly 4 per cent of disposable income. By the end of the 1990s this share had fallen by more than a third to just over 3 per cent, where it has remained until recently. The UK has a relatively high proportion of households with no one in work. Relative poverty in 1997 was twice the level it reached in the 1960s, and three times what it had been in the late 1970s. A larger proportion of children in the UK were poor by the mid-1990s than in any other EU country apart from Italy and Spain. The pattern of change over time has not been uniform. In the early 1980s poverty rose against a fixed standard as well as a relative standard. In the following decade, absolute poverty fell while relative poverty continued to rise steeply.

New Labour since 1997

The 1997 government consciously adopted a strategy distinct from its Labour predecessors, including its approach to poverty and inequality. Economic stability and stable economic growth, New Labour argued, are the key to social policy. Moreover, programmes concerned with social justice must be related to issues of economic dynamism and employment creation, an outlook reflected in the extensive use of tax credits that mark Labour's reform model.

Previous Labour governments had foundered in economic crises of one sort or another. Some on the traditional left had imagined a postwar age where more radical measures were adopted to realize the goal of equality. But like most 'golden ages', such a time never existed. Until the current one, Labour governments had been in power for relatively brief periods. Brave talk about social justice had never been much more than that, as fiscal instability constantly derailed Labour's broader ambitions to create a more equal society.

New Labour since 1997 has focused firmly on the poor. The reasoning is that the priority should be to concentrate on the most disadvantaged, rather than worry about overall levels of income inequality. The rich were to be largely left alone: it was far more important to concentrate on raising the floor – improving the economic and social position of the poor both in absolute terms and relative to median income. New Labour sought to break away from the traditional theme of the left that the rich must have become so by exploiting others. Those who are economically successful often bring benefits to wider society as a condition of their drive, initiative or creativity. A prosperous economy requires these qualities; an aspirational society cannot be one in which success is heavily penalized. Controversially, at least on the left, Labour did not raise income tax rates for top income earners, leaving them at a maximum rate of 40 per cent, and significantly lowered capital gains tax rates for entrepreneurs.

In 1999 the government introduced the working families tax credit (WFTC) as a benefit for people in low paid work with children, building on the introduction of the national minimum wage and thereby guaranteeing a minimum income floor of £220 per week for families with a full-time earner. New tax credits to assist with childcare costs (CCTC) have since been set up, and the married couple's allowance has been replaced to facilitate a fully integrated tax and benefits system. A new working tax credit (WTC) extended the principle of the

WFTC to the childless. The pensioner tax credit targets benefit on the poorest pensioners – an important emphasis, because in spite of the looming 'pensions crisis', on average today's older people are doing better than the young.

The government's policy orientation has met with considerable success. Indeed, it could plausibly be argued that this is the first Labour government to actually achieve a significant and sustained measure of redistribution in favour of the poorest. According to 2003 statistics, one and a half million people have been lifted out of poverty since 1997, where 'poverty' is defined as living at a level under 60 per cent of median income. The traditional social democratic goal of improving the relative position of the worst-off in relation to the average remains a crucial objective. The government is on track to reach its target of reducing child poverty by a quarter by the end of the financial year 2005.

Since 1997, absolute poverty has fallen steadily. Levels of employment stand at a historic high of 75 per cent, and rates of unemployment, including long-term unemployment, are low. The number living in poor households has fallen from 13.9 million in 1996–7 to 12.4 million in 2002–3. Median incomes have grown by 2.6 per cent per annum since 1997, compared with 0.7 per cent under John Major, and 2.1 per cent under the Thatcher governments.

Poorer pensioners have also done far better than under previous governments, although the new provision – including new universal payments, the minimum income guarantee, a new tax credit and the new 'second state' pension, all on top of the basic state pension – is highly complex and might usefully be simplified. Some experts also question its sustainability for the future.

However, several core weaknesses remain in the architecture of welfare state modernization and social policy enacted by New Labour since 1997.

One area concerns the strains that have emerged at the local community level in the UK. Even in the most deprived areas, more families have at least one member in work than was the case in 1997, and support for children, and the performance of children at school, is improving dramatically. But the community space that these families inhabit too often remains blighted. Official statistics suggest, for example, that 42 per cent of all burglaries happen to 1 per cent of all homes, principally those belonging to the poor and to single parents. For all the action zone policies and strategic partnerships, too many of the worst estates and most deprived communities in Britain remain largely unchanged – bleak ghettos depressing the spirit of those who live in them, dominated by fear of crime and by racial tension, including areas of real fear and desperation.

Governments in the future will need to be far bolder in tackling neighbourhood renewal, and in reshaping the future of social housing, if they are to succeed in limiting the social exclusion that arises from concentrated disadvantage, as Anne Power argues. The same remains true of health inequalities, as Richard Wilkinson shows in this volume.

Egalitarianism – old and new

In the discussion that follows, we focus on economic inequality, especially inequality of income and wealth. The new egalitarianism has to reach out more extensively, however, covering the various dimensions of inequality discussed by other authors in this book. The priority is to invest in human and cognitive capacities that promote individual opportunity, rather than in reparation after the event.

We need a new egalitarianism for several reasons. First, Labour has made no commitment to the pursuit of egalitarian goals remotely comparable to its emphasis on the revitalization of Britain's public services. It is time that it did so. Increasing economic equality is as necessary for rebuilding solidarity as are effective public services.

Second, it is true that Labour's policies since 1997 have not only had a significant impact on poverty, they have also brought to an end the persistent rise in income inequality that has occurred since the early 1980s. The incomes of the bottom 10 per cent of earners grew by an average of 2.8 per cent each year in real terms from 1996–7 to 2002–3. This compares to 2.6 per cent growth among the top 10 per cent. But, as mentioned earlier, there are still serious reservations about how far existing policies will reduce inequalities further.

Moreover, the government has been haphazard in its approach to reducing poverty and curbing inequality. There have been many policies introduced to counter poverty, but there have been *so* many it is difficult to see the wood for the trees. Even policy experts have a hard time assessing what it all adds up to. More integration is surely required.

Finally, there are reasons to be cautious about the guiding metaphor used by New Labour to orient its efforts to pursue social justice: the concept of social exclusion. We discuss this point further below.

In our view, the contemporary left needs to develop a dynamic, life-chances approach to equality, but outcomes and opportunities are of course closely connected. It is hard to envisage a more mobile, dynamic society where individuals have greater respect for each other in the context of an ever increasing income gap between rich and poor. There are still important distinctions between these egalitarian commitments, however. We can distinguish between egalitarianism as it used to be understood, the egalitarianism of the traditional left, and the new egalitarianism, in the following ways.

(1) Old egalitarianism treated economic dynamism as incidental to its basic concern with economic security and redistribution. New egalitarianism holds that expanding the productive efficiency of the economy is necessary for governments to have a long-term impact on the distribution of income and wealth. Social democrats such as Anthony Crosland in *The Future of Socialism* recognized this fact, but his writings lacked a coherent economic theory of the mixed economy, as growth was largely taken for granted in Britain during the late 1950s.[3]

The Thatcherites – quite rightly – placed competitiveness and the generation of wealth at the forefront of their philosophy. The left should never have surrendered this ground. The new egalitarianism posits enhanced economic efficiency created by a flexible and dynamic economy as the necessary precondition for future redistribution. Economic dynamism and fairness must go hand in hand.

(2) Old egalitarianism was concerned with removing class distinctions, and the pursuit of equality of status. New egalitarianism is about equalizing life chances across the generations by levelling up more than levelling down, in the context of a far more diverse society than existed in the past. Since 1945, the British class structure and social stratification has grown more complex as a consequence of occupational changes. The traditional sociological conception of a society marked by a rigid class hierarchy looks less plausible than it did. The large-scale entry of women into the labour force and the rise of mass consumerism have also disrupted earlier patterns of class affiliation. The 'standard' postwar family is in rapid decline, superseded by a plurality of household formations with greater instability and fragility. Dual earner and lone parent households are increasingly polarized. Child poverty in Britain drops to 3 per cent where both the mother and the father work. Lone parents, on the other hand, face a considerable risk of falling into poverty,

and sole breadwinner families with a low skilled earner are losing ground.[4]

(3) Old egalitarianism held that social justice could be achieved within the boundaries of the nation-state, and that support for its reforms would come by forging a national coalition based on class solidarity. The new egalitarianism recognizes the impact of globalizing influences, and accepts that there may be a trade-off between support for ethnic and cultural diversity and the social solidarity necessary for strong welfare states.

There is no irreducible conflict between the core social democratic values of solidarity and diversity, as David Goodhart demonstrates in this volume. However, we do need a renewed focus on integration, finding ways to incorporate newcomers and constructing forms of national identity that sustain social solidarity. These tensions relate to the clash in contemporary societies between the cosmopolitan middle class, who tend to benefit from the 'new economy', and those who lack the basic skills and qualifications to advance up the economic ladder.

(4) Old egalitarianism was inclined to treat rights as unconditional claims. New egalitarianism ties rights to corresponding responsibilities. The new egalitarianism thus introduces two elements of conditionality into the means-tested welfare system. Benefits depend not only on a person's means but also on his or her behaviour. For example, failure to accept one of the New Deal options leads to deductions in benefit. It is worth considering the case for a wider range of conditional rights in the welfare state, such as withdrawing child benefit from the uncooperative parents of truants, or reducing housing benefit to unruly tenants.

(5) The new egalitarianism focuses primarily on widening opportunities rather than traditional income redistribution – equality of outcome – *per se*. Yet to a large extent, as we have argued, one reinforces the other. The left's traditional distributive goals should be pursued not only through income distribution or solidaristic wage policies, but through more concerted action to change the initial distribution of assets and productive endowments.

A purely meritocratic model would be not only impractical but also incoherent. Impractical, because most social mobility is, and is likely to remain, structural – brought about by shifts in the occupational structure. A high level of 'exchange mobility' where many individuals exchange positions over time would in all probability be socially destructive. No society could cope easily with large degrees of downward mobility that promote widespread feelings of disaffection or despair.

This scepticism as to the virtues of a meritocratic society stretches back to the British tradition of ethical liberalism propounded by T. H. Green, R. H. Tawney and Leonard Hobhouse.

Pure meritocracy is incoherent because, without redistribution, one generation's successful individuals would become the next generation's embedded caste, hoarding the wealth they had accumulated. Social justice demands that high incomes and large concentrations of wealth be spread more widely, in order to recognize the contribution made by all sections of the community. The new egalitarianism should have more modest, and realistic, ambitions however – to redistribute the balance of opportunities and life chances in favour of those lower down the social scale, while narrowing the gap between rich and poor through high, universal social standards.

The new egalitarianism embraces the 'New Labour approach', but seeks to extend, entrench and deepen it. Further progress will not be achieved simply by consolidating existing tax, welfare state and labour market reforms. Work and employment, however, must continue to be central. Promoting high levels of employment, above the floor of a minimum wage, has proved a largely successful strategy. The UK currently has three-quarters of the adult population in jobs. The EU Lisbon Strategy published in 1999 aims to achieve an average employment level of 70 per cent by 2015 in the EU.[5] At present, the average lags well behind the target of 64 per cent. The emphasis on labour market flexibility, far from betraying the ideal of social justice, has directly contributed to furthering it. Full employment is fundamental to social justice, and paid labour remains the most effective route out of poverty.

Policy considerations: a new egalitarian strategy?

A new egalitarianism should be ideologically driven: in other words, open and explicit in its commitment. The authors of a recent report by the Institute for Public Policy Research, *State of the Nation*, accept that Labour since 1997 has successfully reduced levels of poverty. They go on to observe that 'there is a strong sense that Labour's reform programme is incomplete and vulnerable to challenge', as well as 'lacking in vision'.[6] The assessment is a valid one.

But what could such a vision be? The IPPR study does not say. Here we can draw usefully on the writings of reformist social democrats from the continent. The German political scientist Wolfgang Merkel has listed five priorities of social justice in postmodern social conditions:[7]

1   The fight against poverty – not just because of economic inequality itself, but on the grounds that poverty (above all enduring poverty) limits the individual's capacity for autonomy and self-esteem.
2   Creating the highest possible standards of education and training, rooted in equal and fair access for all.
3   Ensuring employment for all those who are willing and able.
4   A welfare state that provides protection and dignity.
5   Limiting inequalities of income and wealth if they hinder the realization of the first four goals or endanger the cohesion of society.

The devil is always in the detail. But this formula provides a sound ideological basis for the new egalitarianism. It is simple and luminous. It recognizes that equality of opportunity must take precedence in a differentiated society, against the backdrop of current economic imperatives. It also makes it clear that reducing child poverty is absolutely crucial. The higher the proportion of those who suffer poverty as children, the more likely it is that all five goals will be compromised. In one recent study, cognitive development tests sat by children at the age of twenty-two months were found to serve as accurate predictors of educational attainment by age twenty-six. The test results were related to the socioeconomic status of the child's family, and it was found that children from more disadvantaged families scored lower than their counterparts from wealthy families.[8]

There are still, of course, major difficulties in living up to this vision. The dramatic growth in income inequality since the late 1970s in the UK won't be reversed overnight, nor will the deeply entrenched problems of poorer urban areas. Inevitably, much of the progress made since 1997 has been achieved by plucking the 'low hanging fruit'. The success of the government's employment policy has resulted in a tight labour market in much of Britain that is advantageous to the economic bargaining power of the lowest skilled. The real challenge is to make significant progress with the 'hardest to reach', including the long-term unemployed, disabled people and some ethnic minority groups.

Moreover, certain structural trends are difficult to counteract. For example, key factors driving the widening dispersion of earnings, such as increasing returns to educational qualifications, are arguably intensifying rather than weakening as the spread of the knowledge economy takes hold. This is one driving force behind renewed inequalities in OECD countries as less skilled workers experience declining real wages, and inequalities in pre-tax household incomes rise sharply.[9] The challenge is to attack the roots of such inequalities, implying a two-pronged strategy biased towards high-risk households with the aim of equalizing the acquisition of educational and social capital.

Labour developed its initial approach to social policy during the 1990s. Initiatives such as tax credits were borrowed from the US Democrats. They have, by and large, been successful. But have we reached the limits of their usefulness? Tax credits have imposed a complicated means-testing infrastructure on the social security system, leading to a higher than anticipated rate of non take-up among eligible claimants. Moreover, tax credits for working people as a long-term approach to labour market participation merely transfer dependency from 'out of work' to 'in work' benefits. A family income raised by £40–50 a week is welcome, but it is not a fundamental life change.[10] Too few families on tax credits believe that they have much prospect of further improving their lives, and low aspirations are often transmitted to children, reflected in their low educational achievements.

Social exclusion as a concept refers not to gradations of income, but mechanisms that act to detach groups of people from the mainstream. Many on the more traditional left have attacked the notion as substituting an anodyne, and therefore more politically palatable, notion for poverty. This sort of criticism does not hold much water. 'Social exclusion' is not a category that was invented by New Labour, but by academic sociologists who pointed out that poverty does not capture the range of deprivations that prevent individuals from engaging fully in the wider society around them. Economic deprivation is only one form that concentrated underprivilege can assume.

The real limitations of the notion lie in its limited applicability. At the time when it was coined, social exclusion was thought by many to characterize the position of an underclass, 5 to 10 per cent of the population, effectively cut off from mainstream society. Labour was guided by this conception in formulating its earlier policies.

Recent research shows conclusively, however, that there is no underclass in European societies, though the position in the United States might well be different. One study reported by the UK government's Strategy Unit looked at four measures of social exclusion, covering people who (1) are not in employment, education or training; (2) have low income (below 60 per cent of the median); (3) have low levels of social interaction; and (4) perceive that they live in an area marked by high crime, vandalism or material dilapidation. Less than 1 per cent of the UK's population is excluded on all four of these measures.[11] This finding does not mean, of course, that multiple deprivation does not exist. It does imply that it tends to be concentrated in pockets, specific streets and neighbourhoods, rather than affecting a whole 'class' of people.

There are some further important considerations relevant to this issue, concerning the dynamics of poverty and inequality. For many years, our understanding of poverty was based on a static, snapshot picture of deprivation. We simply didn't have evidence of how people's lives change over time. As a result of the accumulation of longitudinal data panel studies, we now do. Robert Walker's contribution analyses some of the implications of a dynamic approach to poverty and inequality – and very important those implications are. The prevalence of poverty in the UK, and the other industrialized countries too, is far more widespread than we used to think. Yet, for the large majority, poverty is a transitory phenomenon – most people experience only relatively short spells.

Such findings indicate that rather than simply being preoccupied with social exclusion, we should be looking at how to prevent those at risk of falling into poverty from doing so. This approach may involve active labour market intervention. In the UK, a major problem is the 'carousel effect'. People repeatedly leave poverty, but for short spells, returning later. It is not sufficient simply to get individuals into the labour market. We must seek to ensure that they remain in work and get the opportunity for career progression, not just a job *per se*.

The transition from an industrial to a service or knowledge based economy creates a disproportionate number of skilled occupations. About two-thirds of the jobs created in the service economy are skilled jobs, 'lovely jobs'. However, a third are low skill, routine service occupations, 'lousy jobs' – for example, at the supermarket checkout, or as a petrol station attendant. These occupations are often insecure and poorly paid, offering little or no prospect of career advancement. The implications for widening inequality in the wage and income distribution are considerable.

Active labour market intervention may be part of the answer but so, intriguingly, might automation, as Kenneth Atkinson suggests.

Automation is ordinarily treated as part of random technological advance, but perhaps it could also be guided politically to increase the supply of stable, decently paid jobs. Of course, as Gøsta Esping-Andersen argues, the key question remains not whether an economy is replete with 'lousy jobs', an inevitable feature of a dynamic service economy, but whether citizens can be assured of realistic mobility chances. US and UK data suggest that deregulated, flexible labour markets do not necessarily promote greater mobility; indeed, it often happens to the contrary.[12]

New Labour's policy approach has been concentrated on the poor. What about those at the top? A mass of information is available on the poor and underprivileged. We have surprisingly little reliable information about high earning professionals, and even less about the tiny minority of the rich. Yet the strategies of the affluent in gaining concentrated access to the best housing, health and education plainly affect the life chances of poorer groups.

A fairer society cannot be built from the bottom up alone. This consideration raises the crucial issue of how the overall community itself can be sustained in the face of market-driven economic inequalities.[13] The centre left has long been concerned with the social fragmentation that arises as a consequence of Thatcherite economics and the concentration of wealth. New Labour is understandably wary of antagonizing those sectors of society where it drew supporters it had not had before. But others have argued the case for raising income tax rates to 50 per cent for those earning more than £100,000 a year.

Is this the way forward? We do not think so, for a mixture of economic and political reasons. Such a policy would probably yield an extra £3.5 billion a year in revenue, not the £5 billion that is sometimes claimed. This sum is small beer compared to the total level of government expenditure. Moreover, such a policy could rebound electorally, since it could be attacked precisely as penalizing success. A concerted strategy that addresses 'social exclusion at the top' is required nonetheless. A far more effective approach would concentrate on citizenship obligations, and the reinvigoration of the public good, using a mixture of regulation and positive incentives. Legal tax avoidance schemes for the rich, for example, cost the Exchequer far more than would come from raising top-level rates of income tax.

The top 1 per cent, and even more so the top 0.5 per cent, of individuals have pulled away more sharply from the rest in the UK than in other European societies. This fact is almost certainly related to the aggressive nature of Anglo-American corporate practices, since similar trends have occurred in the United States since the late 1970s. There are many issues here, and we cannot analyse them all in the context of this chapter. However, further encouragement of share-holder activism, and other measures to promote corporate responsi-bility and corporate citizenship might begin to redress this balance. The Treasury has recently begun to clamp down far more forcefully than before on tax avoidance and tax evasion, with some measure of success. The process should continue. We should also pursue fiscal incentives in a more thoroughgoing way to encourage philanthropy, charitable giving and responsible corporate behaviour. But there is also a case for taxing capital transfers, as discussed later in this chapter.

Policy proposals

A realistic centre-left approach requires a new story about social justice that takes account of economic realities and public opinion, while connecting it to a coherent vision of the good society. What about specific policies?

The proposals listed here would not stand alone. The dominant idea uniting these themes is customized, individually tailored measures that carefully identify target groups and objectives: a social investment state. Active welfare replaces the 'one size fits all' postwar welfare state predicated on a stable, mass production industrial economy. The new welfare system is designed to sustain each individual throughout life, concentrating its efforts wherever empirical evidence shows that persistent clusters of economic and social disadvantage are being gen-erated. It makes careful use of the main instruments at the disposal of governments to reduce poverty and inequality. The distribution of income and wealth depends not merely on fiscal redistribution and education, but on economic institutions, and indeed the choices that individuals make themselves.

The policy toolkit has developed rapidly in recent years, from in-work benefits to SureStart centres and 'baby-bonds'; more systemic shifts have been urged by advocates of 'stakeholder capitalism'. We would include the following ten areas in this discussion, with the fol-lowing aims for action.

(1) Place a continuing premium on job opportunities, with routes to career progression, and springboards to further decently paid and stable jobs. This endeavour requires governments to foster

intermediate labour markets, including more public sector jobs programmes, the expansion of Employer Training Pilots, the extension
of the 'Ambition' programme giving skilled individuals access to
jobs above 'entry level' with structured training, and widening the
availability of modern apprenticeships, including adult apprenticeships.

(2) Widen access to lifelong training and education. The UK government should extend adult entitlements to free tuition and training at
level 2, 3, and 4 in underperforming areas, tackling regional inequalities in educational qualifications. Serious investment in early years
education – as the basis for lifelong learning – has at long last been
embraced. The challenge for governments is to create a universal
under-fives service with responsibility shared between the state,
employers and individuals for every child between three and five years
old. But participation of women in the labour force also depends
on families having day-care options for children between one and
three years old, though the fiscal implications are considerable. For
example, expenditure on child-care provision in the fifth of neighbourhoods that are the most deprived, and related services, currently
amounts to 0.5 per cent of GDP in the UK. In Sweden, the universal
early years infrastructure costs approximately 2.5 per cent of GDP.
To meet these ambitions without raising taxes or introducing extensive charges, Britain would need to radically shift the balance of public
expenditure away from present priorities to address the needs of
children and families.

(3) Transform the public sector housing mix, identifying new mechanisms to restore social cohesion and control on chaotic estates. This
approach would attach greater conditionality to the availability of
social housing. It would ensure that tenants previously evicted from
local authority properties agreed to a behavioural contract and attendance at regular interviews, subject to sanctions if they persistently
infringed agreed rules. Public agencies must be wary, however, of
intensifying the polarization between 'respectable' and 'sink' estates.

(4) Invest in social capital – the civic leadership of poorer communities
as much as their physical capital – while providing further ladders of
opportunity to strengthen 'welfare to work' and career progression
objectives. The opportunity to participate in volunteering should be
extended radically, and the chance for local people to be involved
directly in the governance of public projects – pioneered, for example,
by the SureStart programme – could be expanded to other spheres of

neighbourhood provision such as the police, parks and local transport. This also helps to forge renewed bonds of citizenship, facilitating deeper social integration.

(5) Switch the focus of investment from ameliorating symptoms towards preventative programmes that have an impact on the underlying causes of poverty and deprivation, and block the slide into precarious and poorly paid employment. Key groups that should be targeted include those in low skilled, casual contract jobs with weak literacy and numeracy skills; offenders and ex-offenders who are returning from prison; and young people who leave school with no formal educational qualifications, and weak social and cognitive skills. This approach requires preventative screening programmes to be embedded in Jobcentreplus, the Prison Service, and in cooperation with employers, for example through the Employer Training Pilot initiative.

(6) Expand initiatives that tackle inequalities in the utilization of public services. This point follows from Julian Le Grand's substitution theory, where higher public expenditure on the welfare state since 1945 has disproportionately favoured the middle class.[14] We need to build, for example, on the health inequalities programme in the NHS, and initiatives such as Excellence in Cities in education. Such proposals could mean developing more community based health programmes; expanding vocationally orientated education and training schemes in impoverished areas; and introducing new measures to strengthen parental involvement in schooling, such as school–parent contracts. Specific curriculum initiatives are also required in schools. For example, improving maths teaching in the most deprived schools by offering special incentives to talented maths graduates, as Howard Glennester argues, is essential to narrow the achievement gap by social class.[15]

(7) The tax system should be further reformed, abolishing national insurance altogether for the lowest paid, and comprehensively restructuring national insurance contributions. Two out of the three most regressive elements of the contributions in the UK have already been eradicated: the lower threshold, and the lack of an initial tax-free allowance. But the old ceilings remain intact. The rich make no contributions on earnings over £32,000, with the exception of the 1 per cent addition introduced in 2003. Is it not time to remove this ceiling altogether? The costs of employment for the low skilled have to be cut both to promote work, and to reduce poverty in the long

term. The lowest fifth of taxpayers still pay a higher proportion of their earnings in income tax than the top fifth, and this clearly violates the principle of progressive taxation. There is a long-term debate about whether national insurance contributions as a whole should simply be abolished to create a fully integrated tax and benefits system; and also about how to make consumption taxes in the UK less regressive.

(8) Labour market institutions could be strengthened to tackle exploitation and rising wage inequalities. There should be legal protection ensuring that workers are employed on 'no less favourable terms' where public services are contracted out to private agencies. Wages, terms and conditions must not be cut in the drive for short-term profit maximization. This framework also involves the reintroduction of wages councils into the most casualized sectors; raising the minimum wage in line with earnings, and abolishing the youth differential; and encouraging the development of union organization in low skilled sectors of the economy through the government's union modernization fund. In the US in the 1980s the minimum wage was kept at a fixed nominal level and consequently declined in real terms – and this decline caused a rapid rise in inequality, particularly in the bottom half of the distribution.[16]

(9) Economic inactivity could be reduced by reforming invalidity benefit through positive incentives that stem the initial flow on to the benefit. Otherwise individuals will remain trapped outside the labour force, spending their lives in a state of benefit dependency. Take-up levels have increased steadily in the UK since the 1980s. There should be greater use of employment creation schemes that create long-term benefit savings, including public sector jobs for the low skilled, such as park attendants and community wardens. The activation of the unemployed requires more than supply-side measures where the demand for low skilled labour in a region is low. Targeted measures to create jobs in these regions raise employability levels, promoting long-term integration into the labour market and providing springboards of opportunity, while enabling the regeneration of local areas. The labour market flexibility agenda needs to be reformed to provide decent employment opportunities for all.

(10) The steady rise of inequalities in the distribution of wealth must be tackled, in part through asset-based redistribution and the democratization of market capitalism, but also by containing the excessive accumulation of wealth by a few individuals. Just as Edwardian social

policy drew a distinction between the 'deserving' and 'undeserving' poor, these categories might be applied to the concentration of wealth in the global economy. The accumulation of wealth is excessive and unjust where it arises not from hard work and risk-taking enterprise, but from 'brute luck' factors such as rising returns to property and land. Inheritance itself is a form of brute luck inequality, enabling citizens to share in the social product while violating the principle of reciprocity: if one enjoys the fruits of other citizens' labours, a good or service should be provided in return.[17]

The case for liberty does not therefore defeat the case for taxation of wealth transfers. The present inheritance tax regime in the UK still offers loopholes for the affluent, and is inequitable in its impact on the modestly well-off. The government should look again at a capital transfer tax extending beyond simply inheritance, and including all lifetime gifts. The capital transfer tax proposal introduced by the Labour government in 1974 was full of holes; the exemption made for gifts between husband and wife, during lifetime or on death, made it a sieve. It was barely redistributive, and did not yield much additional revenue.[18] However, a similar approach, more carefully designed and implemented, could still be effective.[19]

There is also a strong case for hypothecating the funds from the taxation of wealth transfers to the funding of a universal capital grant scheme. Such an arrangement can strengthen the perceived legitimacy of taxing concentrations of wealth. This capital endowment or 'participation account' would provide a time-limited basic income to the individual. It is a flat-rate benefit paid to adults who are 'participating'. This rewards a wider range of activities than paid work alone, and embodies the principle of reciprocity: the right to an income in return for the responsibility of contributing to society as a whole in a number of recognized ways. It thereby endorses the notion of active citizenship. Eligibility would be linked to a productive contribution to the community such as education, training, setting up a business, or parental leave.

The question of taxation

We conclude by making some general points about taxation and inequality. Can we make further inroads into economic inequality in the UK without a significant rise in rates of taxation? Many would say no; but there are reasons to suppose that we can.

In the first place, when developing economic and social programmes it is crucial to concentrate on the tax base, rather than on tax rates as such. Many factors influence the size of the tax base, including economic growth, since a growing proportion of individuals come within the higher tax bands as economic development progresses. Taxation as a proportion of GDP since 1997 has grown from 35.0 per cent to 39.6 per cent in 2002–3; some of this rise is explained by the increase in national insurance contributions introduced in 2002, but most emanates from growth.

In assessing the relationship between taxation levels and social programmes, especially in relation to the tax base, we have to be careful about the comparisons usually made between countries. At first sight, it appears as though more economically egalitarian societies have far higher rates of social expenditure than less equal societies, since taxation levels as a proportion of GDP are higher. Willem Adema's research at the OECD has shown that comparisons based on gross rates of taxation in relation to GDP between countries can, however, be misleading.[20] This is because some countries claim back more through taxation on benefits than others, especially in Scandinavia.

If we compare Sweden and the UK, for example, it appears as though the Swedes allocate far more in social and welfare benefits than the UK. If we look at net rates, however, the difference is far less stark, in part because the British welfare state is more effective at targeting benefits. Gross public expenditure in Sweden stands at 36 per cent of GDP. In the UK, it is only 26 per cent. The net rate for Sweden, however, is 25 per cent, compared to a net rate of 22 per cent in Britain. The real difference in expenditure is much less than the gross figures imply. These figures remind us that the way expenditure is allocated can be as significant as the total level of public expenditure in improving the public infrastructure and poverty reduction.

Conclusion

The new egalitarianism thus affirms a significant role for the state in tempering the inequality of earnings that results from market-driven employment growth, and in pooling resources to meet risks. It demands that the state regulates the distribution of endowments and assets among the least advantaged, and spreads these assets more widely. Such social investment is not only good for equity, but is a source of efficiency. Finally, the new egalitarianism is more receptive to the problems arising from state failure than traditional social democracy. But it also stresses the potential for market failure. Neither market nor state instruments are privileged: they have to be balanced and integrated with non-state, non-profit instruments in the voluntary and mutual sectors. Many tools exist to promote greater economic equality, as we have shown, that can be used to sustain a new egalitarianism in the future.

7

Inequality and recognition: pan-European social conflicts and their political dynamic

Ulrich Beck

This chapter examines two key questions. First, what is the *pan-European dynamic of inequality* that results from European integration? Secondly, is a Europe of conflict the end for Europe, or is it the point at which a single European society is conceived?

At the outset, it is important to judge the epistemological quality of this problem correctly. The question of a pan-European inequality dynamic relates not simply to those conflicts that are already apparent, but primarily to dynamic, pan-European concepts and indicators. Can it simply be assumed that the same inequality patterns – such as class or stratum differences – which apply in the nation-states and national communities also operate at European level? Charles Taylor's 'The politics of recognition' refers to the paradigmatic conflict line at the beginning of the twenty-first century.[1] Today, we should ask, will the call for the 'recognition of difference' made under the banner of nationality, ethnicity and religion also determine Europe's future conflicts, and if so, in what form? The question of cultural dominance conceals and relegates to second place the issue of socioeconomic redistribution; 'injustice' is no longer understood just materially, but culturally too. We must thus evaluate how the issues of material and cultural (in)justice relate to one another at the European level.

Enlargement of the European Union to central and eastern Europe does not involve the colonizing of countries, nor are unforeseeable migratory flows likely. But something much more serious may be happening: whole countries are 'immigrating' into the EU. European 'foreigners' are becoming European 'nationals'. Voluntary collective immigration by states is historically a new phenomenon. The issue is what it means for the EU's 'ethnic' self-definition, which has hitherto been marked by a kind of 'Western European racism', albeit scarcely needing to or able to perceive itself as such. And what does it mean for webs of inequality within the nation-states and at the pan-European level?

The European Union is a club of ageing societies, confronted in many developing countries by extremely young societies. The antagonism of the age pyramid could signify either good fortune or doom for Europe. One way or another, the balance between migrating pressures from the outside and the internal need for immigrants will become the central topic of political debate, as suggested by David Goodhart in this volume. Only if the Europeans can overcome their rigid, *quasi* ontological differentiation between Us and the Others, between Europeans and non-Europeans, can the ageing continent subsist in the long term in competition with the world's youthful powers and regions. Europe's cosmopolitan opening up is becoming both a prerequisite for survival and an opportunity. Only thus can grey-haired Europe simultaneously rejuvenate itself and regain its world economic prosperity. What therefore are the effects superimposed on the conflicts over cultural recognition and material redistribution in a Europe open to the world and cosmopolitan? Will Europe become more European, or more national, or more neonational?[2]

Today, answers to these questions are characterized by two national perspectives: the methodological nationalism in the sociological approach to inequality and the study of migration and minorities; and the national view of state politics. These forms of myopia have, hitherto, complemented one another perfectly. Cultural distinctions and social inequalities have been perceived (almost) exclusively within national boundaries, and have only really been taken seriously and handled politically within this framework. This is certainly the case for the material core of the welfare state (in whatever variant form), with its comprehensive social security systems, which remain almost exclusively *national*. In the past fifteen years the European institutions have admittedly gained sociopolitical powers,[3] but these powers are purely regulatory. The European welfare state is a 'regulatory state',[4] not an institution for redistribution. The key function of European institutions in this area lies precisely in *not* redistributing money.

In the case of intergovernmental institutions, and agreements relating to redistribution between states, the most important organizational principle is the 'juste retour'. For example, institutions like the European Space Agency operate on the basis that each country gets back (for example, in orders for industry) what it paid in (contributions to the programme).

Here, the EU is an exception, and from the outset it was evident that it was not organized according to the 'juste retour' principle. Redistribution of funds was expressly provided for, albeit within a strictly limited scope. This has meant that in the EU there have always been two groups of countries, so-called 'net contributors' and 'recipients'. It is well known that the Federal Republic of Germany has always been the largest 'net contributor' to the European Community's budget. This transfer centred for a long time on agricultural policy, which continues to make up the largest proportion of the EU budget. The redistribution logic of the 'agricultural community' was simple: the Community's more industrialized countries, Germany in particular, subsidized the agriculture of the less industrialized countries, obtaining in return a large market for their industry. A second sphere of redistribution was created in the 1980s through Regional and Structural Policy, which allocated funds to development programmes of the economically weaker regions of the Union. The Regional and Structural Policy was also based on a simple logic: the economically weaker member states (primarily southern Europe) assented to the formation of the European internal market on the condition that they received development funds from the economically stronger member states to help them improve their economic infrastructure and development.

Overall with this and countless other programmes (in the field of research and development policy, among others) an undoubtedly substantial level of redistribution has been established between the states at European level, albeit one which differs markedly from national transfer systems. The area of welfare state redistribution is entirely excluded and remains under the member states' exclusive control.

From the national perspective, this combination of circumstances gives rise to two main problems. First, governments face the challenge of protecting the national welfare states from the expansion momentum of the neoliberal market logic embedded at the European level. Here a European–national contradiction becomes apparent, one which may have grave consequences for the policy competence of nation-states in Europe. How can national social security systems be protected from suffering the same fate as the former government owned enterprises (telecommunications, electricity, etc.) – that is, how can we guarantee they are not considered as distortions of competition and market hindrances, then liberalized and privatized?

Second, were we to succeed in protecting these systems, a complementary problem would arise: how might we conceive a minimal *European* welfare state that does not eventually place too heavy a burden on the fragile national welfare states of the 'rich member countries', causing them to collapse under large-scale European transfers? Is it conceivable or indeed realistic to believe that self-contradictory Europeanization of both markets *and* welfare states can be coordinated?

One impression that is often given is that these problems only have perverse – and therefore equally undesirable – alternatives. One option is to restrict the scope of Europeanization drastically to preserve the margin of manoeuvre of national economic and social policy. This would be the neonational option. A second option would be to dismantle the national welfare states in order to improve the European market's functional efficiency. This would be the neoliberal option. Is there also a third, *cosmopolitan* option? And, if so, what might it look like?

What social conflicts then characterize cosmopolitan Europe? And how can these conflicts be handled? However these questions are answered, or, more modestly, made answerable, one thing is certain: the sociology of social inequalities and the political science approach to welfare state research are poorly equipped to address them, let alone resolve them.

Critique of the methodological nationalism of inequality sociology and welfare state research

The methodological nationalism of inequality sociology and welfare state research is just as obvious as the self-affirmation effect between these two sociological disciplines. One starts from the nation-state as the basic unit for social conflicts and their governmental control – mostly without wasting a single thought on the presuppositions which guide research. The problem in this congruence of social science based perspective is that it transforms practical categories into analytical ones without questioning them. The conceptions and self-perceptions of those active in social welfare are thus implicitly transposed on to the empirical enquiring into social inequalities and the welfare state. It is thanks to this analytical mindset that this kind of theory and research is Europe-blind. Moreover, the failure to appreciate that the confusing, blurring and redrawing of frontiers between member states, as between Europeans and their Others, has far-reaching consequences in the pan-European conflict dynamic in questions of social recognition, social inequality and social redistribution. Likewise, the problems and dilemmas resulting from the intersection of these issues are not appreciated.

To gauge the scope of our critique of methodological nationalism we must question one intersection which materially affects the sociological and political debate about the stability of societies, namely that between the *reproduction* and *fragmentation* of societies. At the level of methodological nationalism, social reproductions – that is, processes by which societies maintain themselves over time – and social fragmentations – that is, processes which endanger the social reproduction of societies – are quite naturally directed solely at *national* communities and *national* states. Europeanization however is associated with a *revaluation* of the positive connotation of reproduction and of the negative connotation of fragmentation. Europeanization *demands* 'fragmentation' of Europe's system of nation-states and also new social differentiations and conflict dynamics. It is not social reproduction but *non*-reproduction of national societies and nation-states that opens the latter up for Europeanization. In a nutshell: it is not the conflict over Europe but the self-reproducing integration of national societies that is Europe's downfall.

Two problems arise from this dilemma. First, which pan-European conflict dynamics *promote* and which *impede* the advance of European integration? This question must not be understood too narrowly. The incidental consequences of conflicts that are missed, glimpsed or unexpected could favour the development of political Europe. The architects of the euro, for example, must have foreseen the consequences of this process, namely the further political integration it necessitates.

Second: how can *Europe's reproduction* as an integrated society be conceived and what does it mean for the 'integration' or 'fragmentation' of Europe's national communities? What new forms of differentiation arise in the pan-European area of social inequalities which contribute to buffering or counterbalancing Europe's national divisions? What kinds of European conflict and conflict dynamic can stimulate European alliances across national frontiers, with the result that both the pros and cons drive Europeanization (in terms of denationalization and transnationalization) forward? To rephrase the question: must pan-European conflicts always endanger Europe, or can they not also contribute to its construction? Can, for example, neonational, isolationist tendencies within Britain, France, Spain, Italy, Germany, Poland, etc., be tempered by a pan-European pro and contra?

These problems will be analysed below on the basis of four questions: (1) How does European frontier mobility affect the European inequality dynamic (assuming that the conventional inequality concepts are provisionally accepted)? (2) What new patterns and coordinates of social inequality arise? (3) Given Europe's variable geography, how do inequality and recognition conflicts relate to one another? (4) To what extent do these conflicts lead to a recognition–inequality dilemma?

Mobile frontiers, mobile inequality patterns?

How does the national perspective affect the perception of social inequality? What do national frontiers accomplish for the perception and legitimizing of social inequality?[5] The critical factor is that it causes the perception of social inequality to appear curiously distorted: inequalities within national societies have been grossly *magnified*; inequalities between national societies are *diminished* beyond recognition. This is the prerequisite for the political legitimation of sociopolitical activities at home and passivity towards others abroad. If the political criterion were 'need', then it could hardly be justified that affluent European societies organize – at enormous cost – their own country's financial systems based on national poverty and need criteria, while a large part of the world's population daily faces a very real threat of starvation. What consequences does the 'European border' and border policy have for social inequality patterns in Europe? Two answers, which relate to the different ways of pluralizing and relativizing frontiers, are 'normally' given to this question:

- *First*, Europeanization changes the nature of European borders. Inside they become low and porous, and outwardly they become mobile, flexible and imprecise – but also higher and less porous.
- *Second*, frontiers between (national) societies lose their significance; the barriers between societies (especially their economies, education systems, etc.) are removed.

One could thus argue that previous distortions in the perception of social inequalities – that is, the making and maintaining of the incomparability of identical inequalities within and across national borders – *disappear* in the course of the border altering process of Europeanization. Europe thus becomes enmeshed in inner contradictions which hold enormous potential for political conflict.

The problems may be illustrated by a simple example: the claim 'equal pay for equal work' was one of the central demands of the workers' movement – and so it still is. In the highly industrialized countries with a strong trade union organization this principle has been very largely realized, not just within enterprises, but also far beyond them. The trade unions' campaign for equality ended however at a 'natural' limit: the border of the nation-state. In the same manner it is natural to campaign within Germany for the upholding of the nationwide collective wage agreement, and, after Germany's unification, for equalization of pay in east and west Germany; it was also natural for a long time to ignore differences in pay relative to other European countries. Viewed from such a national perspective, differences in pay between Bavaria and Saxony are illegitimate, whereas the same differences between Bavaria and Belgium are legitimate. What happens then if the same differences are viewed and judged from a European perspective? Are differences in pay between the European countries not illegitimate? Ought not the European trade unions to want *all* European workers to demand 'equal pay for equal work'? Or must this principle be abandoned? And if it is abandoned, how can the differences be legitimized?

These questions are anything but academic! This was made clear by an example in January 2004 when there was heated argument among the general public of the various countries over the initiative by a number of members of the European Parliament to strengthen it's identity by standardizing parliamentary attendance fees. The inequalities for the same work in a very limited area are huge: an Italian MEP receives 11,000 euros gross, his German party colleague by contrast about 7,000 euros; the Spanish party colleague alongside him has to make do with 3,000 euros, while the new colleagues from the new central and eastern European accession countries will receive no more than 1,000 euros. For the present, there will be no mitigation of this extreme inequality in attendance fees for the same MEP activities, since under public pressure the EU foreign ministers have rejected this initiative.

How explosive these matters are is also evident from the fact that they form one of the main battle zones between neoliberals and neonationalists in Europe. Neoliberalism has tried systematically in the last few years to delegitimize the differences between levels of pay. The intention was not to lift the low pay in Portugal and Greece to the German level. Quite the reverse: it was meant to criticize the level of pay in Germany.[6] Neoliberalism thinks in European, indeed global terms, in the categories of a European, global *market*. Social differences are thereby reduced to simple cost–benefit calculations and recorded as differences in wage costs. Neoliberalism has now appropriated the old workers' movement slogan: 'equal pay for equal work' – but at the lowest level!

This means that the trade unions appear to face two equally unacceptable alternatives. One alternative is to hold out and demand 'Equal pay for equal work' – but at a high level. This is the alternative chosen after Germany's unification;[7] that it is economically disastrous and politically utopian is probably not in dispute. The second alternative is no more appealing; it puts the trade unions in the perverse position of adopting their opponents' old catchphrase and demanding

'Unequal pay for equal work'! – in effect, defending the existing differences in pay between the European countries. The societies are thereby forced into a neonationalist position, for the existing differences in pay can be maintained only if national frontiers are preserved and effectively controlled.

This example shows that with the dismantling of the frontiers the explosive potential of European inequalities is not defused. Rather, conflict threatens to flare up because the perceptual barriers of national incomparability are being dismantled, and comparable inequalities are therefore assessable and commensurate adjustments sued for. Thus the present Europeanization policy has led us into a paradoxical situation: the Europeanization of markets, but also of societies, appears actually to bring about a neonationalist reaction such as force. To date there has been no success in defusing the conflict potential of European inequalities by other means such as force.

Moreover, this pattern of conflict holds enormous political potential, not yet at the present time clearly specified.[8] It can be utilized by both post-Communist parties and right-wing neonationalist movements. The right-wing populist parties could thereby come into possession of a second 'winning formula'. In the 1990s their 'winning formula' consisted of a combination of neoliberal economic policy and authoritarian domestic policy (for instance, restrictive towards foreigners).[9] In a new 'winning formula' the authoritarian domestic policy would be combined with a neonationalist economic and social policy. Even social democratic parties are not really immune to this neonationalist temptation. All these parties and movements may make themselves the advocates of those whose possessions are endangered by neoliberal Europeanization.

European regions as conflict patterns of European inequalities

It was stressed early on that inequality may relate to different parameters. From the Enlightenment onwards discussion of inequality was marked by the juxtaposition of *individual* and *social* inequality. This applied not just to the causes of inequality, but also to its manifestations. Manifestations of social inequality were generally *social* aggregates such as classes, strata, social environments, personal circumstances, etc. It was through these aggregates that the classification of equals and unequals was regulated. The individual was 'equal' in terms of a stratum or class, and the relevant inequality existed between these. If one analyses European inequalities, it becomes clear immediately that we need a third category: *geographically/territorially* defined inequalities. This means first and foremost inequalities between states and regions. In this case individual life chances are determined not by class or stratum membership, but by membership of a nation or region.

Of course geographically defined inequalities already existed even within the old nation-states, for example between Italy's 'rich north' and 'poor south'. And conflicts between centre and periphery were one of the characterizing forces in the formation of nation-states.[10] These regional disparities within the nation-states are comparable only to a limited extent, however, with the new forms of inequality in Europe. Within the nation-state these disparities were *illegitimate*; at least in principle the nation-state raised the claim to 'identical social and economic conditions', as the old Article 72 of the German constitution put it. Government policy was to be based on this principle of identity, and that also means that it had to intervene supportively where this identity did not exist.

With the intensification and multiplication of regional inequalities the identity principle can no longer be sustained in this form. This already applies within the nation-state. Not surprisingly Article 72 was amended and watered down in Germany following unification. The new version no longer refers to 'identity', but only to 'equivalence' of social and economic conditions. Apart from the obvious definitional difficulties – when are social and economic conditions 'equivalent'? – enormous problems arise in applying even such a compromise formula on a European scale.

Inequality thus constitutes in Europe a *three-dimensional stress field* in which individual, social and geographical differences collide. The first, immediate consequence of this new combination of circumstances is a pluralization of forms of inequality. Individual, social and territorial disparities can be combined, broken and played out against one another in many different ways. Inequality in Europe resembles a large hall of mirrors in which the proportions and perspectives are constantly changing. Moreover, they must be redefined politically; Europeanization is accompanied by *politicization* of inequality. An inequality meta-power game has started in which differences are legitimized and delegitimized, equalities constructed and deconstructed. In this power game everything seems open and a whole series of fundamental questions are thrown up: Is it possible to define a poverty line for the whole of Europe? Or must there be multiple poverty lines between different national and regional contexts? Who decides on the basis of what authority and with what arguments for or against which of these alternatives? And if poverty is relative, what are the reference figures for relative poverty in Europe? And here too the same question again: who decides how, on the basis of what evidence and authority, which reference figures are relevant and which irrelevant for determining poverty in Europe?

At this point it is now possible to further develop some central assumptions made by the theory of reflexive modernization. They can be grouped into three scenarios:

- *First scenario* With Europeanization the importance of social strata and classes is further moderated. For example the life chances of a factory worker in Munich may be far better than those of a factory owner in southern Spain or eastern Poland.
- *Second scenario* Europeanization moderates and reactivates individual inequalities. Social inequalities which have been levelled out inside a country by welfare state policies may gain importance through comparison with other countries.
- *Third scenario* Through Europeanization, geographically defined forms of inequality (regions) gain importance, also as targets of government policy. Regional policy becomes European social policy. In this way the European institutions stoke up regionally oriented allocation contests, which 'fragment', moderate and relegate to secondary importance the national conflict lines and internal differentiations.

The argumentation which now follows draws attention to how close the connection is between policy and inequality even in the European conflict scenarios. For all these questions can ultimately be resolved only through political decisions. In the past the European Regional and Structural Policy has had a markedly national bias: on the one hand, the 'poor' member states asserted the nation-state claim to uniformity on the European level as well, that is, they Europeanized the national perspective. On the other hand, out of 'national interest' the 'rich' member states adopted a stance of great reserve towards European redistribution programmes. Between these extremes the European Regional and Structural Policy has been transformed into a huge bazaar in which there is constant haggling over budgets and development zones – with, in many cases, absurd results.

One should note that this is not just further evidence of the ineptitude of European bureaucracy or of the irreconcilability of the conflicts of interest between the member states. In fact, it is possible to analyse some of the central contradictions which, with Europeanization, are breaking up the familiar patterns of social inequality. These contradictions will become considerably more intense with the EU's eastward expansion. For if the previous criteria of the European Regional and Structural Policy were to be applied to the enlarged EU, then a far-reaching redefinition of social and economic conditions would be the result. The 'poor' Spanish farmer would suddenly be relatively 'rich', without anything having changed in his conditions of life. He is no longer being compared only with a farmer in Germany, but also with a new fellow EU citizen in the Baltic states, Poland or Slovakia. This raises another problem however: how can such political decisions on the EU's inequality and conflict dynamic be legitimized?

Mobile Us and mobile Others?

We have seen how the pan-European conflict dynamic is produced by the denationalizing and transnationalizing of social inequality conflicts and of conflicts over the recognition of differences. The questions raised concern firstly the relationship of recognition conflicts to inequality conflicts, and secondly the differences which emerge in the dynamic of recognition and inequality conflicts when they are viewed through the European lens.

Recognition conflicts and inequality conflicts are two linked but nevertheless analytically distinguishable ways of understanding *injustice*. In the one case it is *socioeconomic* injustice, which is grounded in a society's politico-economic structure. The other understanding of injustice relates to *society's treatment of otherness*. Here injustice is rooted in the devaluation and shutting out of minorities, different national, ethnic and religious traditions and identities resulting from the 'sectional universalism' of the dominant group.

The resolving of material inequality and justice issues rests on redistribution policy. The resolving of issues of social recognition of otherness, by contrast, generally involves fundamental social transformations and reforms in participation, representation and self-interpretation in history, politics and religion, which ultimately change the self-conception of each individual.

Of central importance now is the realization that the relationship between inequality/redistribution and recognition issues appears entirely different at national and at European levels. In the methodological nationalism of inequality sociology and welfare state research, redistribution means *national* redistribution and therefore presupposes the recognition of equality, or more precisely, the recognition of national equality. Inequality conflicts and redistribution issues are raised and investigated both socially and sociologically solely within national frontiers – in the sense of inequality/redistribution between nationally equal classes, between nationally equal men and women, nationally equal minorities and majorities. Inequality and allocation conflicts have, to the extent that they are conducted and investigated within the confines of the nation-state, an *ethnic* background component which is both concealed and constitutive – not recognition of others' otherness, but the converse principle: recognition of the (national) equality of the equal is the *sine qua non* which establishes the difference between the worlds of inequalities which actually exist and politically relevant inequalities. Recognition and redistribution are, even where redistribution and not recognition is at stake, in a certain way fused with one another. It is the national framework, the national view, which simultaneously makes redistribution possible and limits it. The methodological nationalism of sociology puts its seal on the concealing, forgetting and the contrived naturalness of 'national recognition' as a background prerequisite for inequality and allocation conflicts.

It is precisely this nation-state fusing of recognition and inequality conflicts which shatters at European level. The pan-European conflict dynamic can, accordingly, be developed and investigated theoretically and empirically as a conflict-rich decoupling of

- postnational, transnational struggles for recognition;
- postnational and transnational inequality and redistribution conflicts; and
- the intersections of recognition and inequality conflicts together with the dilemmas resulting from them.

The conflict dynamic of cosmopolitan Europe – this is the scenario for which the case will be made in what follows – results from the fact that the *social dynamic of recognition conflicts is gaining a new explosiveness in relation to redistribution conflicts*. At the same time, this is not only bad news. *In a Europe capable of conflict, a cosmopolitan sensitivity to recognition of the Others' otherness might well contribute to tempering the intensifying redistribution conflicts in Europe and, moreover, to helping Europe become more European.*

Europe's ethno-cultural self-conception – measured by the criteria set by political Europe itself – bears *perverse* traits. The more the frontiers inside the 'us Europe' are dismantled, the more forcefully they are invoked and strengthened in relation to Europe's others. EU citizens enjoy the right of free movement internally, and at most internal frontiers there are, thanks to the Schengen Agreement, no longer any personal checks. In anticipation of this free movement, a securing of the external frontier, checks to counter illegal migration, and also a residual exclusion of persons belonging to third-party states are being vigorously pursued.

This can be designated as the *paradox of 'frontier mobile' Europe*. While the frontiers between 'Europe' and 'non-Europe' are being rendered *mobile* as nowhere else in the world, social integration is being re-ontologized to exclusion mode in order to secure the frontiers. Is the European Union to remain a Christian club? Will it define its outer territorial limits by renewing what Europe wants to and is intended to overcome: the 'transcendental community of common descent'? This is now being called for by national politicians and historians to fend off membership of Turkey, or, at yet greater distance, Russia. Are the frontiers between 'Europeans' and 'non-Europeans' to be determined by, of all things, religion and ethnicity? Are we threatened at European level with the repetition of the mistake which has just been more or less overcome at nation-state level and which is altogether so profoundly contrary to the cosmopolitan founding principle?

In this way, moved by the European discussion of common parentage, the power shifts are already being acted out preventively. Should Turkey join the European Union, a substantial transfer of power within the European Union would follow because of its demographic growth. As an EU member Turkey would soon 'disempower' the currently most densely populated country in the EU, Germany. It would also end the dominance of the Christian religion in Europe. There is thus a fair amount of hypocrisy behind the concern over human rights and democracy in Turkey.

Considerable differences between Turkish society and most European countries cannot be denied. Those who stress these differences and advance them as a reason for rejecting Turkey's application to join the EU misapprehend European reality: the number of Muslims in Europe is now approaching the population count of some European countries. A total of 15 million Muslims live in western Europe, more than 5 million in France alone and more than 3 million in Germany. The issue initially is thus not recognition of difference at all, but recognition of reality. Those who would keep Turkey out of the European Union would – for consistency – have to do away with the real Turkey within the European Union.

Secondly, the criterion of cultural difference is an inappropriate yardstick for drawing the frontier between Us and the Others in Europe. After all, it is precisely the differences that also exist between the member states which make Europe attractive. But just let us assume that Canada or the US were flirting with the idea of joining the EU. It would then be inadvisable to stress the 'cultural difference' between these countries and Europe to make a case for rejection. A membership application from the US would probably be a chess move by which the European Union could be checkmated through 'over enlargement' – so at least many Europeans would think and react. At the same time, however, the differences between Amsterdam and Philadelphia, Frankfurt and New York or Paris and Montreal are slighter than those between many parts of the EU. What then does recognition of Others' otherness mean in the relation of 'Europeans' to 'non-Europeans' – given that this frontier structure is in principle intended to be variable and is also politically determined?

There are two temptations which cosmopolitan Europe must guard against. The first is the idea that ethnic identity is an *essence*, something which is predetermined, specific and objective. And the counter temptation is to assume that ethnic difference is nothing more than *pure illusion*, which with advancing modernization – Europeanization – will become transparent as such and dissolve.

To raise the question of Europe's ethnic identity some distinctions are necessary. The first concerns the 'multinational', 'polyethnic' and 'multination' state. A country which is home to more than one nation is in this sense not a nation-state, but a multination state, and smaller cultures are designated 'national minorities' and integrated with greater or less conflict. The incorporation of different nations in a state can be brought about *forcibly*, for example when that nation is conquered or colonized. Many Western democracies are in this sense multinational (for instance, there is a whole series of national minorities in the US, the American Indians for example or certain Mexicans who were living in the south west when the United States annexed Texas, New Mexico and California after the Mexican war).

A second source of cultural diversity is *immigration*. The more immigrants with different cultural and religious provenance come into a country, the greater the country's cultural and religious diversity becomes (again exemplified by the US).

A third reason however – and this reason represents the EU's internal plurality – lies not in the conquest or colonization of other nations, nor even in mass immigration, but in the fact that ever more countries and states are joining a community of states. In this process the people remain where they are, but the collective entities – countries, states – 'immigrate'.

The American experiment runs as follows: how can immigrants, that is, deterritorialized groups, be reterritorialized, rooted nationally in a 'new country', and fused into one nation? The European experiment runs differently: how can historically deep-rooted territorial ethnicities, nationalities, regional and religious identities, whose differences are written down deep in people's memory in the blood language of power, be opened to one another and woven together so that a cosmopolitan empire, or state cooperative, is formed? In the American case people are mobile, in the European case states are mobile while the people remain rooted in their own territorial allegiance.

The EU is of course permanently wrestling with the immigration issue and policy, but it did not – as the US did – come into being as an immigration country, but rather as an immobile community of 'immigration *states*'. In this sense the EU is not a multinational large nation-state, not a 'crucible', but rather a mosaic of states and societies brought about by a radical contradiction between mobility and immobility. These states and countries are completely immobile, but they are at the same time also (often without being really aware of it) completely mobile. It is in making this permanent contradiction liveable, indeed grasping it as a solution, that the political innovation, the political 'invention' of Europe, lies. *The European miracle is the reconciliation of traditional enemies!* This kind of 'enemy plurality', 'enemy integration' in a cooperative network of states, in a 'consensual empire' is something utterly different from a multinational, multicultural, polyethnic state entity as represented for example by the US, Canada or Switzerland.

At the same time the EU is paradoxically 'racist' in its conception. This statement may surprise and appear exaggerated to many. But we are dealing here with a (Eurocentric) racism of a white-skinned world minority still largely undiluted by doubt, in which dominance, invisibility and ignorance cause one another. The campaign for recognition in Europe is directed against the (concealed) racism of Eurocentrism: the authoritative construction of norms which accord with the 'whiteness' of the Western Europeans' appearance and being, as well as give it a privileged status. The other side of this coin is the entirely self-evident exclusion and devaluation of people and projects regarded as 'black', 'brown' and 'yellow', and therefore of all 'non-whites' as 'non-European' or 'un-European'. The notion of black Europeans, Turkish Europeans, Muslim Europeans, etc., is perceived in this white racism as 'absurd', as 'contradictory', and thus dismissed and devalued. Two strategies can be distinguished in which this European racism is recognized and reacted to.

For one thing there is the position of *colour-blind universalism*. Here it is assumed that race or ethnicity is not a morally acceptable reason for treating one person differently from another. One may of course notice ethnic differences (like difference of sex etc.), but these must not lead to differences in treatment and action. The basic principle is: *Our actions must be colour-blind.* This position gets caught up in the contradictions of universalism: on the one hand the Other's otherness is overcome by regarding and treating that person as an equal. On the other hand, however, the reality of the otherness is simultaneously denied. Those unwilling to quit the position of otherness are shut out. People defend the ideal of others' equality, while simultaneously spreading the cloak of secrecy over the fact that blacks, coloured persons, Muslims, etc., are excluded from Europe's participation opportunities precisely by its social structure. The ideal of universal humanity without social distinction allows the dominant groups to ignore their own particularity. Blindness to difference perpetuates cultural dominance.

The second position could be called *self-critical racism*: here it is recognized that ethnic and religious differences play a central part in both the attitude of Europeans and in the European institutions. The criticism is made that serious differences exist within European institutions. There are those that, intentionally and unseen, discriminate according to ethnic attributes, and those that seek to minimize or overcome such ethnic discrimination. Here the focus is on the fact that European civil society has a fundamentally ethnic conflict dimension – in the interactive relationship between social players, just as in the attitude of the European public authorities and their representatives. European decisions and actions in the past and present have treated people very differently depending on their ethnicity. The European authorities cannot therefore simply shirk their responsibility in this matter. Europe cannot suddenly declare itself 'colour-blind' – without in reality prolonging the cultural imperialism which has hitherto prevailed in invoking 'colour-blindness'.

In this sense, the following questions will become a key pan-European conflict: 'What's your attitude to Others' otherness?', 'How should and can the frontiers between "Europeans" and "non-Europeans" be drawn and legitimized without a political Europe based on human rights blatantly contradicting itself?'

The recognition–inequality dilemma: on the intersection of inequality conflicts and conflicts over recognition of difference

In methodological nationalism the conflict dynamic of modern national societies is conceived as the dynamic of the *inequality of equals* – in practice as well as in scientific theory. This means that in nation-state inequality sociology and welfare state research the issue is always exclusively inequalities between fellow citizens and the recognition of difference between fellow citizens. Even in relation to territorial and geographical inequalities the national *a priori* dominates. Territorial inequalities are discussed only within national frontiers and as a derived subdifferentiation of national class and stratum differentiations and differentiations in social and economic conditions. The line of argument outlined earlier runs accordingly: the pan-European conflict dynamic is characterized by the fact that what appeared fused once and for all time in the national *a priori* becomes uncoupled. The results of this process may be illuminated under three spotlights.

(1) The campaign for recognition cannot be silenced either by 'national assimilation' or by 'European descent'. It erupts transnationally in the European area and in the European sense, that is, beyond differentiation between national and international. In this way a dialectic of cosmopolitanism and anti-cosmopolitanism has begun.[11] The careers and career setbacks of Jean-Marie Le Pen and Jörg Haider, for example, show both how spectacular and how flawed the actions are of the anti-cosmopolitanism movement. In many countries, defensiveness to hostile responses to cultural, linguistic and religious differences and an almost fascist enthusiasm for 'cultural purity' are close to one another in patriotic rhetoric and appeals to national equality. These are reactions to the emerging future and not, as often suggested, about bringing the past back to life. But the demand for the new 'purity of Europeanism' by which Europe's Others are construed and shut out is encouraged not least by official European policy, which is building a 'Fortress Europe'. And that means that a *perverse coalition* comes about *between the official multiculturalism of the European fortress builders and the anti-cosmopolitanism of the European neonationals*. Both groups are complemented by indifference and intolerance towards the presence of refugees, asylum seekers or 'other immigrants', many of whom – looked at more closely – are not immigrants at all, but recognized/non-recognized 'resident citizens' whose living and employment conditions have long been deeply linked to the history and culture of their inhospitable host country, Europe.

The absurdity of the 'Fortress Europe' project is seen not least in the fact that Europe's former and new 'barbarians' have lived behind their doors for a long time. Huntington's 'clash of civilizations' forecast is wrong not least because it ignores the fact that it long ago ceased to be possible to make the frontiers of cultural differences congruent with nation-state borders. In the European capitals – London and

Paris, Berlin and Madrid, Athens and Warsaw – (ex-)colonizers mix with the (ex-)colonized, European applicant nationalities with ethnic groups and nationalities 'not yet' and 'never to be' members. The cosmopolitan atmosphere of these cities is generated precisely by the legitimately illegal variation of cultural crossings – intermixtures and movements – which derive precisely from coexistence and an increasing indistinguishability from the so-called 'Others of Europe'. It is apparent here that Otherness is not only marketable, not only yields economic added value, but also delivers cultural and political added value. These are after all liberal-minded places where the important future experiment is being conducted into how human rights and citizens' rights can be linked to one another again in the public arena across the frontiers of nations, ethnic groups and religions.

(2) To the extent to which Europe becomes real as a society, the exclusion of nation-state inequality areas in Europe is eroded. An environment of comparison of hitherto nationally incomparable inequality is emerging, containing immense explosive political material. A *pan-European* inequality and conflict sociology might well also play a part in this, not just by waking sleeping dogs, so to speak, but rather by preparing methodologically a neither-nor and both-and-also point of view. It should neither simply adopt the categories of nation-state politics nor simply adopt those of European politics, but would have to incorporate both European and nation-state perspectives in its own autonomous conception of pan-European conflicts and develop these conceptually as well as examine them empirically from that point.

(3) Beyond the nation-state *a priori* not only do the European recognition conflict and the transnational inequality dynamic become independent, but a new *territorial-geographic* conflict pattern also develops. This pattern – depending on European policy – intensifies, disrupts or tempers the recognition and inequality conflicts. Thus, one must pose the urgent question of how these different conflict dynamics relate to each other.

There are good reasons for studying such intersection effects. Conflicts which have flared up over recognition of difference aim to eliminate the distinctiveness and high cultural value of this group and its traditions. To put it differently, recognition presupposes (the construction of) group frontiers. On the other hand, those who address the issue of inequalities appeal to the recognition of equality; for only on this condition do inequalities become a political problem, a political question of the redistribution of resources and rights that is politicizable.

In other words, the politicizability of recognition conflicts presupposes the (construction of) *diversity*, the politicization of social inequality the (construction of) *equality*. Recognition politics and redistribution politics – it becomes apparent here – pursue conflicting aims. Nancy Fraser speaks accordingly of a *redistribution-recognition dilemma*: 'People whose circumstances are characterized by both – cultural injustice and economic injustice – need both – recognition and redistribution. Of course they need both things in order to simultaneously emphasize and nullify their distinctiveness. But how, if at all, is that possible?'[12]

There are two possible strategies for dealing with this dilemma. One might be designated as *strategic essentialism or multiculturalism*. Here the difference is 'essentialized' in order to establish the basis for its recognition.

A second strategy turns against this affirmative recognition of existing group frontiers and distinctive group features. This *transformative* strategy of recognition of otherness aims at destabilizing the existing differences and directing attention at the actually existing instances of penetration and intermixture.[13] The affirmative strategies are traditionally associated with the national welfare state. The transformative strategies on the other hand can be linked to cosmopolitan realism. After all they aim:

- *first*, to focus attention on the actually existing cosmopolitanisms in Europe; and
- *second*, to alter the self-conception of *all* the groups involved in accordance with a cosmopolitan 'common sense'.

For a European perspective and policy these transformative strategies hold a double opportunity: first, they are not tied to the welfare state, whose development in the EU is only rudimentary; second, a pan-European conflict (within Europe and among the general public of the nation-states) in which the struggle is for recognition of otherness might bring about a 'fragmentation' of nation-state integration which will help to popularize a European awareness of society in recognizing the Others' otherness.

But even if this assessment of this pan-European conflict scenario is overoptimistic, the intersection of recognition, inequality and redistribution conflicts nevertheless offers scope for a *cosmopolitan option* which is clearly distinct from the neoliberal and neonational options. This cosmopolitan option rests on three principles:

- *First*, redistribution conflicts endanger, while recognition conflicts may hone, the European identity; politically they have top priority over inequality and redistribution conflicts. A policy of recognition may invigorate political Europe.

- *Second*, recognition conflicts, to be at least partially detached from conflicts over material inequality and redistribution, open up for European politics new opportunities for action *beyond* welfare state responsibilities and resources. These lie principally in the development of a European civil society, which is perfectly feasible through fragmentation of national society.

- *Third*, this cosmopolitan Europe is characterized not by what it wants, but by what it does *not* want: no universalist levelling, no essentializing of difference; no violation of human rights and human dignity either inside or outside Europe; but also no besmirching of human dignity through 'absolute' poverty. A welfare state minimum is integral to the European understanding of political freedom and democracy.

The idea of absolute poverty as negative consent given by European cosmopolitanism may be surprising. As used here 'absolute' denotes a standard which counters the pluralism and relativism of the 'relative' poverty lines in Europe with a clear-cut conventional stipulation applicable to all Europeans: *no political freedom without basic subsistence*.

The universal content of cosmopolitanism is thus preserved in the negative, in what must on no account be allowed to come about. *Only* (but this 'only' covers a massive political programme) in the setting of a universalist minimum are recognition, inequality and redistribution issues enmeshed with one another in Europe.

The strategy of selective uncoupling and restricted coupling of these different dimensions of pan-European conflicts might be used for and lead to a situation where conflict-shy Europe discovers and develops the politically productive force of conflicts. To what extent this is successful and 'realistic' is, however, a matter which can only be resolved *politically*.

To what extent can and should a cosmopolitan Europe be solidary?

The extent to which Europe should and can be solidary is one of the key questions in the European project. It is striking that this question is discussed principally by Eurosceptics concerned for the national welfare state. In the prevalent neoliberal discussion this question is by contrast not asked at all. The result is that not even the rudiments of a positive vision of a *social* Europe in which the *European* dimension is taken seriously are as yet discernible!

Such a vision is, however, indispensable. The claim to social solidarity – to 'fraternity' – is part of Europe's stock of indispensable values, just as the ideas of liberty and equality are. A European civil society and a cosmopolitan Europe are conceivable only if they are solidary. First, however, this must be clarified: What does 'solidarity' mean, what does 'fraternity' mean? How can and must national and cosmopolitan conceptions of solidarity be distinguished? Only then can the following question be discussed: 'To what extent can and should a cosmopolitan Europe be solidary?' The question of a cosmopolitan understanding of solidarity can be formulated more precisely in demarcation *vis-à-vis* Claus Offe.[14] Europe, Offe argues, is not a historically evolved community of common destiny, from which it follows that solidarity between Europe's citizens is only weakly developed, and redistributive welfare state policies at European level are consequently not possible. The logic goes: Europe can be solidary only in a very limited sense – and for the foreseeable future this cannot be changed – because the notion of Europe as a meta-nation is unreal. A second inference runs: because Europe can ultimately not be solidary, it should not be overloaded with political expectations.

We are dealing here with a theoretically ambitious concept of national solidarity, which is however entirely in the grip of methodological nationalism. Lack of solidarity and anti-solidarity towards the culturally different, which is linked to it both inwardly and outwardly, are tacitly masked. Not being solidary towards people born outside one's own officially set regional borders is part of the integral concept of 'national solidarity'. This solidarity of *equality* must be distinguished from the solidarity of *diversity* associated with a concept of 'cosmopolitan solidarity'.

The understanding of national solidarity is complex, because what is distinguished in the concept of cosmopolitan solidarity is taken for granted:

- *First*, the national concept permits no differentiation between solidarity among equals and solidarity with the others brought into view by the cosmopolitan perspective. For there is only either solidarity or none – only this solidarity monopoly of the national analytically excludes the question: 'How solidary are you towards the cultural Others?' In the cosmopolitan view the understanding of solidarity is thus *expanded*. In addition to the question of solidarity with equals, these questions arise: What consequences does this solidarity with equals have for those thereby culturally shut out and excluded? To what extent can and must solidarity with the culturally different be made an integral part of solidarity with equals?

- *Second*, national solidarity with equals, precisely because with it the ethnic constitutive element implicitly exists, concentrates primarily or exclusively on the dimension of *material* justice. By contrast, in the cosmopolitan view the questions of cultural recognition of otherness appear, sometimes intertwined with it and sometimes independently. For one thing the concept of national solidarity is thus blind to the ethnic recognition issues which it itself presupposes; for another the complexity and dilemmas arising from the intersection of material and cultural justice issues are left aside or played down. The question 'How do national redistribution campaigns relate to campaigns for recognition of cultural distinctiveness?' can be treated systematically only within a cosmopolitan conception of solidarity.

- *Third*, national and cosmopolitan solidarity also rest on a differing valuation of sameness and diversity. In the cosmopolitan view it is not sameness and unity which merit the highest value (as is assumed in the concept of national solidarity), but multiplicity. The aim is not to suppress or gloss over the differences (for instance, within the EU) in order to maximize the differences between an 'essential' community of nations and its Others. Cosmopolitan solidarity is directed against overintegration into a nation and is sensitive not only to particular sectionality, but also to the particularity of all Europeans! This is a community of particularity, a solidarity of particularity which does believe in the equality of the equal as the paramount aim and supreme value. At the same time, this community of particularity puts a high value on equality within diversity and the equality of the otherness of the Others, as well as seeing in it a source of pleasure and cultural productivity.

- *Fourth*, while national solidarity is essentially concerned with the material justice issues and largely disregards cultural justice issues, cosmopolitan solidarity campaigns for a new kind of historical compromise between material and cultural justice. To measure these by the criteria of national solidarity and to reject them (as Claus Offe does) betokens a fundamental misapprehension of European reality. Here, surely, only the concept and criteria of cosmopolitan solidarity are capable of modelling appropriately the more complex relations between transnational inequality conflicts, redistribution conflicts and recognition conflicts.

To arrive at a vision of a solidary Europe two steps must therefore be taken: first, the concept of national solidarity must be stripped of its claim to monopoly and its inadequacy for explaining European conditions must be convincingly shown. Secondly, there arises the problem of how resilient a cosmopolitan, European solidarity actually is in view of the tensions, dilemmas and contradictions inherent in it. How much solidarity can we expect in a cosmopolitan Europe from the citizens in the two dimensions – love of recognition of otherness on the one hand, and willingness to accept redistribution on the other – to obtain a *social* Europe?

8

New global classes: implications for politics

Saskia Sassen

Since the 1980s we have seen the formation of new global classes.[1] The formation of these classes points to dynamics that partly disaggregate the national state from the inside and weaken the grip that national politics and national policy concepts have historically had over the particular groups involved in these new global classes. At the same time, the particular features of these classes, especially their ambiguous position between the global and the national, point to the possibility of a type of policy work that, although global, can get done inside national domains. This interpretation contests the widespread notion that global classes will tend to be cosmopolitan, and hence outside national reach.

The issues

When it comes to global classes, most of the attention has gone to a new stratum of transnational professionals and executives.[2] But I see at least two other global classes. One of these arises out of the proliferation of transnational networks of government officials: among these networks are those formed by experts on a variety of issues critical to a global corporate economy, judges having to negotiate a growing array of international rules and prohibitions that require some measure of cross-border standardization, immigration officials needing to coordinate border controls, and police officials in charge of discovering financial flows supporting terrorism. The other is an emergent class of disadvantaged workers and activists, including key sectors of global civil society, diasporic networks, and transnational immigrant communities and households.

A second issue concerns the prevalent tendency to equate the globalism of the transnational professional and executive class with cosmopolitanism. A more careful examination of that class raises some doubts about their cosmopolitanism. This is also the case with the other two global classes. All three of these classes evince forms of globality that, in my reading, are not cosmopolitan. Each of these three global classes remains embedded, in often unexpected ways, in thick localized environments: respectively, financial and business centres, national governments, and the localized microstructures of daily civic life and struggles. And each of these classes is guided by a single logic rather than the multiple logics at the heart of genuine cosmopolitanism: profits in the case of the new professional elites (no matter how cosmopolitan their tastes for, say, culture), specific and narrow governance issues in the case of government networks, and specific local struggles and conflicts in the case of global civil society, diasporas and immigrant networks.

The fact of global classes that are not necessarily cosmopolitan and that remain partly embedded in localized environments raises a host of issues when it comes to the concerns of this volume. In so far as these classes are part – indeed, constitutive parts – of current forms of inequality, they and the underlying socioeconomic structures may well be more subject to government policy and governance mechanisms than the imagery of globality typically allows for. The political options will be different from those involved in the case of genuinely cosmopolitan classes. At the same time, although not cosmopolitan, their incipient globality does make a difference.[3] One way of thinking about them is as bridging between the thick national environments within which most politics, economics and civic life still function, and the global dynamics that are 'denationalizing' particular components of those national settings.

Emerging global classes

There are a variety of economic, political and subjective structures underlying the formation of these three global classes. We are seeing the emergence of global networks with variable degrees of formalization and institutionalization for each of these three classes. These global networks are not seamless as is often thought. They are lumpy: they contain nodes (global cities, major supranational institutions, particular activist networks) and it is here that much of the global action gets done. Further, contexts such as the global corporate economy or the international human rights regime also play critical roles in the proliferation of these global networks. These and other globalizing dynamics have contributed to the weakening of the exclusive authority, both objective and subjective, of national states over people, their imaginaries, and their sense of where they belong. This facilitates the entry of non-state actors into international domains once exclusive to national states. Economic, political and civic processes once confined largely to the national sphere can now go global, even when this is only an imaginary, or a subjective disposition, rather than a daily reality for many of these actors.

It is, at this time, only in particular domains that these globalizing processes generate actual new social forms. In my research experience it is largely at the top and at the bottom of the social system that the national state has weakened its grip in shaping the experience of membership and identity. Vast middle strata – whether workers, firms, or places – have not been particularly affected by these processes of transformation. Similarly most of the work of governments has not either, even though there is a specific type of government official that is at the forefront in the work of developing the technical infrastructure for corporate globalization and key aspects of global governance.

Thus the emergent global classes I focus on here are partial and specific outcomes. They are not necessarily new social forms as such; they can also arise out of a subjective, self-reflexive repositioning of an old social practice or condition in a transnational framing. For instance, transnational immigrant households have long existed, but today this condition assumes a whole new meaning and the immigrants themselves know it and act on it. Similarly, an international class of powerful elites has long existed, but in today's context it carries novel implications. It is partly their objective systemic position and partly this subjective interpretation that give these new global classes their political import, as I will argue in the conclusion. In my reading one of the crucial dynamics at work here is a process of incipient denationalization, a changed attachment to the national.

Transnational elites and agendas

National attachments and identities are becoming weaker for global firms and their customers. This is particularly strong in the West, but may develop in Asia as well. Deregulation and privatization have weakened the attachment to the *national* economy. The nationality question simply plays differently in these sectors than it did even a decade ago. Global financial products are accessible in national markets and national investors can operate in global markets. For instance, some of the major Brazilian firms now list on the New York Stock Exchange, and bypass the São Paulo exchange, a new practice which has caused somewhat of an uproar in specialized circles in Brazil. While it is as yet inconceivable in the Asian case, this may well change given the growing number of foreign acquisitions of major firms in several countries. Another indicator of this trend is the fact that major firms set up key operations in one or another leading business centre, regardless of what country it is in. Thus, to a much larger extent than in the past, the major US and European investment banks have set up specialized offices in London to handle various aspects of their global business. Even French banks have set up some of their global specialized operations in London, inconceivable a decade ago and still not avowed in national rhetoric. Japanese firms also have opted for London to set up some of their financial operations aimed at the continent of Europe. Finally, most major firms now have vast worldwide networks of affiliates and other types of collaborative arrangements with local firms, as when they subcontract manufacturing production.

The proliferation of these worldwide activities and networks can be seen as a kind of operational infrastructure for corporate economic globalization. For the latter to exist and function it takes vast numbers of professionals, managers, executives and technical staff. A good part of this high level workforce is quite mobile and gets easily represented as a new transnational professional class. The basic agenda for this class is profit-making, today contingently embedded in transnational work. However, through this work they are also contributing to the instituting of cross-border transactions and standards. Further, this work requires a whole physical infrastructure – the hyperspace of global business – of state-of-the-art office buildings, residential districts, airports and hotels. At its most developed this is the worldwide network of about forty global cities that functions as an organizational infrastructure for the management side of the global corporate economy. The new transnational professional workforce both navigates through, and contributes to constructing, this cross-border corporate economic space.

It is important to capture three sets of distinctions here. One is that the driving force that feeds the emergence of this cross-border domain has few resemblances to the forces driving and constituting cosmopolitanism in the rich sense of the word. While this new transnational professional class may open up to diverse cuisines and urban landscapes, the particular condition that constitutes it as a global class is a rather narrow utility logic – the drive for profits. In itself, this is not a cosmopolitan drive, even though it may help these professionals become a bit more worldly. The second set of distinctions concerns the fact that through its work this new global class shapes an increasingly significant change in its relationship to the system of national states. That is to say, as a class it does not have the same systemic position as that of a country's national business community, even though particular individuals may circulate in both. The third set of distinctions concerns the fact that this class and its work are partially embedded in national terrains – most conspicuously the network of global cities. To be global and hypermobile this class actually needs a state-of-the-art infrastructure.[4] From here then comes a particular type of engagement and partial dependence on national states, a fact easily obscured by the language of the new cosmopolitanism and hypermobile capital.

One way of describing this process is as a partial, often highly specialized, denationalizing of particular institutional domains. It can be argued that such denationalizing is a necessary condition for economic globalization as we know it today. For instance, a global market for capital requires the adoption of international standards in all participating countries, which in turn often entails a reorienting of various policies (on taxation, monetary policy, accounting norms, and others) away from the national economy and towards the global economy. The sophistication of this system lies in the fact that it only needs to involve strategic components of the pertinent institutional domains – most national systems can be left basically unaltered. China is a good example. It adopted international accounting rules in 1993, necessary to engage in international transactions. To do so it did not have to change much of its domestic economy. In fact most firms in the domestic economy did not even know such accounting standards had been implemented, because it did not affect their operations. Japanese firms operating overseas and wanting to list on the New York Stock Exchange or the London Exchange adopted such standards long before Japan's government considered requiring them. In this regard the 'wholesale' side of globalization is quite different from the global consumer markets, in which success necessitates altering national tastes at a mass level. This process of specialized and partial denationalization has been strengthened by state policy enabling privatization and foreign acquisition. In some ways one might say that the Asian financial crisis has functioned as a mechanism to denationalize, at least partly, control over key sectors of economies which governments, while allowing the massive entry of foreign investment, would not relinquish before.

The network of global cities produces what we could think of as a new subculture, a move from the 'national' version of international activities to the 'global' version. The long-standing resistance in Europe to mergers and acquisitions, especially hostile takeovers, or East Asia's resistance to foreign ownership and control both signal national business cultures that are somewhat incompatible with the new global economic culture. I would posit that global cities, and the variety of global business meetings (such as those of the World Economic Forum in Davos and other similar occasions), contribute to partly denationalize corporate elites (as well as government elites). Whether this is good or bad is a separate issue; but it is, I would argue, one of the conditions for setting in place the systems and subcultures necessary for a global economic system.

A key feature, then, of this new global class is its intermediate position between the national and the global.

Transnational networks of government officials

Transgovernmental networks have existed for a long time. But there are novel types of networks that emerged in the 1980s and 1990s clearly connected to corporate globalization and the globalizing of other governmental responsibilities and aims, for instance regarding human rights, the environment and, now, the fight against terrorism.

An older and common type of international government network is to be found within international organizations. The key actors are government officials from the pertinent national ministries or agencies. Transgovernmental regulatory networks can be found among trade ministers in the General Agreement on Tariffs and Trade (GATT), financial ministers in the International Monetary Fund, defence and foreign ministers in the North Atlantic Treaty Organisation, and central bankers in the Bank for International Settlements, as well as various efforts within the OECD and the EU Council of Ministers. These are often enormously powerful networks of government officials in charge of critical work in the development of a global corporate economy. In some cases the secretariat of an international institution explicity tries to form a network of officials from specific governments to act as a negotiating vanguard in developing new rules that are to apply eventually to all members; examples of this are the negotiations for the TRIPS (Trade-Related Aspects of Intellectual

Property Rights), for the World Trade Organization, for the governance of the internet, and so on.

What is critical about these transgovernmental networks as an emergent global class is the change brought on by globalization dating from the 1980s, when a tipping point was reached.[5] This is no longer the post-Second World War Bretton Woods decade of intergovernmental collaboration. The aim is not simply intergovernmental or international communication and collaboration. It is, rather, a deregulatory project that aims at denationalizing those components of state work that are necessary for corporate globalization (or, in other settings, for implementing global treaties about the environment, human rights and other non-economic efforts). In the early Bretton Woods period the project was one of global governance to protect national economies; by the 1980s the goal was to open up national economies and create hospitable and institutionalized environments for global firms and markets. This brought a proliferation of highly specialized transgovernmental networks: good examples are the worldwide efforts to institute compatible competition policies, accounting standards, financial reporting standards, and so on. The work of the pertinent, typically highly specialized government officials began to get oriented towards a global project. One consequence was an increased commonality among officials within each transnational network and a growing distance with colleagues from the national bureaucracies back home. In this sense then, we can speak of an incipient global class that occupies, again, an ambiguous position between the national and the global.

There are also government networks within the framework of executive agreements,[6] which function outside a formal international institution. Members operate within a framework agreed on at least by the heads of their respective governments. Good examples are a variety of executive agreements between the US and EU Commission presidents to foster increased cooperation, including the Transatlantic Declaration of 1990, the New Transatlantic Agenda of 1995 (with a Joint US–EU Action Plan attached) and the Transatlantic Economic Partnership Agreement of 1998. Each of these meetings in turn produced ad hoc meetings among lower level officials, firms and environmental and consumer activist groups, around shared issues.

Finally, a very new development is the formation of informal networks, operating outside intergovernmental agreements (that is, outside treaties and executive agreements). Among these are the Basel Committee focused on financial governance, the international arbitration community, high-level members of the judiciary, and experts from both the private and the government sector working on international standards. What they do is not legally binding on the members but it is often the preparatory work for eventual formal arrangements. The turbulence of financial markets and the market uncertainties confronting global firms have fed the weight and strategic importance of these informal deliberations. Most recently we have seen a proliferation of agreements between domestic regulatory agencies of two or more countries; they have shown far sharper growth than traditional treaty negotiations. These are agreements that can be instituted by the domestic regulators themselves and in this sense they are an interesting instance of denationalized state work; they do not require approval by national legislators.[7]

The new global class of disadvantaged

We see emerging today a distinct global formation comprised of a mix of individuals, population categories, and organizations. Notwithstanding sharp internal diversity and mostly lack of interaction, there are shared objective conditions and subjective dynamics. It cannot be thought of as equivalent to global civil society, even though part of it is at specific times, and even though the imaginary about such a global civil society is a significant subjective condition shared by some of the people and projects involved. What is of particular interest to the concerns of this volume is the fact that most of the people involved are quite immobile. They are not part of a travelling transnational class or the new global civil society international elites. Yet they are either objectively or subjectively part of specific forms of globality.[8] For the sake of brevity, I confine myself to some of the key features of this emergent global class.[9]

One of my concerns has been with the types of cross-border networks that resource-poor people and organizations can construct and join even if they are not mobile. The key here is that localized activist struggles can be global even if completely engaged locally and without the means or permission to travel. We can think of these as localizations of global civil society. Important spaces for such localizations are global cities, home to multiple diasporic and activist networks and organizations. The actors can include disadvantaged sectors: a variety of groupings and organizations that have limited resources, no or little power, often lack the proper documentation, are often invisible to national politics and national civil society, are unrecognized as politico/civic actors or are unauthorized to be such by the formal political system.[10]

Cities, critical to global civil society, contain at least two key spaces: the concrete space of the city as a space for politico-civic activities (as distinct from the highly formalized space of national politics and national civil society), and the state-of-the-art built environment for the command functions and social reproduction of global corporate capital. Critical also is the partly deterritorialized space of global electronic networks. Here the public access internet is enormously important. It allows easy, low cost communication, distribution of information and, crucially, the formation of electronic domains where multiple actors from many different localities can join in.

Among the issues that arise out of these conditions we can identify the following. One concerns the forms of politico-civic engagement that are made possible for the disadvantaged in global cities; these are at least partly enabled by globalization and the human rights regime. A second is that the presence of immigrant communities produces specific transnational forms of engagement, including the formation of globalized diasporas. For instance, we see a growing number of immigrant networks concerned with specific struggles, such as exposing illegal trafficking groups and brides-by-mail organizations, which have the effect of partly reorienting these communities away from a one-to-one orientation to their home countries and towards other immigrant communities in the city, or co-nationals in other immigration countries.[11] A third is the modes of engagement made possible in the global city between the disadvantaged and global corporate power, for instance anti-gentrification struggles or fights against transforming industrial districts into luxury office districts. A fourth is the extent to which access to the new media, specifically the internet, allows/induces various types of groups to transnationalize their efforts (such as poor women's organizations, environmental activists and human rights activists).[12] Many of these groups have begun to connect up with other such groups in other countries where before they were purely local. The binding is through the shared objectives rather than through travel and meetings. A fifth concerns the extent to which these multiple activities and engagements contribute to denationalize the global city and thereby enable more global forms of consciousness and of membership/belonging even among the disadvantaged. These are all elements that are part of the localized microstructures of global civil society.

The large numbers of people from all over the world who often encounter each other for the first time in the streets, workplaces and neighbourhoods of today's global cities produce a kind of transnationalism right there *in situ*. These encounters can include encounters with co-ethnics who are in high professional jobs (that is, a class encounter).

We see an emergent recognition of globality, often shaped by knowledge about the recurrent struggles and inequities in city after city. This knowledge, enabled by both global media and the rapidly spreading use of the internet among activists, functions both as fact and as subjective formation. In my travels around the world I have found that this subjective dimension increasingly enables the disadvantaged and the localized to recognize the presence of the global in these cities and their participation in it; the global becomes visible. This then also produces an ambiguous position for these, mostly activist, disadvantaged and localized actors between the national and the global.

Conclusion: political implications

These new global classes are probably best thought of as emergent social forces. Their points of insertion into our societies are today not primarily through established policy frameworks and the more typical political struggles – those enacted through party politics and union politics. But a key point of the analysis in this chapter is that, even though global, they are, to variable extents, embedded in national settings. This is critical in considering policy options for national and local governments seeking to address the new inequality.

A first issue is, then, the relation of these classes to national settings. There are clearly significant differences among these three classes when it comes to their insertion into national contexts. The new transnational professional class has far more exit options than the other two. But, as the analysis in this chapter seeks to show, this class is ultimately far more placebound than one might think from the imagery about it. The reverse is the case with the amalgamated class of disadvantaged workers: here it becomes important to recognize that this class is far more embedded in what we might think of as the global workplace and transnational politics than the imagery associated with these workers. Finally, the proliferation of networks of specialized governmental officials can be seen as building international social capital for the governments involved; but to extract the utility that this might carry will take building some bridges between international and national policy around questions that have typically been thought of as national, that is, recognizing that the global gets partly played out within national settings.

All three in their own distinctive ways have a strong insertion into territorially bounded contexts – global cities and national governments. One might say that each makes the global partly endogenous to specific national settings. My assumption here is, then, that this carries implications for national government policy when it comes to matters pertaining to these new global classes. This is the opposite from what might be the policy implications coming out of notions of free-floating cosmopolitan classes with no national attachments or needs.

A second issue concerns the relation between these new global classes and domestic class structures. This holds largely for the professionals and the disadvantaged working class. There is much to be said on this subject, but given space limitations let me focus on two critical aspects. One is that these two global classes are part of a deep economic restructuring that has contributed to a growing demand for both high-level professionals and low wage service and production workers. Nowhere does this become clearer – both on the street and in statistical datasets – than in global cities. In this regard current forms of globalization add to inequality and indeed produce new types of inequalities. One challenge for analysis is to recognize the interconnections of social forms and outcomes that we usually think of as unconnected. For instance, the state-of-the-art international financial centres in cities such as New York and London actually depend on a far broader range of workers and firms than is usually assumed: all kinds of low wage service workers labour in the global workplace that is the financial centre in these cities. Public opinion and policy frameworks classify these low wage workers as belonging to backward economic sectors. That is a mistake. For policy to address some of these forms of inequality will require a correct analysis.

The other is that these new segmentations get filtered through distinct political and policy cultures: a neoliberal policy culture that opens up a country to the upper professional circuits of global capital, on the one hand, and immigration policies that close a country to lower labour market circuits. Filtering these novel processes through these in many ways older policy frames has the effect of obscuring precisely those features this chapter thought to illuminate: the greater than evident placeboundedness of the new global professional classes, and the greater than evident globality of the new disadvantaged workforce. These two unconnected policy frames basically contribute to strengthening the new types of segmentations these two global classes introduce into the political and civic fabric of a society. Policy aiming at reducing these new inequalities can only begin to address the matter if it recognizes the interconnections between these two classes and the fact, as indicated above, that one is more placebound and hence susceptible to policy interventions than is typically assumed, and the other is more global and hence more indicative of the future rather than a backward past than is usually assumed.

9

Britain's glue: the case for liberal nationalism

David Goodhart

In the past few years the cluster of issues that are often grouped together under the heading 'security and identity' have loomed ever larger in the minds of voters and politicians in most European countries. The category includes (with different emphasis in different countries) asylum and immigration; European integration, national sovereignty and regionalism; violent crime (or the fear of it) and rising incivility; the changing character of local communities, especially in big cities; Islam and the problem of parallel communities.

The security and identity issues have emerged in response to real events such as the decade-long rise in asylum-led immigration starting in the early 1990s, and the continuing arguments about the speed and desirability of European integration. The higher profile of these 'who are we?' and 'how can we live together?' issues may also reflect the declining force of class-based distributional questions and the state versus market conflict related to the Cold War that dominated European politics in the second half of the twentieth century. Indeed, partly thanks to the new salience of security and identity issues and the populist parties that have emerged to exploit them, the main political party of the left no longer commands a majority of the working-class vote in the Netherlands, France, Belgium or Italy. A 'new politics' that cuts across established left–right boundaries is upon us.

In Britain there has been no equivalent of the Front National or Pim Fortuyn, but here security and identity issues similarly emerged from a position of very low visibility ten years ago, according to pollsters, to become by 2001 the second most pressing political theme for ordinary citizens (after the NHS). The British National Party and the UK

Independence Party (UKIP) have also started to win sizeable shares of the vote in some elections, and can no longer be regarded as politically irrelevant.

Indeed the combined UKIP/BNP share of the vote in the last European election was over 20 per cent in most of the regions of Britain, rising to 32.6 per cent in the East Midlands and 25 per cent in the West Midlands and the south west.

The Labour Party's working-class vote has not deserted it to the extent of some of the European countries mentioned above; nonetheless it is now commonplace to hear expressions of anxiety about sections of the white working class from Labour politicians and rueful reflections on the large gap between the London-based cosmopolitanism of much of the party's elite and the far more conservative attitude of traditional party voters on security and identity issues.

Most people assume, not unreasonably, that security and identity issues are likely to benefit the political right (both moderate and extreme right) with its historic claim to speak with the nation's ancestral voices, its simplistic approach to national identity and crime reduction, and its historic reservations about immigration. But it is the aim of this chapter to argue that security and identity issues can, with the application of some hard-headed liberalism, be at least neutralized and perhaps even turned to the advantage of the centre left.

The security and identity field has in the recent past been a self-imposed weakness for the left partly because of the influence of a set of myths and half-truths that insist, among other things, that human beings are purely rational creatures with a propensity to treat all other humans (apart from close family) with equal regard; that nationalism and national feeling are necessarily a belligerent and negative force; and that Western countries, especially those like Britain with a colonial past, remain responsible for most of the ills of developing countries.

It is time to abandon these myths but also to acknowledge more openly the moral and political dilemmas for the left thrown up by the fusing of two historic social experiments of the past fifty years. The first is the still extraordinary fact of the modern welfare state in which we are compelled to share a large slice of our incomes with fellow stranger-citizens whom we are also entreated to regard as equal citizens. The second experiment is the growth and celebration of difference and diversity of many different kinds – social, sexual, ethnic, racial – and the more open national borders which have contributed to the greater human variety in modern liberal states.

These two overlapping experiments give rise to at least two 'progressive dilemmas' for the centre left. The first[1] concerns the potential tension between solidarity and diversity. The argument is simply that the more different we become from one another and the less we share a moral consensus or a sense of mutual obligation and belonging, the less happy we may be to support a generous welfare state. One should not exaggerate the degree of homogeneity or moral consensus that existed in, say, 1950, or the inevitability of a growth in diversity translating into an unwillingness to share. But coming on top of all the other strains on the welfare state, from rising individual affluence to an ageing society, it would be foolish for the centre left not to keep a close eye on the interaction between diversity and welfare over the next two or three decades.

The second progressive dilemma concerns the nation-state itself. The left has historically struggled for a 'universal' notion of equal national citizenship that is blind to wealth, status and, more recently, race and ethnicity, and one that promotes a high degree of sharing and engagement with our fellow citizens. Yet this idea of citizenship is not really universal at all, it stops at our national borders. Notwithstanding the much greater cosmopolitanism of modern life, we continue to favour our fellow national citizens over those of other countries – hence our readiness to spend twenty-five times more each year on the National Health Service than on development aid. This does not mean that we have no obligations towards humanity as a whole, and especially towards citizens from former colonial countries whose countries we exploited in the past. But those obligations that we express through development aid, fair trade rules and a properly policed asylum system are a small fraction of the mutuality expressed in the political, legal, economic and welfare rights and duties which we daily maintain and reinforce in relation to our fellow national citizens. The uncomfortable truth to many progressives – and something which the Human Rights Act sometimes seems to overlook – is that the modern nation-state is based not on a universalist liberalism but on an idea of exclusive membership. This is neither arbitrary nor capricious. If we did not exclude most of the rest of humanity from those national rights and duties they would very quickly become worthless, especially those welfare rights with a financial cost attached to them that progressives value so highly. And it also follows from a progressive, active notion of citizenship that we should be far from indifferent about who becomes a fellow citizen.

Yet a studied indifference to who is becoming a fellow citizen has in the past been expected of progressives in relation to immigration.

Sweep away the old myths of the left and face up to these progressive dilemmas and it becomes possible to construct a liberal, progressive nationalism or 'integrationism' for a country like Britain that gives priority to its existing citizens and communities – and indeed is happy to acknowledge the existence of a majority culture and set of values, however loose – but is also open to newcomers who play by the rules, and is generous in trade and aid relationships with developing countries.

Of course such general statements leave many questions begging. But it is my belief that the centre left cannot afford to be squeamish about nationalism and feelings of national solidarity; the alternative to a mild, progressive nationalism is not internationalism, which will always be a minority creed, but an exclusive and inward-looking nationalism. As Richard Rorty has written: 'National pride is to countries what self-respect is to individuals: a necessary condition for self-improvement. Too much national pride can produce bellicosity and imperialism just as excessive self-respect can produce arrogance.' [2]

National feeling has always been a Janus-faced phenomenon. Alongside the hatred and aggression it has generated, it is also responsible for many of the most positive aspects of modern industrial society: the readiness to share with and make sacrifices for stranger-citizens, the strong feelings of belonging and membership beyond one's own kin group that it generates. It was sentiments of national solidarity as much as class solidarity, a feeling that 'we are all in this together', that helped to build and sustain the welfare state. It is the core belief of the left, against the individualism of free market liberals, that there is such a thing as society – but in the modern world that always, everywhere, means a specific national society.

Nationalism was, of course, a highly destructive force in European society in the first half of the twentieth century. But war within Europe, at least between the big powers, is unthinkable in 2004. And feelings of national solidarity can now usually coexist comfortably with many other ethnic, class or regional identities. Security and identity issues of course throw up many complex and difficult questions about citizenship and membership and how much continuity a society needs and how much change it can bear. But two basic points for the centre left are surely clear.

First, the security and identity issues are mainly questions about community. By placing these issues so high on their list of priorities some voters may well be registering an objection to the speed at which their town or community has changed, including an objection to the number of outsiders (of people who are 'not like us') who threaten to turn the familiar into the strange. But most voters are also sending a broader signal about how important they continue to regard the idea of society and citizenship to be, and are implicitly rejecting a Thatcherite idea of society as nothing more than a collection of individuals. Second, as greater mobility means that membership in the national or local community becomes no longer so self-evident, we require a renewed emphasis on the conditionality of citizenship. The social, political and welfare rights of citizenship need to be 'earned' through appropriate behaviour (such as the unemployed, or single mothers, being ready to seek work in return for welfare support). This 'rights and duties' approach on domestic issues has been a central plank of New Labour's mainstream appeal. It now needs to be extended more overtly to immigrants. A more visible programme of 'earned citizenship' is required in which access to full citizenship and welfare rights for migrants is phased in over time. Much of this phasing already happens, but if citizens were more aware of it, it might help to reduce the widespread anxiety about free riding among newcomers.

These last two points stake out a territory that the centre left can make its own, indeed must make its own, as it seeks to channel feelings of national belonging in a benign direction and away from the xenophobia and racism that is the expression of national and communal feelings turned sour.

Creating a modern sense of membership

Many people in Britain, especially those living in run-down areas, with little money and few opportunities, look back nostalgically to a time of more tightly knit and supportive communities. Since industrialization and the growth of big cities this golden age has seldom actually existed. And to the extent that it has existed it is wrong to place the central focus for its demise on post-Second World War immigration, as many people, especially the elderly, tend to do. There are in fact many other economic and social trends over the past fifty years that have contributed to the disappearance of micro-communities capable of generating strong feelings of stability and belonging: social and geographical mobility (according to Britain's Office of National Statistics, 11 per cent of the British population moved region in 2000); the erosion of collectivism and class feeling; the rise of lifestyle and value diversity. Most of these developments are welcome and represent a step forward in human freedom, but some of them have also come at the cost of eroding traditional communities.

The ubiquity of the mass media and the sameness of many aspects of modern urban life act as a countervailing force to atomization and social fragmentation. We are less likely to know our neighbour but we are more likely to have something in common with any given stranger, because of the similarity of work and consumption patterns (including media consumption) across the country. Nonetheless, the priority now given by voters to security and identity issues is perhaps an indicator that in the contest between fragmentation and homogenization, many people think that fragmentation is winning and regret the fact. But the fragmentation of local communities that is an inevitable, if unintended, consequence of modern life makes even more important a strong sense of British national identity and solidarity: it provides a kind of 'roof' under which the other more particular identities of class, region, race and religion can shelter.

A liberal nationalism may even be part of the answer to one of the great paradoxes of modernity: the fact that although many of the forces of modern life have been successfully designed to give citizens greater control of their destinies and their environments, the means by which that control is achieved, such as the increasingly internationalized market economy or international political institutions like the European Union, leave people with the feeling that their destinies are subject to forces outside their national, territorial and political communities. As a consequence of rising affluence and modern technology, most of us can control our individual destinies to a far greater extent than our parents or grandparents, but it may be that the price of such control is the loss of a clear sense of our collective destinies.

A liberal nationalism/integrationism for our cosmopolitan age would, of course, look very different from the kind of nationalism that most British citizens would have instinctively signed up to in 1950. The English, Welsh and Scots were more socially and ethnically homogeneous in 1950 than they are today; British political institutions were far less entwined in international institutions such as the EU; and in 1950 feelings of national solidarity were at a peak after two hundred years of homogenization through industrialization, urbanization, the creation of Britain itself and its international empire, the emergence of democracy and mass literacy, and then the two world wars of the twentieth century.

Some people argue that this feeling of national solidarity was a kind of historic blip: it had never existed before on such a large scale and it will never exist again as we evolve in a more individualistic and transnational direction. But while it is surely true that it is neither possible nor desirable to recreate the strong and often exclusive feelings of national membership that existed in 1950, a milder version of membership is still required to realize many of the goals of social democracy.

But what should this milder, modern form of membership look like?

Constitutional patriotism, the view that a citizen must merely embrace the rules of the national political system, is surely too thin.

For any national society to function well some minimum membership rules are required on a number of other issues: language, legitimate authority, the role of religion, some aspects of gender relations and perhaps a very basic moral consensus on the broad contours of right and wrong. A stronger sense of national belonging, although one which it is harder for recent citizens to share, may also come from consciousness of a shared history, traditions, conventions and customs. Of course, membership rules will have fuzzy edges and will change over time. Nations are not static things, they evolve constantly with or without immigration – but by stretching backwards and forwards in time, in some recognizable way, they also provide a reassuring framework for people's lives.

Different people will, of course, express their British identity in different ways. A recent immigrant is likely to have a more abstract, rational identification with the country, with the economic opportunities it provides, with the laws and political traditions that have made it a desirable place to live. A citizen from one of the long established, indigenous ethnic groups – the English in England or Scots-Protestants in Scotland – is likely to have a more automatic, even ethnic, sense of belonging to Britain. There is no reason to think of either sense of being British as superior to the other. Many on the left are suspicious of the idea of an unreflective sense of national belonging, but this is invariably the form it takes for most people in most countries and there is no reason why, especially in Britain in the early twenty-first century, the instinct should be a menacing one. Nor is there anything inherently illiberal about belonging to a majority ethnic group: an ethnicity is simply a group of people with loosely shared ancestry and common historical myths. In the case of the ethnically English, who probably still make up about 75 per cent of the population of England, that would include descendants of the Vikings, Normans, Huguenots and some of the Jews, Celts and even Africans who have blended in over the centuries with the Anglo-Saxons who became the dominant group in England in the sixth century.

A liberal nationalism merely requires that a citizen from the majority ethnic group acknowledges that ethnicity and citizenship are not the same thing and that it is possible to be a full and welcome citizen of Britain while belonging to a minority ethnic, racial or religious group. In Britain this is easier than in many other countries because, despite English dominance, Britain is already an amalgam of four different ethnic nations. And the Mori poll which found that 86 per cent of British people do not think you have to be white to be truly British is reassuring evidence that most people do not have a racial view of citizenship.[3]

When people of very different backgrounds come to live together one would expect some initial distrust, suspicion and even hostility. One would also expect time and shared experiences to iron out most of that distrust and suspicion. But strong communities require continuity in space and time: I know that I can trust my neighbour regardless of markers of difference such as accent or skin colour because we have lived next door to each other for many years, he has sometimes helped me out and I have done the same for him. But the modern world is very bad at creating this kind of trust-generating continuity, either locally or nationally. Many of the trends of the past fifty years have increased social distance and eroded moral consensus – and the left too, with its stress on a universal humanism and its suspicion of the nation-state, has helped to chip away at the special solidarity we feel towards a fellow national citizen.

Of course, generous social programmes can help to reduce group-based conflicts over welfare and housing resources in particular communities, and can perhaps even help to increase trust. But that begs the question of who will pay for these generous programmes? Can we hold on to the level of sharing and redistribution at national level that grew out of the stronger sense of national membership of fifty years ago even as our societies become more diverse and our attachments to one another become thinner?

As critics of my *Prospect* essay 'Too diverse?' pointed out, the size of the welfare state remains at historically high levels throughout Europe even as diversity of all kinds has continued to rise. And it is certainly true that the welfare state has powerful forces preserving it at its current levels. But the scholarly work of Robert Putnam,[4] Alberto Alesina[5] and most recently Stuart Soroka,[6] has reluctantly concluded that there is often a negative trade-off between racial/ethnic diversity, on the one hand, and levels of trust and, in some cases, welfare spending, on the other. Some critics argue that much of this work is based on the very specific and unrepresentative experience of the United States. It is certainly true that the experience of countries like Canada, Australia and even Britain suggest that quite high levels of diversity can be compatible with European-style welfare states. And it is also true that there are often bigger factors contributing to reductions in trust and solidarity such as city life itself. But the most recent work of Soroka, based on a broad international survey, concludes:

> International migration does seem to matter for the size of the welfare state. Although no welfare state has actually shrunk in the face of the accelerating movement of people, its rate of growth is smaller the more open a society is to immigration. The typical industrial society might spend 16 per cent or 17 per cent

more than it does now on social services had it kept its foreign-born percentage where it was in 1970. [7]

Moreover, the solidarity versus diversity trade-off is likely to be a long-term trend manifesting itself over the next thirty to forty years. Over that period, affluence, the ageing of society and the erosion of historic class and national solidarities are all likely to squeeze welfare, particularly redistributive social spending. It is therefore all the more important to establish clear and transparent rules of national membership and citizenship entitlement to help sustain at least a minimum of the solidarity needed to underpin a generous welfare state.

It is not enough to point out, as many multiculturalists do, that there is no simple moral consensus any longer in a country like Britain. Of course that is true. The political challenge is to create a minimum degree of moral consensus and solidarity in an otherwise highly pluralistic society. When it comes to migration this means picking a path between the assimilationism of the Republican French model and the subsidized multiculturalism that was the Dutch way before the emergence of Pim Fortuyn. Both approaches have failed in the context of the modern European nation-state.

An approach that seeks to integrate outsiders without assimilating them is clearly the most viable model, at least for liberal countries like Britain that for economic reasons (among others) are likely to remain open to quite high levels of migration over the next couple of decades. Newcomers must be encouraged to integrate and be given special financial help to do so where necessary. But sometimes in discussions on the left about migration to Britain there is an underlying assumption that Britain must radically adapt its majority way of life or reach out to meet the newcomers halfway. This is surely disproportional. Britons must adapt to the extent of treating a new group of citizens with fairness and dignity, and it is of course especially important that institutions like the police and the criminal justice system are sensitive to difference. In the longer run, as different ethnic groups grow in size and importance they will, willy nilly, change the host society. But in the nature of things most of the adaptation will, initially, be on the side of the newcomers who have chosen to live in an already existing society with a majority way of life and at least some sense of itself. There is no compulsion to fall in with every aspect of that way of life – it is in any case too varied to describe – but it is important that newcomers acknowledge that Britain is not just a random collection of individuals, and that they are joining a nation which, although hard to describe, is something real. British citizenship makes us special to each other. And notwithstanding many blemishes, it is by international standards a possession to prize.

Clearly, a developed, liberal society like Britain can and does sustain a huge variety of beliefs and lifestyles all of which are compatible with an adequate sense of Britishness. We do not all have to like each other, or agree with each other, or live like each other for the glue to work. Indeed, as philosopher David Miller has written:

> Liberal states do not require their citizens to believe liberal principles, since they tolerate communists, anarchists, fascists and so forth. What they require is that citizens should conform to liberal principles in practice and accept as legitimate policies that are pursued in the name of such principles, while they are left free to advocate alternative arrangements. The same must apply to immigrant groups, who can legitimately be required to abandon practices that liberalism condemns, such as the oppression of women, intolerance of other faiths and so on.[8]

Similarly, many on the left confuse political principles or laws with attitudes or emotional states. So, for example, whereas the principle of equal citizenship requires that the state and its agencies treat gays and non-gays with equal respect, this does not require that all Britons should be indifferent as to whether their son or daughter becomes gay. The principle of equal citizenship can coexist with a vast array of attitudes and emotions about other types of people and ways of life; Michael Ignatieff has made the useful distinction[9] between negative tolerance (conforming to liberal norms in public but not necessarily in private) and positive tolerance (embracing diversity both in public life and in private attitude). (The gap between public behaviour and private attitudes does, of course, become more problematic in the case of agents of the state such as police officers.)

Dealing with the free-rider anxiety

The 'roof' of national identity and citizenship is not there only to help straddle the divide between ethnic majorities and minorities. It is the glue that connects a working-class person and a middle-class person, a northerner and a Londoner, a Scot and a Cornishman, and across the racial minority divide, say, a British Pakistani with a British Arab. The purpose of a politics of liberal nationalism/integrationism is to reinforce a strong sense of membership among all citizens in an increasingly complex and socially fragmented world. And as Antonio Vitorino, the European commissioner for justice and home affairs, has put it: 'The integration of migrants works better if one has a clear vision of oneself.'[10]

But this rather general political rhetoric needs to be combined with a more concrete political campaign to reassure the majority population, especially the least well-off, that other citizens are not 'taking advantage' in some way. An important part of the rise of security and identity issues in welfare states is connected to this powerful feeling that other people, especially newcomers, are unfairly jumping ahead in the queue of life. Recently the other person said to be taking advantage is likely to have been an asylum seeker from abroad, but twenty years ago the culprit would most likely have been a white working-class single mother on benefit.

Clearly much of the disproportionate passion invoked against the 'other', and indeed the very identity of the other, is connected to media reporting. But it is not enough to say that people are suffering from *Daily Mail* induced false consciousness. The form of this anxiety can perhaps be influenced by newspapers but the content of the emotion seems to be quite deeply ingrained. Many people in welfare societies have an acute sensitivity to 'free riders'. A recent *Prospect*/Mori poll asked whether people felt that other people were taking unfair advantage in their use of public services and benefits, and 45 per cent of respondents said yes. (The groups most commonly blamed for taking unfair advantage were asylum seekers and recent immigrants, but, more optimistically, the long established minorities of blacks and Asians featured hardly at all, suggesting that given time people do extend their idea of the 'we'.)

This sensitivity to free riding seems to have something to do with the opacity of our developed urban societies and the fact that even people on low incomes pay large chunks of their income to the state but cannot clearly see how much of the money is coming back to them and where the redistributed part of it might be going. (And people on low incomes pay a larger proportion of their incomes in tax, including indirect tax, than people on high incomes.)

Labour has quite properly responded to these populist anxieties by stressing the conditionality of welfare, in effect readopting the Victorian distinction between the deserving and undeserving poor that had been submerged by several decades of universal welfareism. John Denham, the influential Labour chair of the home affairs select committee, has defended this shift in a *Prospect* essay describing an extended focus group he conducted in his Southampton constituency:

> Fairness comes up in every important area of public policy: what happens at
> work; access to public services and communal goods; the way public services

are delivered. It's not a selfish 'I should get more' reaction, but something broader and more complex. Is good behaviour rewarded? Do I get a fair return for what I put in? Are some people getting something for nothing? There's a sense of fairness that comes out in many conversations, the belief that there is a set of obligations and opportunities that should underpin British society. When people say 'it's not fair', it is usually because they believe that the balance of duties and rewards – 'the fairness code' – has been upset.

The fairness code cuts across the values of left and right. Few people express the left's traditional concern about income equality and there is little interest in the right's individualistic, self-reliant model of social and economic policy. The fairness code is concerned with what rights you have earned, not just what your needs are today. Public services should be for people who are entitled to them, need them, and use them responsibly. People should be expected to exercise personal responsibility and be rewarded for it, but they must be given a realistic chance to do so.

Some of this – with its strong echoes of the deserving and the undeserving poor – will sound discomforting to progressives who also fear the stigmatisation of those, like recent immigrants, who have not yet had a chance to contribute. But in most cases the fairness code is a simple assertion of an appropriate connection between effort and reward. [11]

But there is a growing problem for those of us who wish to reassure Denham's constituents that the fairness code is not being breached on a large scale. The British welfare state has been drifting away from a contribution based system (at least for unemployment benefit and pensions), with its direct link between what you put in and what you get out, to a system based on needs, regardless of what you have paid in. For a 'common pool' welfare system to thrive you need to have confidence in your fellow citizens to play by the rules and not to take advantage. But we have been making this shift to more common pool welfare just at the time when trust levels have been declining and when people believe that we no longer fully control our borders and consequently who becomes a fellow citizen. Unfortunately this latter belief is partly justified. As any migration expert will tell you, it is very hard to keep full control of your borders and remain an open society when there are 90 million journeys into and out of Britain each year.

We cannot return to a more contribution based welfare system because it discriminated against women and others who break their careers. But what politics can and must do is help to neutralize the sometimes irrational anxieties people have about free riding in more morally and ethnically diverse societies. As a liberal realist I prefer measures of majority reassurance rather than a doomed attempt to turn the average citizen into a cosmopolitan.

Majority reassurance

So, if we want a more generous, capacious notion of the 'collective we' allowing for moderate levels of immigration and high levels of welfare, I would suggest the following measures as markers for the politics of liberal nationalism/integrationism.

(1) *Immigration* Mass immigration is not popular, but quite high levels are likely to continue for several decades for reasons of economic demand, family reunion and asylum. Government cannot and should not stop immigration but it can, and is, trying to reduce the quantity and speed of immigration, especially illegal immigration. More resources have to be invested in controlling and counting what is actually happening at our borders, eventually through electronic embarkation controls. Political symbolism is also important here. The government should produce a detailed annual 'migration report' on what we know about those leaving and coming to the country, and in the case of the latter we should be told as much as possible about where they have come from, whether they are settling permanently, what sort of jobs they are going into and what the criterion for entry is. Each report, preferably produced by an independent migration panel, should also be accompanied by a migration target for the coming year. Despite majority scepticism about high levels of immigration, people are happy enough to accept newcomers both nationally and locally if they are seen to contribute (they are least keen on wage-depressing unskilled labour from the developing world). An annual report full of reassuring facts and figures would give an impression of transparency and communicate the idea that we are in control of who is becoming a fellow citizen.

Clearly many migrants, including asylum seekers, do not want to become citizens, preferring to stay for a few years and then return home. But many others do want to stay permanently and become citizens. The important line between temporary residence and permanent citizenship should be more clearly drawn. Indeed, we should not be frightened by a more formal two-tier citizenship: the unfavourable comparison often made with the *Gastarbeiter* experiment in Germany is not relevant – most of the *Gastarbeiter* came from one country, Turkey, and they were *de facto* permanent citizens but *de jure* temporary ones. For those who do become full British citizens it is important for the rest of us to have confidence in them and to feel that they have 'worked their passage', have earned their citizenship. In other words, there needs to be a clearer contract between host country and migrant.

European commissioner Antonio Vitorino again: 'There should be a contract between host societies and migrant communities in which the former should be ready to accept greater diversity and the latter should have to learn our core values.'[12] One simple way of underlining this contract would be to follow the Canadian model and have a more overt probationary period for citizenship of three years, during which time a person would not qualify for full political and welfare rights. (This is already the case but few people are aware of it.) Moreover, anyone who commits a crime above a certain level of seriousness during the probationary period would not be allowed into full citizenship. The idea that it is racist to be anything other than 'blind' about who we accept into citizenship is very peculiar. If we value citizenship, as surely anyone on the left must, then we should take care about whom we share it with, and surely it makes sense to give priority to those who will fit in easily and contribute most. That does not mean a racist 'whites only' immigration policy but it might well mean giving priority to, say, a well-educated Indian electronics engineer over a Bangladeshi peasant. We can more appropriately help the latter through development aid and fair trade rules.

Such an approach would also imply support for the plea of David Blunkett as Home Secretary to the south Asian community to find spouses from within their community here, rather than returning to the subcontinent for them. The latter practice constantly short-circuits the process of integration by bringing in spouses who are often completely new to our culture and language.

(2) *Welfare*   Immigration requires a clearer and more overt contract between new immigrants and the host society, and welfare too requires a more overt contract between established citizens and society. We need to increase the conditionality and transparency of entitlements if we want people to continue paying more than one-third of their income to the state. Citizens need to believe that the vast majority of people are playing by the national 'fairness code'. Where appropriate, benefits should be (as they often already are) conditional on proper behaviour, such as the commitment to genuinely seek a job in return for unemployment benefit. But Britain has an unusually open welfare system, thanks partly to the lack of identity cards.

Almost anyone can access public education and health care if they have an address. In a more mobile society such openness, although attractive, is probably no longer feasible. By connecting your entitlement to your citizenship status, identity cards would go some way to ensuring the fairness code is not breached. Identity cards are also a badge of Britishness which transcends our more particular regional, ethnic or racial identities. John Denham again:

> Nothing is more damaging to social cohesion than the belief that expensive tax-funded services are too readily available to people who are not entitled to them. The legal basis for access to the NHS and education is not clear enough for a modern mobile world; this is unsustainable given our record investments in these services. Citizens must be sure that access to public services is not a free-for-all but is based on a protected and privileged entitlement. Identity cards, supported by legislation to clarify entitlement to services and backed by a beefed-up workplace inspectorate to take action against employers of illegal labour, will demonstrate a commitment to using taxpayers' money fairly. This could also provide a clear framework for phased entitlement for migrants to different benefits and services – a kind of 'earned citizenship'.

(3) *European Union*   There is no reason why strong feelings of Britishness, and pride in British history, institutions and values should not coexist with enthusiastic participation in the primarily intergovernmental association of the European Union. Other countries such as France combine both a stronger sense of national identity and a stronger historic commitment to the EU than Britain. Moreover the national interest argument for Europe is more persuasive now than it was in 1973 when we joined. Since enlargement to an EU of twenty-five the federalist argument has been largely defeated and the organization is far less politically dominated by the Franco-German alliance. And while the EU does, of course, require the relinquishing of some sovereignty, the main issues in British politics – tax and spend, health, education, crime, personal tax levels, asylum and immigration – all remain overwhelmingly national matters. Finally, one reason for Britain's relative lack of enthusiasm for Europe is that compared with many other European countries our national identity has been more bound up with our history and our political institutions, and those institutions are, of course, subject to change and interference from Brussels. Other big European countries, by contrast, express their national identities more through language and way of life, making them less sensitive to political change directed from Brussels.

This, however, seems to be changing. As the importance of politics in general and Parliament in particular recedes in our national life and we, too, come to express a more 'cultural' understanding of our identity, this problem with Europe may fade away.

(4) *Education*   As society becomes more diverse, common values and institutions become more important. The school becomes a key

institution of integration, especially for the children of recent migrants and especially when they may be segregated, often by choice, in most other areas of their life – housing, work, religious worship. Curriculums should obviously reflect the distinct cultural background of pupils when a school draws many pupils from the same immigrant group, but teaching British national history and literature – and more recently British citizenship – must remain a central part of every schoolchild's education. Also, if common schools are important in fostering trust and understanding across ethnic and religious divides, then surely there should be a policy bias against faith schools.

(5) *Symbols of Britishness*   As we can no longer depend on shared assumptions, we need to establish more overt contracts – as we have seen above with immigration and welfare. This also applies more generally to politics and to national symbols. Symbols are important both for integrating outsiders and for validating the identity of the majority population. For historical reasons Britain does not have a national day. We should inaugurate one. Such a national day could also coincide with an American-style state-of-the-nation address delivered by the prime minister, in addition to or instead of the rather technical Queen's Speech. The national flag and the national anthem remain central symbols of Britishness, and particularly in the case of the flag have become more so in the past few years. (One of the most uplifting things about the Athens Olympic games was the way in which medal winners from ethnic minorities embraced the union flag so enthusiastically and talked about their pride in winning for their country.) The citizenship ceremonies initiated by David Blunkett have also been an important small-scale innovation.

Political imagination is required here to create more binding symbols.

Conclusion

The points above are largely defensive measures designed to persuade an anxious public that British citizenship remains a valuable and protected thing. Some of these measures also hint at a less tangible objective: how to deal with the thorny issue of majority needs for belonging. We tend to think about culture and identity issues as something that only relate to minorities, what Eric Kaufmann has described as 'asymmetrical multiculturalism'. [13]

But perhaps the biggest question of all in modern Europe is how majorities can express their local and national identities without alienating minorities? How can outsiders be made to feel at home without making insiders feel that they have become strangers in their own home? It is no longer enough to say that the prevailing society and culture already reflects that of the majority and thus provides identity, meaning and belonging to members of majority ethnic groups. An increasing number of people evidently do not feel this to be the case any longer – this is the virtue and the vice of a more diverse society.

The British state and its mass culture must, of course, strive for ethnic and racial neutrality. But what we also desperately need is a new vocabulary that can acknowledge real affinities of people and place and respect the feelings of solidarity of Britain's historic, majority ethnic communities too. At present there is a large conceptual and linguistic space between racism, at one end, and liberal cosmopolitanism, at the other. Most people reside in this middle space but it is empty of words for us to describe our feelings. 'Preferring your own' is a natural human reaction; we do not consider it racist when practised by minorities, nor should we when practised by majorities. Such feelings may exclude class and ethnic outsiders of all kinds, at least initially, but they are not 'racist' unless they are used to ensure racial purity or erect a racial hierarchy. A politics of liberal nationalism which provides a 'thin' canopy over the thicker and inherently more closed identities of ethnic, racial, class and religious groups is surely the best framework for dealing with the potential conflicts ahead.

There is nothing very new or radical about liberal nationalism; indeed it has probably been the dominant political force of the past 150 years in developed countries. This has perhaps been less obviously true in Britain, which seemed in the postwar period to move from an imperial sense of identity to a post-national one in one bound, leaving the political class – especially the left of centre part of it – with an unusually hostile attitude towards nationalism of all kinds. We now seem to be reaching the end of this British 'exceptionalism'. The political task now is to help shape a non-ethnic, liberal nationalism which is not seeking to rub out the majority ethnicity. Such a refashioned liberal nationalism is surely the best means of appealing to a strong, generous notion of British citizenship.

10

Why gender equality?

Magdalena Andersson

The first question almost everyone asks when a baby is born is whether it is a boy or a girl. Not if the baby is doing fine. Not how the mother is doing. No – it is the sex that seems to be the most absolutely crucial piece of information. How can that be?

From the very first day we are born, our sex defines how people treat us. Girls are encouraged to be sweet, calm and helpful. Boys are encouraged to be strong, active and independent. Old fairy tales as well as new stories teach boys and girls how they are supposed to act in order to keep to traditional role models. Girls and boys who differ from that pattern are often considered strange or odd.

All through our lives, we are constantly reminded how to live up to the traditional roles of men and women. What does this do to us? What would you have been like if you hadn't been pressed into the standard male or female role model? If you are a man and had been encouraged to show your feelings and develop caring skills? If you are a woman and had been encouraged to be independent and stand up for yourself?

The thought is rather intriguing – what combinations of strength, caring and independence would come out? What would we all be like? Nobody knows, we can only guess. We can guess that if children were taught to 'be all that you can be' rather than to 'be as you are supposed to be' things would be a lot different. The way things are today limits all of us from developing our full potentials.

Gender equality is therefore more than liberating women, strengthening the position of women in society. Gender equality is also about liberating men.

Apart from being limiting and, of course, simply unfair, it is easy to argue that gender inequality is bad for economic growth. A reasonable assumption would be that competence is evenly distributed between men and women. It would then follow that jobs that entail important decisions should be evenly distributed between men and women. This in turn would imply a more equal distribution of men and women in decision-making positions. And then that the way most societies are organized today cannot be the optimal one.

Gender inequalities also tend to result in low female labour force participation. Therefore a more gender equal society could liberate a potential labour supply reserve – an important aspect in the light of forthcoming labour supply shortages because of demographic change.

Towards gender equality

There is no single measure that will create gender equality. Rather, gender equality is about changing structures. It is about changing the way children are raised, what decisions we make within our families, how family policy and taxes are formed. Gender equality is also about changing attitudes, within families, within the church, in businesses and political institutions. Last, but not least, gender equality is about fighting trafficking and prostitution, as well as changing attitudes towards pornography.

A methodology has therefore been developed to take on these different issues. Mainstreaming is the method by which all political decisions are analysed from a gender perspective: How will this tax cut affect men and women? How will this labour market programme affect men and women? Earlier, one minister in government was responsible for gender equality policies. The problem was that this person would not be the one who had the tools, since the tools are educational policies, labour market policies, tax policies and so forth. At the UN international conference on women's rights in Beijing in 1995, mainstreaming became seen as an answer to the problem. Gender equality should instead be the responsibility of each and every minister. The minister for gender equality should be responsible for coordinating rather than creating gender equality policies.

Mainstreaming has turned out to be an excellent tool for increasing the awareness of gender inequality across all fields of political action. So successful that it is now being implemented in several other areas, such as the social integration of immigrants, sustainable development and global development.

Even if mainstreaming is the general method, some areas are particularly important to focus on. This paper will cover two areas: economic independence for women, and the representation of women in 'elite' positions. These areas are central since they highlight the structure of power both within families and in public life. The policy measures discussed in this chapter will not create gender equality on their own, but they are tools available for political decision-makers who are intent on continuing the journey towards a more equal society.

Economic independence for women

Being able to live on your own income is crucial for the independence of all individuals – and therefore also for women. When you are able to support yourself, you increase the possibility of making your own decisions. The power of other people to influence important decisions decreases. Two incomes rather than one also change the structure of power within a family. Neither individual is economically fully dependent on the other. This shifts the balance of bargaining power within the family.

Women have made fantastic progress in the labour market during the last forty years. Still, the statistics clearly show the link between gender and income. First, women participate in the labour force to a lesser extent than men. In EU-15 (the fifteen EU states before expansion) the overall employment rate for men is around 75 per cent; for women it is around 55 per cent. The numbers vary between countries, but in all EU member states the employment rate is higher for men than for women.[1]

Second, women who do participate in the labour force are more likely than men to work part-time. Approximately 30 per cent of the women in EU-15 who participate in the labour force work part-time; only 7 per cent of men do. The figures for levels of part-time work vary greatly between countries, though the statistics should be read carefully. Some countries with low labour force participation rates for women also have low part-time figures. The Netherlands leads the female part-time league in Europe. The lowest figures for female part-timers can be found in Spain and Finland.[2]

There are at least two dimensions of part-time working. Working part-time can be considered much better than not working at all. This is probably true because women who are completely absent from the labour market, for instance during their children's first years, might have problems re-entering the labour force. Their skills and qualifications may be outdated, and general labour market competence might have been lost. On the other hand, working part-time reduces employers' incentive to invest in promotion and training. Further, combining part-time work and a senior position can prove impossible.

Third, women on average earn less. Women's wages are about 15 per cent lower than those of men with similar skills and characteristics.[3] Comparing wage statistics is not easy. For instance, many women likely to suffer low wages are not in the labour market at all. And men have, on average, better qualified and higher skilled jobs. But when economists try to take all possible variables into account, including education and experience, they still cannot explain the wage difference between men and women.

Wages also work differently for men and women. Men who are married and have children earn more than their single, childless counterparts. Married mothers earn less than their single, childless counterparts.

We also know that the higher the proportion of women in a sector or occupation, the lower the hourly earnings for both men and women.[4] This also seems to work dynamically – as more women move into a sector, the earnings there gradually fall behind other sectors.

There are many explanations as to why women's position in the labour market is worse than men's. Perhaps women do not want to work, or maybe they prefer to work part-time because of the political system or because their husbands do not do their share of the household work? This chapter argues that the latter is a stronger explanation.

The systems we see across the world today are not gender neutral. Together with history and culture, they force women into economic dependence and lack of power. There are policy measures that can make our systems more gender neutral – and in countries where these measures have been adopted, women choose to work more.

So what changes may increase female labour supply?

Parental leave

Paid parental leave makes it possible for parents to stay at home with their children while retaining an income and job security. It is an opportunity for the baby and the parent to get to know each other.

There are parental leave systems of many different sorts. Parental leave can be short with lower benefits, as in the US. They can be short with high benefits, as in Denmark. They can be long with low benefits, as in Austria. And they can be long with high benefits, as in Sweden.

Systems with very short leave are problematic since mothers are forced to go back to work earlier than they may consider acceptable. The alternative would be to quit work and try to find a new job later.

Systems with long parental leave have two dimensions. On the one hand, parents (which most of the time means mothers) can spend a lot of time with their children while retaining job security and keeping some income. On the other hand, generous parental leave systems keep mothers away from the labour market for long periods – especially if the family decides to have more than one child. This means that employing, promoting and training any young woman will be a risky business for an employer, since the return on investment will be lower on average for women than for men. Politicians must therefore be very careful when designing parental leave systems.

Where there is long parental leave with low benefit levels, the mother often takes all the leave, since wives tend to earn less than their husbands. She therefore risks staying away from the labour market for too long. But models with long parental leave and high benefit levels are also problematic. Take Sweden as an example. Parental leave is long, thirteen months, with two months designated directly for the father (if the father does not remain at home during this time, the benefit freezes). Levels are high at 80 per cent of salary, but with a ceiling slightly above 2,000 euros a month. Still, fathers take only 16 per cent of the parental leave – a figure that is steadily, but slowly, rising.

If parental leave is not to become a reason for employers to cease investing in young women, a substantial part of parental leave has to be designated to each parent – at least when parental leave is generous in time.

Is that not intruding too much into each family's private decision? There are two strong arguments that it is not. First, no system is gender neutral. As long as women earn less than men and parental leave does not fully compensate the wage loss for high income earners, there will be economic incentives for fathers to take less parental leave. Second, this isn't a private decision made by each family. It is implausible that it is in reality each family's own decision, when the choice is almost always that the mother is going to remain at home. It is a structural problem, and progressive politics has an obligation to fight old-fashioned structures.

Child care

Across the OECD, around 75 per cent of children from the age of three are enrolled in early education and child care institutions.[5] But for children under three, enrolment is much lower in all countries and very low in some. In Austria, for instance, only 10 per cent of children under three have formal child care arrangements.

In Europe, there are high ambitions to change this situation. Within the EU's 1999 Lisbon Strategy there are goals regarding the number of children enrolled in child care institutions: one third of the children under three, and 90 per cent of children above three will be eligible for child care by 2010.

High quality, heavily subsidized and full-time child care for children by the age of one is an excellent tool to increase mothers' potential to work. Full-time is an important dimension. Some countries have universal child care, but it is either only four days a week or only part-time. This, of course, makes it difficult for parents to combine work and family life. These countries also have low female participation in the labour force – especially considering the amount of tax revenue invested in child care.

Availability from an early age is crucial. Looking at European statistics the lesson is very clear – the correlation between the availability of child care for children under three and female participation in the labour force is striking. The argument that it makes sense for employers not to invest in young women, if women on average stay away from the labour market for long periods when they have children, also carries weight. But the primary reason for providing universal child care is not merely to enable parents to work. High quality child care is primarily an efficient investment in our children's future. Decent child care centres provide a pedagogical platform especially designed for younger children. They are the first step in a lifelong learning process. They are a place for children to practise their social skills, not only with other children, but also with grown-ups other than their parents.

Teachers in a day-care centre can recognize children with special needs early on, and provide pedagogical methods suitable for these children. Teachers in a day-care centre can also recognize different forms of child abuse and provide early help and intervention.

Economic incentives for women to work

No tax or benefit system is gender neutral. Some countries have systems that provide economic incentives for women to work, others have systems that do not. Accepting this idea, one can start thinking about the combined effect of taxes and benefits in a given country. This chapter will comment briefly on three areas.

First, subsidized child care. High child care costs reduce the economic incentives for mothers to work. In countries with high general taxation levels – such as most European countries – this is especially important. In these countries, high taxes reduce the income that actually ends up in the pocket of those working. If the tax revenue is not used to reduce the cost of child care, income after taxes is even lower. Taking a brief look at the statistics, it is the case that OECD countries with high taxes but low subsidies for child care have lower participation rates of women in the labour force than others.

Second, benefits and taxes that are connected to the family rather than to each individual create disincentives for women to work. For example, tax systems where husbands' and wives' incomes are not treated separately mean that women, regarded as second earners, face artificially high marginal tax rates.

Third, many single mothers have low incentives to work or to increase their working hours. The combination of taxes, housing subsidies and child care costs can reduce the increase in income from work to practically nothing. The poverty trap is a reality for too many single mothers.

Shared responsibilities within the family

To make it possible for mothers to work, and achieve economic independence, fathers have to do a larger share of household work. In contrast to the measures discussed above, this is not a public policy proposal. But it is an important conclusion after having discussed policy measures that enable mothers to work.

Gender equality cannot only mean gender equality in public life – it also has to mean gender equality within the private sphere of the family. It is not possible for mothers to leave children in child care, go to full-time work, pick up the children from child care and then go home and do all the household work. The answer cannot be to be nanny to all, so then it has to be a more equal distribution when it comes to taking care of children – and of other work in the household.

This is not the sole answer to the discussion about the work-life balance, but it is one piece in the puzzle.

Part-time work and job sharing are common means to tackle the problem. Following the argument in this chapter, this is not the best solution for women in the long term, since it reduces their economic independence. Job sharing at home rather than at work is an economically more prosperous path for wives, though not necessarily for their husbands.

The reasons this chapter focuses centrally on economic independence for women are twofold. As argued above, it is concerned with changing the structure of power within families – crucial for women's opportunities to decide for themselves what they want to do with their lives. But it is also a crucial tool for solving the problems of falling birth rates that we see across the industrialized world. Today, no country in the European Union has fertility above its replacement rate.

To the extent that the decline in the birth rate reflects the fact that couples are able through family planning to choose the number of children they want to have, it could be seen as a welfare gain to society. However, it does not seem simply to be a welfare gain. A study shows that European women at the age of eighteen want to have around two children on average. The average outcome is a little over one child. This means that every second wanted child in Europe is never born.

It seems to be that faced with the choice of either working or having children, European men and women choose to keep working. Progressive politics should seek to make it possible to combine the two. This is also an argument for directing subsidies towards enabling both partners to work and have children, rather than enabling mothers to stay at home with their children. The argument becomes even stronger when it is considered that the demographic challenge ahead will create labour shortages. It is therefore wiser to spend tax revenue in ways that make more people work, rather than in ways that make fewer people work.

Women in high positions

To transform structures, political and economic power must be more evenly distributed between men and women. Being in a leading position gives you power and the ability to influence how work is organized, and in what direction an organization should develop. Since men are overrepresented in senior positions, they also have greater access to economic and political power. Men formulate and have the power to determine a number of important decisions that influence the lives of both men and women.

Despite dramatic changes in women's social and economic position since the Second World War, the world average representation of women in parliaments has remained stable since the 1960s, at around 10 to 15 per cent. Variations between countries are enormous, with representation in Nordic countries at around 40 per cent and average representation in Arab states at below 10 per cent.[6]

Several factors influence the number of women in parliament: female labour force participation, women's movements, cultural history and the electoral system are all decisive.

There is clear evidence that the number of women in parliament is directly affected by the political system. Countries with proportional electoral systems have on average twice as many women in parliament as countries with 'first past the post' two-party systems. Thirteen of the fifteen countries in the world with the highest representation of women use some form of proportional representation. At the other end of the spectrum, the fifteen countries with the lowest representation of women use 'majority' systems.[7]

There has been increasing impatience with the slow progress regarding the representation of women in parliament. The argument historically has been that there were no women to be found with the right competencies. But now that more women work and have educational qualifications this situation will change. The problem is that over time very little has changed at all.

If decision-makers keep looking for competence in the male sense, it is no surprise that they have a problem identifying competent women. Apart from strengthening the position of women in general, there also has to be a more balanced definition of 'competence'.

One way to increase the speed of change is to introduce quotas into electoral systems. This is being done in a number of countries. There are essentially three different types of quota system:

1   *Voluntary quotas within parties*   There are 129 parties in sixty-one countries that have voluntarily introduced quotas, for example in Germany, Italy, Norway, the US and South Africa.[8] The quotas differ from party to party. In some instances, every third candidate should be a woman; in another example there should be at least 40 per cent of each sex represented on all decision-making bodies.
2   *Legislated quotas of women candidates*   These can be constitutionally binding, or legislated in electoral law and adopted in the constitution of each party. This is largely used in countries with

proportional representation, for instance several Latin American countries. A common result has been that the female candidates have been placed too low on the lists, or in regions where they have no chance of being elected. Argentina and Belgium therefore have systems with strict placement rules guaranteeing that women are put in electable positions.

3   *Quotas of seats in parliament*   In this case a certain number of seats are reserved for women. Reserved seats typically exist in two-party systems, for instance in Afghanistan, Uganda and India at the local level.

Evidence suggests that where quotas are implemented and properly enforced, they are an effective way to increase female representation in parliament. Of the fifteen countries with the highest representation of women, twelve have quotas of some sort. The other three are Denmark, which had quotas earlier, Finland and Cuba. Eight of the twelve have voluntary party quotas.[9]

At the same time, the picture is not that simple. Taking the example of the Nordic countries, all with high representations of women, we can see that other factors are also important. None of the Nordic countries has had quotas enforced by law. Some parties have voluntarily introduced quotas, but others, also with high representations of women, have not. In Finland, where 37 per cent of representatives in parliament are women, there is no quota system.

One conclusion is that quotas do not work in isolation. They interact with a political and cultural system which influences whether and how quotas are formed, and how successful they will be.

If the proportion of women in leading positions is low in politics, it is even lower in business life. The proportion of women who are members of the highest decision-making body in the top fifty publicly quoted companies in Europe is around 10 per cent. The number of women presidents in the same companies is as low as 2 per cent.[10]

What about quotas in the business sector? In Norway the parliament recently passed a law regarding the percentage of women among board members in publicly quoted companies. If the proportion of women is still below 40 per cent by 2005, the parliament will enforce a law to ensure that it is a minimum of 40 per cent. This has so far led to an increase of 8 per cent to 13 per cent women.

If quota systems are controversial in politics, things are no less complicated in the private sector. The democratic argument for intervention in corporate governance is a lot weaker. From a democratic perspective, it is easy to argue that women should be represented equally in parliamentary institutions. There is certainly a democratic argument that business power should be more evenly distributed between men and women, but it is substantially weaker.

In addition, companies can choose to leave the country, and register with another stock exchange. It may be that a law requiring a minimum proportion of women would not force companies out of the country on its own, but together with other rules and regulations regarded by companies as hostile it could be one factor that drives global relocation, to the detriment of higher employment and living standards.

Men – security in change

In order to achieve gender equality it is not only women but also men who have to change. The model of what it is to be a man and the role of a husband has to change. It must be possible to be a 'real' man and do 50 per cent of household work: pick up kids at day-care, do the dishes, the laundry, the vacuum cleaning and so forth. This change has not proved to be easy, or quick.

Role models are clearly important. This is valid for both men and women, of course. But there has been more focus on alternative role models for males. Potential role models who do take responsibility for their families change institutions. This is a challenge not only for sportsmen, rock stars, politicians, journalists, writers and filmmakers, but also for teachers, doctors and social workers.

Security at a time of change is an expression we normally use for periods of labour market transition. But it can also be used in this context. Change can bring new opportunities, new visions and new ideas. But to appreciate the benefits of change, it has to be combined into new forms of security.

Men in today's industrialized world have experienced several important transformations. The labour market is undergoing structural change. The traditional male jobs are disappearing as factories are relocated to Asia; the wharf is long gone, the mine has closed. At the same time, the traditional role models within their families may be changing. Women are moving to regions with more job opportunities, or going on to gain further educational qualifications and new skills in the 'feminized' knowledge economy. There may be a conflict between what is traditionally expected to be a man's life and the lives that men actually have the opportunity to lead.

Policies that increase security for these men may not only improve their lives, but may also improve gender equality in the long term.

Security in this context has to mean high quality labour market pro-grammes, opportunities for adult education and retraining, and measures that increase labour market opportunities for these men.

The policy measures described in this chapter are not a fully fledged road-map towards gender equality. They are paths to take on the journey towards it. There will be obstacles on the way – some we have not yet even anticipated, some we have already experienced. Let us discuss one.

If both men and women have to change in order to achieve gender equality, are they really changing and do we know whether they are changing in the right direction? For instance, we observe tendencies that some young women are adopting what is considered bad male behaviour, such as acts of aggression and violence, often fuelled by alcohol. They smoke more, they drink more and they commit more crimes. This can very well be one result of increased gender equality. We will probably see women gradually adopting positive and negative 'male behaviour'. And we will see men picking up good – and bad – 'female behaviour'. How will the total sum of good and bad social behaviour develop?

No matter what the answer is, I still believe increasing gender equality is the right path. The justice argument, not displayed heavily in this chapter, is the most compelling reason. It is not fair to keep half the population apart from important decision-making, in their own lives or in society in general.

Behavioural development will largely be influenced by general changes in society, where increased gender equality is only a small component. Fighting income inequality, discrimination and injustice reduces 'bad behaviour' among both men and women.

To summarize, gender equality is right for both men and women, and central to the social democratic conception of the 'good society'. To achieve it, men and women both have to change. Politics alone will not achieve gender equality, but politics can make a decisive difference in transforming economic and social structures. Parental leave, child care, the tax and benefit systems, and selective quotas are all tools politicians can use to increase gender equality. Too many politicians still choose not to use these tools. This must now change.

11

Social corrosion, inequality and health

Richard Wilkinson

During the last quarter of a century there has been a concentrated research effort to try to understand why even the richest countries continue to be marked by large social class differences in death rates. According to recent figures for England and Wales, *average* life expectancy in social class V (unskilled manual occupations) is more than seven years shorter for men, and almost six years shorter for women, than it is for men and women in social class I (professional occupations). These differences mark the most important social injustice in modern societies. Indeed, as life is short where its quality is poor, they mark a double injustice.

These differences in life expectancy are not merely differences between the poor and the rest of society. Instead there is a gradient in health across all classes. Despite not including the poor, the homeless and the unemployed, the Whitehall studies which have followed up many thousands of civil servants found threefold differences in death rates between people at different levels of seniority working in the same government offices, almost all of whom would call themselves 'middle class'. (All comparisons of death rates in this chapter are adjusted for age and sex differences between the groups compared.)

As the evidence from many different sources has accumulated, we have been forced to recognize that the *direct* effects on health of differences in physical living standards have been of declining importance among the rich developed countries. The so-called epidemiological transition, which saw a decline in the infectious diseases still rooted in poor and unsanitary material conditions in the less developed countries today, left us in need of a new epidemiology to serve public health in the rich countries. The epidemiological transition marks the stage in the long history of economic growth when most people have attained a threshold level of living adequate for good health. With the dramatic decline in deaths at younger ages, we have been left with the degenerative diseases and 'diseases of affluence' which kill predominantly in old age. Interestingly, even the diseases of affluence reversed their social distribution during the epidemiological transition: instead of being more common among the rich, conditions such as heart disease and obesity become diseases of the poor in affluent societies. Rather than the rich being fat and the poor thin, as had been true throughout human history, in the rich countries the poor now tend to be fatter than the rich.

Having undergone this transition, standards of health in the rich countries are no longer related to differences in gross national income per head. Across the twenty-five or thirty richest countries, there is no relation between life expectancy and average income at purchasing power parities.[1] Yet *within* each of these countries, health remains strongly related to income or any other socioeconomic marker. The paradox that health is related to income within the rich countries but not to income differences between them almost certainly arises because we are dealing with the health effects of *relative* income, social position, or class.

Because health research is concerned not only with the health of individuals, but also with health and health inequalities at the societal level of public health, we have begun to be able to integrate our understanding of the individual's sensitivity to the social environment with our understanding of what it is in the wider structure of societies which triggers these sensitivities and creates health differences between whole populations.

It turns out that health is highly sensitive to psychosocial stressors, and to the nature of the social environment in particular. A very substantial contribution to health inequalities results from the psychosocial effects of social status differences. Partly because of the power of psychosocial risk factors, the social determinants of health provide a lens through which we get a clearer picture of a wide range of the social problems which, like health, show a social gradient and are most common in the deprived areas. Rooted in the psychosocial effects of low social status, the processes affecting health have much in common with those responsible for poor educational performance of schoolchildren, for violence and depression – to name but a few. What comes out of this is an identification of some of the dimensions of social life which are most important to people's social well-being.

I will start by outlining the evidence suggesting the nature and power of the three most important categories of psychosocial risk factors affecting health at the individual level. They are low social status, having few friends, and stress in early life. After that, we shall then describe, at the societal level, the growing body of evidence showing that more unequal societies – with larger income differences between rich and poor – tend to have lower average life expectancies. To understand why that is so means understanding how individuals are affected by inequality. The key here is provided by the evidence showing that the quality of social relations is strongly affected by the amount of inequality. More equal societies tend to have higher levels of trust, more involvement in community life, and lower levels of violence, than less equal ones. The data show that inequality is, as many have suspected, socially divisive. Finally, we shall move on to suggest a view of human sociality which explains how and why all this fits together. What we end up with is an understanding of our sensitivity to the social environment, and to social dominance in particular, which integrates observations at both the individual and societal levels.

Psychosocial risk factors: vulnerability to the social

The three most important categories of psychosocial risk for poor health are low social status, weak social affiliations, and stress in early life. As we discuss each, it is important to see them as pointers to human *social* needs and to remember that they are discussed here as a preparation for understanding the effects of inequality.

Low social status

Death rates in different societies are commonly two or three times as high among those lower down the social hierarchy as among those nearer the top. Even though differences in material conditions within a society are powerful indicators of social status, there are numerous reasons for thinking that health is affected more by the psychosocial effects of low social status than by the direct effects of poorer material living standards. I shall mention three of the most important. First, as we have already seen, the weakening impact of material conditions on health during the epidemiological transition as living standards have risen has left health related to income within, but not between, the rich developed countries. This is why, as a recent comparison showed, it is possible for black American males who have a median real income four times as high as men in Costa Rica to have nine years shorter life expectancy.[2] The power of the psychosocial effects of relative deprivation and stigmatization can outweigh the direct effects of material conditions.

Higher social status and better material conditions are usually so closely related that, but for examples of this kind, it would be impossible to distinguish unambiguously between their effects. It has however been possible to separate them among non-human primates. The social status of macaques has been manipulated by moving animals between groups while at the same time ensuring that they all have the same diets and live in the same enclosures.[3] In this way, changes in social status take place in the absence of changes in material conditions. What makes the results of such observations particularly interesting is that animals which move down the dominance hierarchy under these conditions suffer many of the ill effects known to be associated with low social status among humans. Low status animals show a much more rapid build up of arteriosclerosis, they have a worse ratio of high to low density lipoproteins, a tendency towards abdominal obesity, higher levels of stress hormones, higher blood pressure and heart rates, and behavioural signs of depression. In the animals all these effects clearly result from the stress of low social status. Subordinates tend to be small, nervous animals who have to keep a constant lookout for dominants, keep out of their way and show submission signals to avoid getting attacked. Although among some species of non-human primates which form dominance hierarchies stress levels may be higher at the top than the bottom, especially when dominance is being contested, the work on macaques shows that stresses of low social status can have serious physiological consequences. This is the second reason for thinking we are dealing with the psychosocial stresses of low social status rather than the direct effects of material standards.

The third reason is that psychosocial variables such as depression, anxiety, hostility, hopelessness, low sense of control and many others seem particularly successful in explaining health differences among humans. Low sense of control is particularly relevant to social status. In the Whitehall studies, having little control over one's work explained a substantial amount of the overall social gradient in health across the office hierarchy, and this was true not only after controlling for other psychological characteristics but also regardless of whether control was assessed independently or by the person doing the job.[4] If you have low control at work it is probably because you are being told what to do. Such subordination infringes one's sense of autonomy and often leads to hostility – itself a risk factor for heart disease. It is perhaps an inherent part of the experience of low social status in modern societies.

Weak social affiliations

Moving on from low social status, weak social affiliations seem to presage poor health. Review papers suggest that a doubling or tripling of death rates among people with few friends is not an unusual finding.[5] Everything from close 'confiding' relationships to involvement in community life seems to be protective. Because these links have been found even in prospective studies which exclude those initially sick, we can be sure that this is not just a reflection of how illness curtails social life. As well as observational studies, experiments in which people have been exposed to a measured dose of cold viruses have shown that people with friends in fewer areas of life are four times as likely to develop colds, despite exactly the same exposure to infection.[6] This study controlled not only for socioeconomic differences, but also for pre-existing levels of antibodies which might reflect that people with a more active social life had encountered more cold strains and so had already acquired immunity to them. Even studies looking at survival rates among those suffering from a serious illness (such as a heart attack or breast cancer) have shown that social support is associated with substantial improvements.[7]

Stress in early life

After low social status and lack of social affiliations, the last major category of psychosocial risk centres on stress in early life – both prenatally and in early childhood. The identification of the processes started with David Barker's finding that people who had been smaller as babies were more likely to get diseases such as heart disease, stroke, and diabetes in later life.[8] Although Barker initially assumed he was seeing the effects of poor maternal nutrition in pregnancy compromising foetal growth, it is now clear that in the developed countries – if not elsewhere – low birth weight is much more often the result of maternal stress in pregnancy. Mothers of small babies give histories of stressful pregnancies; several of the biological pathways through which stress would slow foetal growth are known; and experiments show that if animals are stressed in pregnancy, they have smaller offspring.[9]

It looks as if responses are tuned early in life in accordance with maternal stress in pregnancy *and* infant experience. Early childhood experience also has important consequences for health later in life and seems to centre on stress – on the stresses of poor attachment, domestic conflict, loss of a parent, etc.[10] Although psychologists have always told us that early experience is important in the development of life-long personality characteristics, we have only recently begun to appreciate the biological side of this. The effects of this early tuning of stress responses show up, among other things, in higher levels of cortisol (one of the key stress hormones) and a faster age-rise in blood pressure – both of which rebound on health in later life. Indeed, cortisol levels in middle age have been found to be correlated with birth weight.[11]

Stress: biological effects, social causes

We know that psychosocial factors damage health in so far as they are causes of chronic stress. Stress responses involve a shift in biological priorities from processes which could be seen as health maintenance or housekeeping functions, to the 'fight or flight' responses which enable us to deal with an imminent threat or emergency.[12] Priority switches from processes which are not essential in dealing with an emergency – such as tissue maintenance and repair, growth, reproductive functions, digestion and (if the stress goes on for more than about an hour) immunity – in order to increase resources available to support muscular activity, reducing reaction times and making us mentally and physically ready to respond quickly to anything. Because the exact timing of the housekeeping functions is less critical, resources can be concentrated on dealing with the emergency and, if it is over within ten or twenty minutes, nothing is lost. However, if the stress goes on for weeks, months or years, we become more vulnerable to a wide range of diseases, so much so that the effects have been likened to more rapid ageing.

Low social status, weak social affiliations and stress in early life are such important influences on population health not only because the relative risks between those who are or are not exposed is so great (two or threefold differences in death rates) but also because such a large proportion of the population is exposed to them. As determinants of population health they are more important than things like occupational exposures to toxic materials because only tiny proportions of the population are exposed to dangerous materials at work and, even when they are, they rarely produce differences in death rates like those found up and down the office hierarchy among civil servants.

If these intensely social risk factors are such important influences on population health and they work through chronic stress, it suggests that they are the most important sources of chronic stress in modern societies. That is a point worth bearing in mind. Furthermore, it looks as if they are all indicative of one underlying source of stress. The stresses and insecurities that we may carry with us from early childhood are in some ways similar to the insecurities which can come from low social status. It looks as if one can exacerbate or offset the other. Some studies show interaction effects and both early insecurity and low social status are associated with higher basal cortisol levels. Friendship fits into this picture because, unlike low social status or poor early attachment, friends make us feel valued and appreciated. They provide positive feedback: friends enjoy our company, laugh at our jokes or find us interesting. But if we feel excluded or unwelcome, if we are not included in invitations, or people do not choose to sit next to us, we easily become filled with self-doubts. We worry that we are boring or unattractive, that we are gauche or stupid, and end up feeling tense, insecure and socially anxious.

These forces are so strong in human beings because, as social beings dependent on a learned culture and way of life, we are reflexive. We know ourselves partly through each other's eyes and depend on monitoring others' reactions to us in order to shape our behaviour appropriately. Our capacity for shame and embarrassment and our desire for approval are the keys not only to conformity and 'proper' social behaviour but also to a great deal of the imitative learning which is so crucial to our cultural way of life. And just as these processes are central to socialization and to the way society gets into us to shape our behaviour, so too they are the way society gets under the skin to affect our health. That is why the most important psychosocial risk factors for health are as intensely social as low social status, poor social networks, and insecure early childhood.

Health and inequality

With this picture of individual vulnerability to our social environment in mind, I want now to change gear and discuss how the amount of inequality in society as a whole affects this vulnerability. Almost any social problem such as violence, poor educational performance, unemployment or ill health can be approached from an individual or a societal perspective. We can discover risk factors which help explain why some individuals have any of these problems and others do not. But if we are to understand why some societies have 2 per cent unemployed while others have 20 per cent, we have to understand the workings of the economy – even though those affected will always be the most vulnerable 2 or 20 per cent.

Although it has not gone unchallenged, a large amount of evidence has accumulated that more egalitarian societies tend to be healthier than less egalitarian ones. Using data for 528 cities from five different countries, studies show a clear tendency for more egalitarian cities to be healthier.[13] Similar relationships have now been shown in many different contexts, including the richest developed countries,[14] the countries of central and eastern Europe,[15] among the fifty states of the US, and among the eighty-eight regions of Russia.[16] In a forthcoming review, Pickett and I identified over 140 published papers on income inequality and health, containing over 150 separate analyses.[17] Three-quarters of them found *only* statistically significant associations between greater equality and better health. Most of the rest reported a mixture of significant and insignificant associations. Only eight found *any* significant associations between greater equality and worse health – even after the use of whatever control variables the authors thought relevant.[17] Only analyses of much smaller areas, such as counties, parishes or census tracts, have tended not to support the conclusion that greater equality is good for health. This is because the poorer health found, for instance, in the small deprived inner city areas is not the result of the inequality *within* them, but of how much poorer people in them are compared to the rest of society. Indeed, income inequality in the larger areas can be considered as being composed of two elements: the inequality in and between their smaller constituent areas. But the smaller the areas you look at, the greater the residential segregation of rich and poor tends to be, and so the more closely health is related to the differences in income between – rather than within – the small areas. In the largest areas the situation is reversed: health is related to inequality within, rather than between, them.[18]

Social relations and inequality

The tendency for more unequal societies to have worse health might initially be attributed to a bigger burden of relative deprivation creating more of all the social and health problems we often associate with poor inner city areas. However, there is more to it than that. A number of indicators suggest that the quality of social relations is less good in more unequal societies. They tend to have lower levels of trust, more violence, less involvement in community life, lower electoral turnout and more discrimination against women and minorities.

There are over fifty studies showing that violent crime and homicide rates are higher where income inequalities are greater. As long ago as 1993 a meta-analysis of some thirty-four of them showed that this was a robust relationship.[19]

In a footnote, Putnam records the fact that his index of involvement in community life in the twenty regions of Italy is closely correlated ($r = 0.8$) with income inequality.[20] Referring to an egalitarian social ethos rather than to income inequality as such, he says that 'equality is an essential feature of the civic community' and he contrasts the 'vertical' 'patron–client' relationships up and down the social hierarchy in the less civic regions of Italy with the more egalitarian 'horizontal' relations in the more civic regions. He shows similar cross-sectional relationships between income inequality and the strength of community life among the fifty states of the US and says, 'Community and equality are mutually reinforcing . . .'[21] In addition, he points out a relation over time in the US. He says, 'Social capital and economic inequality moved in tandem through most of the twentieth century.' After describing how income differences narrowed and social capital strengthened until the 1960s, he observes that 'record highs in equality and social capital coincided.' But then, 'somewhere around 1965–70 America reversed course and started becoming both less just economically and less well connected socially and politically.'[22] These trends continued for the rest of the century and, as Putnam remarks, 'the [simultaneous] timing of the two trends is striking.'

Measures of trust show the same pattern. Kawachi and colleagues[23] showed that the proportion of people who feel they can trust others varied from only 10 or 15 per cent among the most unequal states of the US to as much as 35 or 40 per cent among the most equal. About half of this variation seemed to be related to inequality. Excluding the ex-Communist countries of central and eastern Europe, Uslaner has shown similar relationships internationally.[24]

Whether we look at trust, violence or the strength of community life, the evidence suggests that the quality of social relations is better in more egalitarian places. This is what many early socialists recognized intuitively. Rather than valuing greater equality simply as a fairer share-out of goods between self-interested individuals, they believed inequality was a barrier to greater human harmony, to comradeship or brother- and sisterhood. Interestingly de Tocqueville had the same intuition. Often cited for his writing on the strength of civic life in the United States when he visited in 1830, he made it clear from the first page of his *Democracy in America* that he thought it was based on what he called 'the equality of conditions'. On the very first page of *Democracy in America*, he says:

> I easily perceived the enormous influence that this primary fact [the equality of conditions] exercises on the workings of the society. It gives a particular direction to the public mind, a particular turn to the laws, new maxims to those who govern, and particular habits to the governed. I soon recognized that this same fact extends its influence far beyond political mores and laws, and that its empire expands over civil society as well as government: it creates opinions, gives rise to sentiments, inspires customs, and modifies everything that it does not produce.[25]

As well as proving these intuitions right, modern statistical analyses seem to be telling us that it is not all or nothing: even the small differences in inequality between different American states or market democracies have important implications.

Returning to the three categories of psychosocial risk with which we started, we should note that inequality affects two of them: it creates a bigger burden of low social status and, at the same time, leads to a deterioration in the quality of social relations. If that is true, it would be surprising if inequality was not associated with poorer health.

Two sides of the coin?

However, if our aim is to understand the effects of inequality, there is another step we should take towards explaining these relationships. The important question to ask is why are social status and friendship linked in what are two very different ways: first, with lack of them being risk factors for poor health in individuals, and second, as varying inversely at the level of societies (the association between inequality and the quality of social relations which we have just seen)? The answer is not difficult to find: they are two sides of the same coin – opposite systems of social relations based, as we shall see, on different methods of resource allocation.

Most fundamentally, human social stratification systems, in common with animal dominance hierarchies or pecking orders, are about the use of status, power and coercion to gain preferential access to scarce resources – regardless of the needs of others. Where the rich get the lion's share, it is inevitable that in times of scarcity it is the weak who go short. Although the development of welfare systems and the rule of law in market democracies means that these patterns are less blatant than they were, the links between power and wealth remain as clear as ever. In addition, we only have to go back a few centuries, or look at some less developed countries, to see examples where the still unbridled use of personal power ensures that great luxury can coexist alongside hunger.

On the other side of the coin is friendship, mutuality, sharing, cooperation, reciprocity and a recognition of each other's needs. Here, instead of depending on strength and ability to win out in conflict, you depend on membership of the cooperative group and on the strength of your social relations.

The two sides of the coin are the two opposite ways people can come together – either in opposition, dependent on power, or through mutuality and social alliances. They have become so important to us because, for members of most species – including human beings – the worst potential competitors are not some other species which might compete for one or two of the same foodstuffs, but other members of the same species who, because they have all the same needs, have the potential to compete for everything. A dominant baboon will even oust a subordinate from a comfortable place in the shade. Human beings may compete with each other for food, shelter, clothing, jobs, sexual partners – everything. But as well as being each other's worst rivals, other human beings also have the potential to be the best source of cooperation, assistance, care, learning and love. In short, other people can be the best or the worst, depending on our relationships.

Hobbes based his political philosophy on the difficulty of maintaining peace between people who, precisely because they had all the same needs, faced the constant possibility of conflict over everything. This was why he thought 'every man was enemy to every man' and why, in the absence of a sovereign power capable of keeping the peace, he thought there was the constant potential for 'warre . . . of every man against every man'. It was Marshal Sahlins who pointed out that hunting and gathering societies, without a sovereign power to keep the peace, used gift exchange and food sharing to keep social relationships sweet.[26] He described the gift as a form of social contract between giver and receiver. The gift is a symbol of friendship because it is a direct demonstration that the parties reject competition between them for scarce resources and instead recognize each other's needs. As Sahlins put it, 'gifts make friends and friends make gifts.' The social contract is completed by the reciprocal gift, prompted by a sense of indebtedness which evolutionary psychologists suggest is a human universal.[27] Similarly, refusal of a gift is a refusal of a social relation which, in some societies, may be tantamount to a declaration of war.

Because other people can be the worst potential threat or the best source of support, the quality of social relations has been crucial to human welfare throughout our evolution. This is why we have become so sensitive and attentive to social relationships, and why the nature of the social environment has become the most important source of chronic stress affecting health. The amount of inequality in a society shows the extent of dominance relationships, creates social distances and feelings of superiority and inferiority. We choose to make friends with our social equals because we find social distances awkward. We feel timid and ill at ease with our social superiors while depreciating and excluding those of lower social status. The extent to which we use affiliative strategies or hierarchical dominance strategies depends on how we read our social environment – on the scale of inequality and social distances, on how much our welfare seems to depend on cooperation and reciprocity, or on competition and individual gain.

Respect

Compared with the mutual support of more affiliative forms of social relations, the opposition of interests among competitors and rivals is stressful. Where there are large differences in social status and some people seem to count for everything and others for nothing, the esteem in which we are held by others matters very much. It was Adam Smith who asked:

> What is the end of avarice and ambition, of the pursuit of wealth, of power and pre-eminence? Is it to supply the necessities of nature? The wages of the meanest labourer can supply them . . . what are the advantages which we would propose to gain by that great purpose of human life which we call bettering our condition? To be observed, to be attended to, to be taken notice of . . .[28]

Just as poverty is shaming and stigmatizing, so loss of face and feeling looked down on and disrespected seem to be the trigger which accounts for why violence is more common in more unequal societies. The violence which increases with inequality is not violence of the poor against the rich, it is violence among the poor.

After working as a prison psychiatrist who saw very violent men in American prisons for almost a quarter of a century, James Gilligan wrote: 'I have yet to see a serious act of violence that was not provoked by the experience of feeling shamed and humiliated, disrespected and ridiculed, and that did not represent the attempt to prevent or undo this "loss of face" – no matter how severe the punishment.'[29] Exactly the same story comes from people like Nathan McCall and Jimmy Boyle who have written autobiographies after being involved in violent crime.

Where greater inequality increases the burden of relative deprivation, more people feel denied access to the jobs, cars, incomes, expensive clothes and housing which are the markers of status in market societies. As a result they are particularly sensitive to being 'dissed'.

There are a number of reasons for thinking that our sensitivity to social status has long evolutionary roots. Most obvious are the implications of social status for access to scarce resources and reproductive opportunities. It is hard not to anthropomorphize de Waal and Lanting's description of dominance behaviour among chimps:

> Chimpanzees go through elaborate rituals in which one individual communicates its status to the other. Particularly between adult males, one male will literally grovel in the dust, uttering panting grunts, while the other stands bipedally performing a mild intimidation display to make clear who ranks above whom.[30]

Low status animals are smaller and have to keep out of the way of dominants and show submission signals to avoid attack. Despite that, they tend to have many more bite marks than their superiors. Interestingly, the Whitehall II study found a clear social gradient in a blood clotting factor called fibrinogen. The lower the status in the civil service hierarchy, the higher the fibrinogen levels.[31] The stress response is a likely explanation. If you risk physical injury it is important that your blood clots quickly to minimize blood loss. Higher levels of fibrinogen, which – as an 'acute phase reactant' – is known to respond to stress, would achieve that. In addition, experiments have shown that blood pressure and heart rate rise when people are interviewed by someone who is of higher social status.[32] Presumably our tendency to feel shy, timid and ill at ease with our social superiors explains why doctors encounter what is known as 'white coat hypertension' in some of their patients.

Summary: liberty, equality, fraternity

In summary then, inequality increases social stress because it changes the nature of social relations as competition and dominance win out over affiliation and cooperation. As social position becomes more important as an indication of people's value or 'worth', our fears and insecurities as to whether we measure up, whether we count, how we are seen, increase. Snobbishness and processes of downward discrimination make society less inclusive and increase social exclusion at every level. Social insecurity and social evaluation anxiety increase and, given the way we know ourselves through each other's eyes and the intensely social nature of the main psychosocial risk factors for health, these insecurities and anxieties are powerful sources of stress which rebound on health and cut us off from the security of knowing we are accepted and appreciated.

Fundamentally, none of this is new. Not only did many early socialists and others (including de Tocqueville) have an intuitive appreciation of how socially divisive inequality is, but the most important dimensions of the social environment to come out of this analysis were expressed in the political demand for 'liberty, equality and fraternity' raised in the French revolution. By liberty, they meant not being subservient to the feudal nobility and landed aristocracy, not being beholden to anyone. This is clearly closely related to the effects of large social status and power differentials and to the concomitant problems of dominance and subordination, superiority and inferiority. The demand for fraternity expressed a desire for a particular quality of social relations – the opposite side of the coin from dominance relations. It expressed a desire for more cooperative and affiliative social relations and for the social inclusion and solidarity which is conducive to increased involvement in community life and higher social capital. Equality comes into the picture because it is the precondition for getting the other two right. As we have seen, greater inequality not only leads to bigger status differentials and problems of dominance and subordination, but is also corrosive of the quality of social relations.

What is perhaps new is that without modern data we might have assumed that the benefits of greater equality would only be apparent if we were able to reach some impractical, utopian level of near perfect equality. What the data tell us, however, is that even small differences in inequality matter. Rather than it being unrealistic to worry, the existing differences in inequality between market democracies or American states have, as we have seen, important implications for health, for violent crime, for the nature of social relations, and so for the real quality of life of all of us.

What can be done?

People sometimes ask whether it is inequalities in power, status, wealth or income which we need to tackle – as if they were all independent of each other. But the reason why socioeconomic inequalities are so important is because these different components are so closely related. The occasional exceptions, where for instance status comes from moral authority and leadership rather than from wealth and power, stand out because they contrast with the rule. But overwhelmingly, the most powerful people are among the top few per cent of income earners, and those with the largest incomes (earned or unearned) tend to be those with the greatest wealth. Interestingly, although people like film stars and celebrities may seem to have status and wealth without power, increasingly frequent examples such as Ronald Reagan and Arnold Schwarzenegger show how status can be used to gain power. Being rich and powerful brings status and respect – as the quotation (above) from Adam Smith shows. The overwhelming sociological fact is surely that the 'high' are the mighty and it often takes little more than expensive cars and houses to win status and at least grudging respect.

These links doubtless run all the way back to the way position in the dominance hierarchy among animals – such as chimpanzees or baboons – approximates a ranking by physical power, which in turn not only ensures prior access to scarce resources, but also elicits the mixture of fear and respect which subordinates show to dominants.

Among human beings wealth is an expression and indicator of dominance, of superiority and power. The rich seem capable and worthy in contrast to the poor, who appear incapable and worthless. At its crudest, second rate goods seem to denote second rate people.

There are of course lots of ways in which governments can reduce socioeconomic inequality. Taxes and benefits, education policy, minimum wages, the management of the economy and levels of unemployment all have important effects. However, in areas such as these, progress made by a government of one political complexion can be easily undone by that of another, and redistributionary governments tend to create their own opposition among those from whom they redistribute.

A more fundamental approach to greater equality involves the extension of democracy into work. Employee ownership and control of the institutions in which people work has the potential to reduce inequalities in income, wealth, power and status, at source. It is also likely to improve economic performance: research which looked at a large number of British companies during the 1990s found that employee share ownership, profit sharing and participation each make an independent contribution to increased productivity.[33] Research currently in progress will show whether employee ownership and control also improve health: studies of job control and institutional justice suggest that they are likely to.[34]

Tax incentives to encourage employee share ownership schemes have been introduced in a number of countries. In the US they already cover 10 million employees in 10,000 firms, with an average employee ownership of 15–20 per cent.[35] In Britain employee share ownership schemes cover almost a quarter of all employees and some 15 per cent of all companies.[36] Though a large majority of these schemes are intended primarily to provide financial incentives to employees and have very little to do with genuine democracy or egalitarianism, they do make it easier to reach the point where control effectively moves from absentee share owners, who are likely to have no knowledge or interest in a company beyond the profit it makes, to the employees who are the people most intimately involved in it. In societies where the vast majority of corporate wealth is owned by the richest few per cent of the population, employee ownership represents an important redistribution of both wealth and the company profits accruing to it.

Perhaps the best institutional structure through which to exercise employee control is for a majority of shares to be held by a trust democratically controlled by employees.[37] Management structures can then evolve to reflect changing attitudes, experience and circumstances – free of the opposition of interests which has necessitated each layer in the hierarchy exercising control and authority over those below it. Where employee-owned companies choose to retain apparently conventional management structures, the fact that managers are democratically accountable to employees binds them to the service of the rest of the workforce. Free of the major source of opposing interests, management no longer needs to function as a force over and against other employees. As a result, the quality of social relations and trust in management improves, enabling it to service and coordinate the productive effort more effectively.

As well as redistributing corporate wealth and the income accruing to it, employee ownership brings earnings differentials ultimately under democratic control. Pay differentials have to reflect not only people's knowledge of the jobs, but also labour market experience. The indications are that pay differentials in employee-owned companies are consistently narrower than in companies controlled by absentee shareholders.

The extension of democracy involved in employee ownership has the potential not only to reduce the concentration of wealth and income, but also to change the nature of power and status differentials at work. In addition, it is likely to improve productivity and health. If governments did more to promote employee share ownership and to encourage the development of democratic institutional structures at work, they would surely be helping to build the foundations of a much fairer, more egalitarian and efficient society. If employee owned and controlled companies were to become widespread, it seems likely that society would became suffused with more egalitarian and progressive social attitudes, with additional benefits for the quality of social relations and other areas of policy.

12

Inequality, choice and public services

Julian Le Grand

In recent years many countries have seen something of a revolution in publicly funded services such as education and health care. Instead of professionals and bureaucrats deciding where children should go to school, or to which hospital patients should be sent, increasingly users of these services are being given the power to make those decisions for themselves – the power to choose. Choice is becoming the watchword of the 'new' public services.

So patients referred for hospital care in Britain under the public system – the National Health Service – are being given the right to choose their hospital. The state still funds the treatment, which remains free at the point of delivery; but the patient has the choice of where the treatment is provided. The public health care systems of Denmark, the Netherlands and Sweden have all recently experimented with extending patient choice in a similar fashion, while the French and German systems have a long experience of choice at all levels of public health care. In England and Wales, parents theoretically have had the right to choose their children's schools within the state system since 1989. New Zealand, Chile, Sweden and several states in the United States have all launched experiments in parental choice, including ones that use public funds to support pupils in independent or private schools as well as public ones.

User choice is also being extended outside the health and education areas. Under experimental schemes in Britain, for instance, disabled people, instead of being simply allocated care by social service departments, are receiving direct cash payments to purchase the assistance they need; and in social housing prospective tenants are for the first time being offered a choice of properties to rent.

Although politically freedom of choice has been traditionally a preserve of the right, the concept is gaining purchase on the left. The choice experiments in health and social care in Britain, for instance, are being pioneered by Tony Blair's Labour government. The Prime Minister himself has said that his government is 'recasting the 1945 welfare state' to base the service 'around the user, a personalized service with real choice'.[1] David Blunkett, when he was one of the most senior cabinet ministers in that government, wrote: 'Many on the Centre Left argue that, whilst services should be responsive and user-friendly, the language and values of choice have no place in public provision. I reject that dichotomy. It would be foolish and politically suicidal, in my view, to reject the concept of choice, and the importance of tailoring services to individual needs.'[2]

But there are also many on the left who do reject the idea of extending user choice. And they do so primarily on grounds that are of direct relevance to the concerns of this book: its impact on equality. Thus the Labour peer, and ex-deputy leader of the Labour Party, Roy Hattersley has argued: 'Choice is an obsession of the suburban middle classes. But when some families choose, the rest accept what is left. And the rest are always the disadvantaged and dispossessed.'[3] The British Treasury has expressed similar anxieties, linking the extension of user choice in public services to its possibly deleterious impact on both inequity and inefficiency: 'Where the Government is committed to public services free at the point of use and available to all on the basis of need, it is important to ensure that choice is not promoted at the expense of equity or efficiency, particularly where there are market failures and capacity constraints.'[4]

Are these fears well founded? Will the 'new' public services, retaining public funding but providing choice to their users, worsen the plight of the poor, and thereby increase inequality? Or might in fact extending choice actually reduce inequality in the use of public services and thereby help create a more equitable and just society? It is to these questions that this chapter is addressed.

Two preliminary points. The first concerns terminology. The concept of user choice comes in many forms: choice of provider (where?), choice of professional (who?), choice of service (what?), choice of appointment time (when?), and choice of access channel, such as telephone, web or face-to-face (how?). The principle of choice in public services includes decisions on all these dimensions. However, most of the debate on the impact of choice on inequality is concerned with choice of provider – choice of school, of family practitioner surgery, of hospital and so on – and it is on this that I concentrate here.

The second preliminary concerns what the chapter does not do. The impact on inequality and inequity of extending user choice is not the only concern about that policy. User choice has been justified on the grounds that it is what users want, and that it helps promote a more responsive and efficient service; its critics have challenged both these justifications, and have added other concerns, such as the impact of choice on social cohesiveness. These arguments have been discussed at length elsewhere,[5] and are beyond the scope of this chapter; instead I concentrate primarily on the relationship between user choice and inequality.

Choice and inequality

Extending user choice creates two kinds of anxiety about inequality. First, there is the argument that the poor and other disadvantaged groups lack the *capacity* to make effective choices. Several commentators[6] have voiced concerns that, however effective extending user choice may be in terms of increasing the efficiency and responsiveness of public services, it will also privilege service utilization by the articulate, confident middle class, and disadvantage the allegedly less capable poor.

The second anxiety concerns what is frequently termed *cream-skimming*, although it is also known as cherry-picking or risk selection. It is argued that extending user choice will result in some providers of public services – some schools, some hospitals and so on – being more popular than others and hence being extensively oversubscribed. These providers will then have the power to select the users to whom they provide services: the easiest, the cheapest, those who are most likely to boost their ratings in any performance league tables. That is, they will be able to skim the cream.

And, at least in the cases of health care and education, the users they select are likely to be the better-off. For people in the middle class tend be healthier and better educated, with more support systems at home. User choice thus turns into provider choice – with adverse consequences again for the poor and disadvantaged.

This worry is of particular concern in the case of education. Opponents of parental choice argue that cream-skimming is likely to exacerbate inequality in educational outcomes, as more affluent families congregate in good schools and less affluent families get trapped in poor ones. In fact, due to the externality effects of pupil mixing, the process becomes self-fulfilling, with good schools in a virtuous circle of improvement, but bad ones in a spiral of decline.

Capacity and the poor

The first point to note with respect to the alleged incapacity of the poor and disadvantaged to exercise choice is the fact that the poor are generally disadvantaged by systems of providing public services that do *not* offer choice. To appreciate the force of this argument, consider the alternative to user choice: a no-choice or monopoly provision of a service. This could be a local hospital to which all patients in the area who are in need of secondary care are automatically referred, or a school system that relied exclusively on fixed geographical catchment areas to allocate pupils. In such situations, with no choice possible, in order to obtain a good service users are reliant upon a combination of (a) the goodwill of the providers concerned not to abuse their monopoly position – that is, in the metaphor of Le Grand,[7] that they are altruistic 'knights' rather than self-interested 'knaves'; (b) 'voice' mechanisms, such as verbal persuasion, complaints procedures, public participation, user consultation or, ultimately, elections, to express their views and preferences; and (c) centrally driven commands and controls over performance, coupled with some form of independent regulation.

While knightliness, central performance management, regulation and voice all have an important place in ensuring public service delivery, the public could be forgiven for feeling them to be fairly distant from their day-to-day experience or personal influence. A knightly or public service ethos undoubtedly forms part of the motivation of professionals and others working in the public service; but it is only a part, with more self-interested or knavish concerns also playing a significant role.[8] Moreover, self-interest and public spiritedness often conflict for public sector providers (as with private practice for hospital specialists), and when they do it is far from clear that public spiritedness always dominates.

Voice mechanisms can be collective, such as voting in elections, or individualistic, such as complaints procedures. Collective voice mechanisms have the advantage that they are indeed collective: they take account of the interests of the community. On the other hand, they are clumsy instruments for dealing with individual dissatisfaction with public services. Parents who are unhappy with their local school, or patients with their local hospital, can vote for local elected representatives who are promising to provide better ones; but, for their votes to be effective, a number of conditions have to be fulfilled. There has to be an election in the offing; the users' views have to be shared by enough other voters for them together to constitute a majority; the issues concerning the quality of schools or hospitals have to be the principal factors affecting the election; politicians promising better schools or hospitals have to be among the candidates; and, if these politicians are elected, they have to have some effective method for ensuring school or hospital improvement. It is rare that all of these conditions will be met.

Moreover, despite their collective nature, these mechanisms are often poor at dealing with underperformance. Voters are rarely faced with the costs of meeting their service requirements. When they are not faced with those costs, they can simply vote to increase or maintain services at other people's expense. Indeed, this often happens when school or hospital closure proposals are put to a vote; the voters concerned usually do not have to bear the costs of keeping the institutions concerned open and in consequence usually vote the closure proposals down. And, importantly from the point of view of inequality, a majority can also vote to segregate a minority, excluding them by formal or informal means from the service concerned.

Individual voice mechanisms such as complaints procedures also have their problems. They require energy and commitment to activate; they take a good deal of time to operate; and they create defensiveness and distress among those complained against. Users who complain are not necessarily those who have the most to complain about; and adversarial relations between professionals and users, especially tied to a threat of lawsuits as they often are, can lead to expensive and inefficient defensive reactions on behalf of providers. Most importantly from the point of view of equity and equality, they favour the educated and articulate.

So, where users do not have choice, it is the bureaucratic system that decides on the allocation of users to providers – that allocates patients to hospitals and children to schools. If the rules of that system do not meet users' wants or needs, then to get what they want, users are reliant on the goodwill of the relevant bureaucrats and/or on their own ability to manipulate the system through their 'voice'. But the voice of the middle class is generally much louder than that of the poor. Their ability to deal with professionals, to articulate their dissatisfactions and to utilize complaints procedures if necessary is significantly greater than that of the less well-off. Voice disadvantages the poor.

That this is in fact a serious problem for no-choice systems was substantiated in a recent review of health care utilization in the current

British National Health Service, where there is currently little choice.[9] This found substantial inequalities in key areas:

- Intervention rates of coronary artery bypass grafts or angiography following a heart attack were 30 per cent lower in the lowest socioeconomic groups (SEGs) than in the highest.
- Hip replacements were 20 per cent lower among lower SEGs despite roughly 30 per cent higher need.
- Social classes IV and V had 10 per cent fewer preventive consultations than social classes I and II after standardizing for other determinants.
- A one-point move down a seven-point deprivation scale was associated with family practitioners spending 3.4 per cent less time with the individual concerned.

Some of these inequalities arose because of difficulties that the poor faced in accessing the system in the first place: high transport costs, the financial costs of taking time off work, and so on. But others – especially the inequalities that arose from differences in referral rates for secondary care – appear to derive from the poor's inability to manipulate the system once they had accessed it, a problem that in turn is likely to derive from their difficulties with expressing their 'voice'.

So systems with no or little choice can also generate inequality – in large part through the relative incapacity of the poor to exercise 'voice'. It is therefore far from clear that things will get worse with respect to inequality in the utilization of services if the poor are offered choice instead of voice. In fact, it could be argued that the shift of power from professional or bureaucrat to user that is implicit in the choice strategy directly favours the less well-off, precisely because it reduces the role of the middle-class voice in allocating public service resources. Ultimately, extending choice to all goes a long way towards equalizing power between users from different social groups; and should therefore enhance equity.

As we saw earlier, there are many who would dispute this conclusion, arguing that poorer groups do not have the ability to make choices that middle-class ones have. However, this argument is usually supported by anecdote rather than evidence.[10] In fact there is no hard evidence that the capacity or willingness for choice of disadvantaged groups is less than that of the better-off. Indeed, there is some evidence to the contrary. For instance, a US study of choices of physician demonstrated that, although a minority of respondents actively searches for a physician, there appears to be substantial variation in the degree of consumer activism across patient subgroups, with greater levels of activism being found among racial and ethnic minorities.[11] Further, some of the biggest supporters of the choice experiments in education in American states have been racial minorities, arguing that the choice programmes have given them power where none existed before.

There is a final point concerning the equity comparisons between choice and no-choice systems. In fact even apparently no-choice systems usually have an element of choice associated with them, one that almost invariably favours the better-off. For instance, in most countries those who are dissatisfied with public health care or public education have the choice of using the private sector. However, since those who go privately have to pay to do so, this is not an option that is open to the poor. Similarly, if fixed catchment areas are used to allocate users to services (as with children to schools, for instance), the better-off can always buy their way into areas where the services are of higher quality. House prices are higher around good schools – a fact that again works to disadvantage the less well-off. As Tony Blair has argued:

> People should not forget the current system is a two-tier system when those who can afford it go private, or those who can move house get better schools. . . . Choice mechanisms enhance equity by exerting pressure on low-quality or incompetent providers. Competitive pressures and incentives drive up quality, efficiency and responsiveness in the public sector. Choice leads to higher standards . . . The overriding principle is clear. We should give poorer patients . . . the same range of choices the rich have always enjoyed. In a heterogeneous society where there is enormous variation in needs and preferences, public services must be equipped to respond.[12]

Cream-skimming

Cream-skimming takes different forms according to the kind of public service involved. In health care systems with consumer choice of multiple insurers, it can arise on the insurance side, where insurers try to select people who are good health risks as enrollees and to discourage those who are worse health risks or charge them higher premiums. In social insurance systems with multiple funds, choice of funds and capitated allocations (such as in Germany, the Netherlands and Belgium), funds try to select enrollees who carry below average risk. In systems such as the UK where health care purchasers are dealing with a defined population, the problem is confined to the provider side, whereby GP practices or hospitals may try to select patients who are easier or cheaper to deal with. The consequence is discrimination against groups with a higher risk of ill health, such as the old and the poor.

The extent of provider cream-skimming in health care is hard to establish. Opportunities to do so exist in most systems with or without user choice. But there are factors that militate against providers exploiting those opportunities. There is first the question of knowledge: can providers effectively distinguish between high and low risk patients before they treat them? Second, there are professional ethics, or 'knightly' motivations;[13] doctors do not like to turn away needy patients. Third, there are professional interests: more difficult patients may present more of an intellectual challenge (although, of course, for doctors in search of a quiet life this could act as a positive incentive for cream-skimming).

It is worth noting that, in hospitals at least, these incentives not to cream-skim are largely associated with clinical specialists, whereas the direct incentives to cream-skim (finance, pressure to meet waiting lists) impact primarily on hospital management. In Britain, much research indicates that it is specialists who are the principal decision-makers in NHS hospitals,[14] suggesting that perhaps the incentives not to cream-skim may currently dominate the incentives to do so.

The situation is complicated further if there is extensive use of private or other non-public providers. For it could be argued that the incentives to cream-skim are intensified in a profit-making context: that private providers are run by 'knaves' not knights, and hence will ruthlessly exploit any opportunity they have to enhance their profits, including the opportunities offered by cream-skimming. This is clearly a danger, although it is likely to be partly offset by the fact that again some of the 'private' organizations concerned are non-profits, and hence likely to have a more complicated (and more knightly) motivational structure than that of simple profit maximization. But again the evidence is lacking.

In education, cream-skimming occurs where an oversubscribed school selects pupils of high intrinsic ability so as to improve the school's performance in examinations at relatively low cost. The problem with cream-skimming in this context is that it can lead to polarization or segregation in terms of ability, with able pupils being increasingly concentrated in high-performing schools and less able pupils in low-performing ones.

Unlike health care, there is evidence that cream-skimming can be a problem for choice in school education.[15] Early research into the operation of the Conservative government's reforms from 1989 in Britain indicated that there was a growth in cream-skimming practices. Subsequent research in Britain has yielded more mixed results, with some arguing that segregation in English and Welsh schools has actually decreased since 1988; but the underlying methodology that led to this result has been challenged. In both Belgium and New Zealand, researchers have found that choice policies led to significant segregation between schools.

However, the evidence is not all one way. For instance, in Milwaukee in the 1990s, a combination of local school supply flexibility via charter schools and pro-poor vouchers led to a marked improvement in results, with the greatest performance gains among the poorest. In Sweden in 1992, reform combined an open supply side (independent profit-making, independent non-profit-making and traditional state schools funded on equal per pupil terms) and universal vouchers. Performance has risen significantly, and there has been a marked reduction in the number of pupils leaving school with no qualifications at all. There has been no evidence of an increase in segregation.

Note that all publicly funded schools in Sweden are barred from selecting pupils on the grounds of ability, religious affiliation or ethnic origin, and independent schools in the state sector are barred from charging extra fees. These features may account for the lack of an adverse equity impact. They also show the importance of proper policy design in the construction of schemes for extending choice; and to this I now turn.

Implications for policy

On balance, it seems as though extending user choice in public services will not necessarily worsen inequality, and indeed, when compared with the operation of no-choice systems, may actually reduce it. However, that is not to say that extending user choice is quite unproblematic from an inequality perspective. Although we have argued that incapacity problems for the poor are likely to be greater for voice mechanisms than for choice, there are still likely to be some difficulties for the latter. And we have seen that cream-skimming is a real danger, especially in education. Choice policies need to be designed with these potential problems in mind.

More specifically, it is likely that extending user choice of provider may create some problems for the exercise of choice by the less well-off, including a need for help with transport and with information and advice. This could involve assistance with transport and travel costs for users and families of users, and perhaps identifying a key worker who would act as an adviser to those users and families. An example of the latter is the highly successful Patient Care Adviser (PCA) scheme that has accompanied some of the choice experiments in the British NHS. Under the scheme each patient confronted with a choice decision to be made is allocated a PCA. These are professionals, sometimes clinically trained, who in practice take on a much wider role than simply advising on choice; they give advice on other matters, including (from those who were clinically trained) clinical ones, and have offered support and reassurance. They are deeply popular with patients.[16]

There are a variety of policy options for addressing cream-skimming. These include:

- stop-loss insurance;
- restricting the admission freedoms of providers;
- weighting funding formulae, so as to favour the less well-off.

Stop-loss insurance is a scheme whereby providers faced with a user whose service costs lie well outside the normal range get allocated extra resources once the cost has passed a certain threshold. This has the advantage of removing the incentive to discriminate against high cost users; but it carries with it the problem that the providers concerned have no incentive to economize on service once the threshold has been passed.

A second possibility is to take the admission decisions away from providers completely. So, in health care, hospitals and other treatment centres would be required to accept anyone referred to them by the relevant referral agency. Schools would have to accept every applicant up to capacity and, once capacity was reached, to allocate pupils by lottery or some other random process, as has been recently suggested by Collins.[17]

A third alternative is to adjust by risk the prices paid to providers under the public funding system. So potentially higher cost users could have higher prices associated with them. If there was full risk adjustment, this could eliminate the incentive to cream-skim completely. However, risk adjustment is a complex and difficult business; perfectly accurate risk adjustment is arguably impossible. And so long as risk adjustment is not perfect, there will remain an incentive to cream-skim.

A form of risk adjustment that would be rather simpler and help assuage any socioeconomic inequities arising from cream-skimming would be to adjust the price by deprivation. The price could be associated inversely with an area deprivation index such that treatments for users from deprived areas would carry a higher price than those from wealthier ones. This could in fact be a form of risk adjustment since it is widely believed that poor users have greater need than better-off ones. If the adjustment was sufficient this would provide a positive incentive for providers to take on poor users in preference to better-off ones.

Conclusion

Extending user choice in public services could have a significant positive impact on inequality in the distribution and outcomes of those services. By giving choice to individuals and groups who previously had none, it extends to all a privilege that was previously confined to those who could go private. Giving poorer groups extra power will advantage them, and diminishing the role of the middle-class 'voice' in determining who gets what will reduce the inequalities in the use of services that arise from this.

On the other hand, there are some potential problems that need to be addressed. The poor and disadvantaged may need extra help in making the relevant choices and in exploiting the opportunities that are offered. These difficulties can be overcome by a package of measures directed at the disadvantaged that would include help with travel costs and the allocation of a special choice adviser. Cream-skimming could be mitigated by stop-loss insurance, by removing provider discretion over admission or by risk adjustment of the relevant price.

So policies designed to increase choice in public services have great potential for promoting equality and equity, as well as efficiency and responsiveness. But to do so they must be properly designed; that is the principal message for policy makers.

Notes

Abbreviations

CASE	Centre for Analysis of Social Exclusion (UK)
CEPR	Center for Economic and Policy Research (US)
CESifo	A joint initiative of the University of Munich's Centre for Economic Studies and the Ifo Institute for Economic Research
CLS	Centre for Labour Market and Social Research (Denmark)
DETR	Department of the Environment, Transport and the Regions (UK)
DSS	Department of Social Security (UK)
DWP	Department for Work and Pensions (UK)
ECHP	European Community Household Panel
EPAG	European Panel Analysis Group
ESRC	Economic and Social Research Council (UK)
ILO	International Labour Organisation
IPPR	Institute for Public Policy Research (UK)
ISER	Institute for Social and Economic Research (UK)
JRF	Joseph Rowntree Foundation
LIS	Luxembourg Income Study
NBER	National Bureau of Economic Research (US)
ODPM	Office of the Deputy Prime Minister (UK)
OECD	Organisation for Economic Co-operation and Development
PSID	Panel Study of Income Dynamics (US)
UNICEF	United Nations Children's Fund

I Inequality of incomes and opportunities

I would like to thank Daniele Checchi, Lane Kenworthy, John Myles, Brian Nolan, Lee Rainwater, Tim Smeeding and Michael Wallerstein for generous comments and suggestions, and Stephanie Brodmann and Cecilie Weatherall for research assistance. The research for this paper was financed by MCyT project no. SEC 2003-02699.

1 A. B. Atkinson, 'Is rising income inequality inevitable? A critique of the transatlantic consensus', Annual Lecture, United Nations University, 1999.

2 R. B. Freeman and L. F. Katz (eds), *Differences and Changes in Wage Structure* (University of Chicago Press, 1995); G. Esping-Andersen and M. Regini, *Why De-regulate Labour Markets* (Oxford University Press, 2000).

3 The Gini coefficient is a summary index of inequality (ranging from zero to 1.0), measuring the degree to which the real distribution of income deviates from what would be perfect equality. A score of zero would imply perfect equality.

4 J. Davies and A. Shorrocks, 'The distribution of wealth', in A. Atkinson and F. Bourguignon (eds), *Handbook of Income Distribution*, vol. 1 (Elsevier, 1999).

5 Ibid.; and W. Kopczuk and E. Saez, 'Top wealth shares in the United States, 1916–2000', NBER Working Paper 10399.

6 E. Wolff, *Top Heavy: A Study of the Increasing Inequality of Wealth in America and What can be Done about It* (New Press, 1995); K. Phillips, *Wealth and Democracy* (Broadway Books, 2002).

7 OECD, *Human Capital Investment* (OECD, 1999).

8 E. Wolff, 'Trends in household wealth in the United States'. *Review of Income and Wealth*, 40 (1994), pp. 143–74; Wolff, *Top Heavy*; Phillips, *Wealth and Democracy*; Davies and Shorrocks, 'The distribution of wealth'.

9 Davies and Shorrocks, 'The distribution of wealth', suggest that the richest 1 per cent in the US is now back to where it left off in 1930. See also Kopczuk and Saez, 'Top wealth shares in the United States'.

10 Davies and Shorrocks, 'The distribution of wealth', table 2.

11 T. Smeeding, 'Government programs and social outcomes: the United States in comparative perspective', paper presented at the Smolensky Conference, University of California, Berkeley, 12–13 Dec. 2004.

12 P. Gottschalk and T. Smeeding, 'Cross-national comparisons of earnings and income inequality', *Journal of Economic Literature*, 35 (1997), pp. 633–87; P. Gottschalk and T. Smeeding, 'Empirical evidence on income inequality in industrialized countries', in Atkinson and Bourguignon, *Handbook of Income Distribution*, vol. 1; L. Karoly and G. Burtless, 'Demographic change, rising earnings inequality and the distribution of personal well-being', *Demography*, 32 (1995), pp. 379–405; F. Levy, *The New Dollars and Dreams* (Russell Sage, 1998); A. Alderson and F. Nielsen, 'Globalization and the great U-turn', *American Journal of Sociology*, 107: 5 (2002), pp. 1244–99; Smeeding, 'Government programs and social outcomes'.

13 But in Sweden inequality continues to rise.

14 Levy, *The New Dollars and Dreams*; Gottschalk and Smeeding, 'Cross-national comparisons of earnings and income inequality'.

15 T. Piketty and E. Saez, 'Income inequality in the United States, 1913–1998', NBER Working Paper 8467; Smeeding, 'Government programs and social outcomes', table 1, shows that the lowest fifth in the US gained a total of $1,100 (or 9 per cent) in real terms, 1979–2000, while the top fifth gained a whopping $576,400 (or 201 per cent).

16 Gottschalk and Smeeding, 'Cross-national comparisons of earnings and income inequality'.

17 M. Forster, 'Trends and driving forces in income distribution and poverty in the OECD area', Labour Market and Social Policy Occasional Paper 42, OECD, Paris, table 3.1.

18 S. Preston, 'Children and the aged in the US'. *Scientific American*, 251 (1984), pp. 44–9; J. Palmer, T. Smeeding and B. Torrey, *The Vulnerable* (Urban Institute, 1988); F. Pampel, 'Population aging, class context, and age inequality in public spending', *American Journal of Sociology*, 100 (1994), pp. 153–95.

19 OECD, *Human Capital Investment* (1999), table 3.4.

20 US studies based on consumption rather than income identify a parallel trend. Johnson et al. show that consumption of families with children, relative to the elderly, fell by 16 percentage points in 1972–90, or by 8 percentage points in 1981–2001; D. Johnson, T. Smeeding and B. Torrey, 'United States inequality through the prisms of income and consumption', paper for conference on The Link between Income and Consumption Inequality, Madrid, 26–7 Mar. 2004, p. 12.

21 OECD, *Ageing and Income* (OECD, 2001).

22 A. B. Atkinson, B. Cantillon, E. Marlier and B. Nolan, *Social Indicators* (Oxford University Press, 2002).

23 G. Esping-Andersen, 'A new European social model for the twentieth century?', in M. Rodrigues (ed.), *The New Knowledge Economy in Europe* (Edward Elgar, 2002).

24 West Pedersen shows, in fact, that public pension transfers in the income package of the elderly fell noticeably in Norway, Sweden and the UK between 1980 and 1995; see A. West Pedersen, 'The privatization of retirement income?', *Journal of European Social Policy*, 14 (2004).

25 These estimates derive from the European Community Household Panel (ECHP), waves 1994 and 2000.

26 L. Rainwater and T. Smeeding, *Poor Kids in a Rich Country* (Russell Sage, 2004).

27 A. Bowlus and J. M. Robin, 'Twenty years of rising inequality in US lifetime labor income values', MS, 2003; at www.restud.org.uk/barlusrobin-res.pdf.

28 I. Bison and G. Esping-Andersen, 'Income packaging, poverty and unemployment in Europe', in D. Gallie and S. Paugam (eds), *The Experience of Unemployment in Europe* (Oxford University Press, 2000).

29 OECD, *Literacy in the Knowledge Society* (OECD, 2000).
30 Freeman and Katz, *Differences and Changes in Wage Structure*; C. Juhn, K. Murphy and B. Pierce, 'Inequality and rise in returns to skills', *Journal of Political Economy*, 101 (1993), pp. 410–12; L. Katz and D. Autor, 'Changes in the wage structure and earnings inequality', in O. Ashenfelter and D. Card (eds), *Handbook of Labor Economics*, vol. 3A (Elsevier, 1999); S. Nickell and B. Bell, 'The collapse in demand for the unskilled, and unemployment across the OECD', *Oxford Review of Economic Policy*, 11 (1995), pp. 40–62; M. Morris and B. Western, 'Inequality in earnings at the close of the twentieth century', *Annual Review of Sociology*, 25 (1999), pp. 623–57.
31 F. Blau and L. Kahn, *At Home and Abroad* (Russell Sage, 2002).
32 Freeman and Katz, *Differences and Changes in Wage Structure*; OECD, *Employment Outlook* (OECD, 1998), *Employment Outlook* (OECD, 2003); M. Wallerstein, 'Wage-setting institutions and pay inequality in advanced industrial societies', *American Journal of Political Science*, 43 (1999), pp. 649–80.
33 D. Acemoglu, 'Cross-country inequality trends', LIS Working Paper 296, Mar. 2002.
34 E. Wasmer, 'The causes of the youth employment problem', in D. Cohen, T. Pikkety and G. Saint-Paul (eds), *The Economics of Rising Inequalities* (Oxford University Press, 2002).
35 Juhn, Murphy and Pierce, 'Inequality and rise in returns to skills'.
36 O. Bover, S. Bentolila and M. Arellano, 'The distribution of earnings in Spain during the 1980s', and A. Brandolini, P. Cipollone and P. Sestito, 'Earnings dispersion, low pay and household poverty in Italy, 1977–98', both in Cohen, Pikkety and Saint-Paul, *The Economics of Rising Inequalities*.
37 OECD, *Employment Outlook* (2003), p. 63; in the US, however, it leaped by 5 percentage points.
38 OECD, *Employment Outlook* (1998), table 3.11b.
39 D. Gallie and S. Paugam (eds), *Welfare Regimes and the Experience of Unemployment in Europe* (Oxford University Press, 2000); OECD, *Employment Outlook* (1998).
40 OECD, *Employment Outlook* (1998), table 3.9; to put this into context, for all ages the unemployment ratio is 2:1 for those with less than secondary education.
41 M. Iacovou and R. Bertoud, 'Young peoples' lives: a map of Europe', ISER Working Paper, University of Essex, Dec. 2001, table 5.9.
42 P. De Graaf and W. Ultee, 'United in employment, united in unemployment', in Gallie and Paugam, *Welfare Regimes and the Experience of Unemployment*; P. Gregg and J. Wadsworth, 'Everything you ever wanted to know about worklessness and polarization at the household level but were afraid to ask', *Oxford Bulletin of Economics and Statistics*, 63 (2001); M. Iacovou, 'Work-rich and work-poor couples: polarization in fourteen countries', EPAG Working Paper 45, University of Essex, 2003.

43 OECD, *Literacy in the Knowledge Society* (2000), table 3.4.

44 L. Kenworthy, *Egalitarian Capitalism* (Russell Sage, 2004), p. 27.

45 H. P. Blossfeld and S. Drobnic, *Careers of Couples in Contemporary Societies* (Oxford University Press, 2001).

46 G. Burtless, 'Effects of growing wage disparities and changing family composition on the US income distribution', *European Economic Review*, 43 (1999), pp. 853–65.

47 L. Karoly and G. Burtless, 'Demographic change, rising earnings inequality and the distribution of personal well-being', *Demography*, 32 (1995), pp. 379–405; M. Cancian, S. Danziger and P. Gottschalk, 'Working wives and family income inequality among married couples', in S. Danziger and P. Gottschalk (eds), *Uneven Tides: Rising Inequality in America* (Russell Sage Foundation, 1993); M. Cancian and D. Reed, 'The impact of wives' earnings on income inequality', *Demography*, 36 (1999), pp. 173–84.

48 G. Esping-Andersen, with D. Gallie, A. Hemerijck and J. Myles, *Why We Need a New Welfare State* (Oxford University Press, 2002).

49 Forster, 'Trends and driving forces in income distribution and poverty'.

50 Rainwater and Smeeding, *Poor Kids in a Rich Country*. Considering that the poverty gap among poor households is often relatively narrow, a modest additional income will easily pull them above the poverty line.

51 OECD, *Employment Outlook* (1998). The percentage living in household poverty follows basically the same country ranking that we find in all income distribution data: 3 per cent in Denmark, roughly 7–10 per cent in continental Europe (and the UK), and a high of 22 per cent in the US.

52 Smeeding, 'Government programs and social outcomes', table 9.

53 Ibid.

54 D. Lam, 'Demographic variables and income inequality', in M. Rosenzweig and O. Stark (eds), *Handbook of Population and Family Economics* (Elsevier, 1997).

55 Cancian and Reed, 'The impact of wives' earnings on income inequality'.

56 C. Goldin, 'From the valley to the summit: the quiet revolution that transformed women's work', NBER Working Paper 10335, 2004.

57 F. Blau, 'Trends in the well-being of American women, 1970–1995', *Journal of Economic Literature*, 36 (1998), pp. 112–65; Blau and Kahn, *At Home and Abroad*; J. Waldvogel and S. Mayer, 'Male–female differences in the low-wage labor market', paper presented at the American Economics Association meetings, New York, Jan. 1999.

58 Blau and Kahn, *At Home and Abroad*; OECD, *Employment Outlook* (OECD, 1995), table 11.4; and (2002), table 7.2.

59 OECD, *Employment Outlook* (2002), tables 2.15 and 2.16.

60 OECD, *Employment Outlook* (OECD, 1996); J. Rubery, M. Smith and C. Fagan, *Women's Employment in Europe* (Routledge, 1999).

61 Calculation from all waves of the ECHP.

62 R. Anker, *Gender and Jobs* (ILO, 1998); N. Datta Gupta, R. Oaxaca and N. Smith, 'Swimming upstream, floating downstream', CLS Working Paper

01–06, Department of Economics, Aarhus University; J. Jacobs and S. Lim, 'Trends in occupational and industrial sex segregation in 56 countries, 1960–1980, in J. Jacobs (ed.), *Gender Inequality at Work* (Sage, 1995); Rubery, Smith and Fagan, *Women's Employment in Europe*; M. Charles and D. Grusky, *Occupational Ghettos* (Stanford University Press, 2004); OECD, *Employment Outlook* (2002).

63 Anker, *Gender and Jobs*.
64 J. Dolado, F. Felgueroso and J. Jimeno, 'Recent trends in occupational segregation by gender', CEPR Working Paper 3421, 2002.
65 Anker, *Gender and Jobs*, p. 412.
66 OECD, *Employment Outlook* (2002).
67 Goldin, 'From the valley to the summit'.
68 OECD, *Employment Outlook* (2002), table 2.10.
69 Ibid., table 2.14.
70 OECD, *A Caring World* (OECD, 1999), table 3.3, furnishes an overview of trends in government redistribution.
71 M. Corak, 'Child poverty in rich nations', paper, UNICEF Innocenti Research Centre, Florence, 7 May.
72 Gottschalk and Smeeding, 'Cross-national comparisons of earnings and income equality'.
73 C. Flinn, 'Labor market structure and welfare: a comparison of Italy and the US', *Review of Economic Studies*, 69 (2002), pp. 611–45.
74 Bowlus and Robin, 'Twenty years of rising inequality'.
75 A. Bjorklund and M. Palme, 'Income distribution within the life cycle versus between individuals', in Cohen, Piketty and Saint-Paul, *The Economics of Rising Inequalities*; Okonomisk Raad, *Dansk Okonomi* (Det Okonomiske Raads Formandsskab, 2001).
76 The Danish lifetime incomes are estimated for a twenty-year period, 1980–2000.
77 Okonomisk Raad, *Dansk Okonomi*, table II.10.
78 S. Haider, 'Earnings instability and earnings inequality of males in the United States, 1967–1991', *Journal of Labor Economics*, 19 (2001), pp. 799–836; Bowlus and Robin, 'Twenty years of rising inequality'.
79 Okonomisk Raad, *Dansk Okonomi*, table II.17.
80 Ibid., table II.16.
81 S. Aaronson, 'The rise in lifetime earnings inequality among men', paper for the Board of Governors of the Federal Reserve System, Mar. 2002; M. Gittleman and M. Joyce, 'Have family income mobility patterns changed?', *Demography*, 36 (1999), pp. 299–314; Haider, 'Earnings instability'; Bowlus and Robin, 'Twenty years of rising inequality'.
82 G. Duncan, B. Gustafsson, R. Hauser, G. Schmauss, H. Messinger, R. Muffels, B. Nolan and J. Ray, 'Poverty dynamics in eight countries', *Journal of Population Economics*, 6 (1993), pp. 215–34; B. Bradbury, S. Jenkins and J. Micklewright, *The Dynamics of Child Poverty in Industrialized Countries* (Cambridge University Press, 2001); L. Leisering

and S. Leibfried, *Time and Poverty in Western Welfare States* (Cambridge University Press, 1999); OECD, *Ageing and Income* (2001).

83 OECD, *Ageing and Income* (2001), tables 2.2 and 2.3.

84 Ibid.; C. Whelan, R. Layte and B. Maitre, 'Poverty, deprivation and time', EPAG Working Paper 48, University of Essex, 2003; The Whelan et al. study, however, uses a high (70 per cent of median) poverty line. OECD, *Ageing and Income* (2001), table 2.12, estimates that roughly half of those who exit poverty in any year will return to poverty subsequently. For the United States, see especially A. Stevens, 'Climbing out of poverty, falling back in', *Journal of Human Resources*, 34 (1999), pp. 557–88.

85 For the United States I use the Panel Study of Income Dynamics (PSID), waves 1993–7.

86 Whelan, Layte and Maitre, 'Poverty, deprivation and time'.

87 OECD, *Employment Outlook* (1998), table 2.10, and *Employment Outlook* (2003), ch. 2.

88 W. J. Wilson, *The Truly Disadvantaged* (University of Chicago Press, 1987).

89 G. Duncan, and W. Rodgers, 'Has children's poverty become more persistent?', *American Sociological Review*, 56 (1991), pp. 538–50.

90 J. Fritzell and U. Henz, 'Household income dynamics', in J. Jonsson and C. Mills (eds), *Cradle to Grave: Life Course Change in Sweden* (Sociology Press, 2001).

91 J. Hills, 'Does income mobility mean that we do not need to worry about poverty?', ch. 3 in A. B. Atkinson and J. Hills (eds), *Exclusion, Employment and Opportunity* (CASE, London School of Economics, 1998).

92 D. Card, 'The causal effect of education on earnings', in O. Ashenfelter and D. Card (eds), *Handbook of Labor Economics*, vol. 3 (North Holland, 1998); S. Bowles, H. Gintis and M. Osborne, 'The determinants of earnings: a behavioural approach', *Journal of Economic Literature*, 39 (2001), pp. 1137–76.

93 R. Erikson and J. Jonsson, in *Can Education be Equalized? The Swedish Case in Comparative Perspective* (Westview Press, 1996), suggest that the Swedish reforms starting in the 1960s probably did help reduce the class bias of traditional tracking.

94 J. Heckman, 'Doing it right: job training and education', *Public Interest* (spring, 1999), pp. 86–106.

95 Y. Shavit and H. P. Blossfeld, *Persistent Inequality: Changing Educational Attainment in Thirteen Countries* (Westview Press, 1993); Erikson and Jonsson, *Can Education be Equalized?*; OECD, *Knowledge and Skills for Life* (OECD, 2002).

96 G. Solon, 'Intergenerational mobility in the labor market', in Ashenfelter and Card, *Handbook of Labor Economics*, vol. 3A; M. Corak, *The Dynamics of Intergenerational Income Mobility* (Cambridge University Press, 2004).

97 D. Harding, C. Jencks, L. Lopoo and S. Mayer, 'The changing effect of family background on the income of adult Americans', in S. Bowles,

H. Gintis and M. Osborne (eds), *Unequal Chances: Family Background and Economic Success* (Russell Sage, 2004). A counterargument is offered by Ichino et al., who argue that despite Italy being a more equal society, Italian intergenerational mobility is lower than in the US; see A. Ichino, D. Checchi and A. Rustichini, 'More equal but less mobile?', paper, Innocenzo Gasparini Institute for Economic Research, Milan, 1997.

 98 R. Haveman and B. Wolfe, *Succeeding Generations: On the Effects of Investments in Children* (Russell Sage Foundation, 1995); G. Duncan and J. Brooks-Gunn, *Consequences of Growing Up Poor* (Russell Sage Foundation, 1997); S. Mayer, *What Money Can't Buy* (Harvard University Press, 1997).

 99 R. Erikson and John H. Goldthorpe, *The Constant Flux: A Study of Class Mobility in Industrial Societies* (Oxford University Press, 1992).

100 C. Jencks, M. Smith, H. Acland, M. J. Bane, D. Cohen, H. Gintis, B. Heyns and S. Michelson, *Inequality: A Reassessment of Family and Schooling in America* (Basic Books, 1972); Haveman and Wolfe, *Succeeding Generations*; C. Mulligan, *Parental Priorities and Economic Inequality* (University of Chicago Press, 1997); P. De Graaf, 'Parents' financial and cultural resources, grades, and transitions to secondary school', *European Sociological Review*, 4 (1998), pp. 209–21.

101 The 'cognitive' returns to cultural capital are substantial when we consider that a one-level jump in the five-level cultural capital variable implies an added 35 points (or an 8 per cent improvement) on children's cognitive score (estimates taken from the US model, but the cultural capital effect is quite similar across countries).

102 G. Esping-Andersen, 'Untying the Gordian knot of social inheritance', *Research in Social Stratification and Mobility*, 21 (2004), pp. 115–39.

103 OECD, *Knowledge and Skills for Life* (2002).

104 Duncan and Brooks-Gunn, *Consequences of Growing Up Poor*; Haveman and Wolfe, *Succeeding Generations*.

105 J. Ermisch and M. Francesconi 'The effect of parents' employment on children's educational attainment', ISER Working Paper 21, University of Essex, 2002.

106 G. Esping-Andersen, 'Untying the Gordian knot'.

107 Ermisch and Francesconi, 'The effect of parents' employment'.

108 For an analysis along these lines, see K. Moene and M. Wallerstein, 'Inequality, social insurance, and redistribution', *American Political Science Review*, 95 (2001), pp. 859–74; and J. Schwabish, T. Smeeding and L. Osberg, 'Income distribution and social expenditures', paper, Center for Policy Research, Maxwell School, Syracuse University, Aug. 2003.

109 A. B. Atkinson, A. Maynard and C. Trinder, *Parents and Children: Incomes in Two Generations* (Heinemann, 1983); Corak, *The Dynamics of Intergenerational Income Mobility*.

110 Wilson, *The Truly Disadvantaged*.

2 Does inequality matter?

I am grateful to a number of people for their invaluable comments and suggestions on earlier drafts of this essay, including Douglas Alexander, Jerry Cohen, Philip Dufty, Ben Jackson, Marion Kozak, Stephen Lambert, Spencer Livermore, David Miliband, Kirsty Milne, Jenni Russell, Paul Segal and, in particular, Martin O'Neill, who commented on two separate drafts. I would also like to thank attendees at a Policy Network seminar who provided very useful comments on an oral version of this paper. Needless to say, responsibility for what follows is my own.

1 T. H. Marshall, *Citizenship and Social Class* (Cambridge University Press, 1950).

2 John Hills, *Inequality and the State* (Oxford University Press, 2004).

3 Anthony Crosland, *The Future of Socialism*, rev. edn (Jonathan Cape, 1964).

4 For an account of the role of changing norms in explaining US inequality, see Paul Krugman, 'For Richer', *New York Times Magazine*, 20 Oct. 2002.

5 See for example John Rawls, *A Theory of Justice* (Belknap, 1971), Michael Walzer, *Spheres of Justice* (Basic Books, 1984) and Ronald Dworkin, *Sovereign Virtue: The Theory and Practice of Equality* (Harvard University Press, 2002). For excellent introductions to the body of work, see Will Kymlicka's *Contemporary Political Philosophy: An Introduction*, 2nd edn (Oxford University Press, 2002), Adam Swift, *Political Philosophy: A Beginners Guide for Students and Politicians* (Polity, 2001) and Matthew Clayton and Andrew Williams (eds), *The Ideal of Equality* (Palgrave, 2000).

6 Amartya Sen, *Inequality Reexamined* (Harvard University Press, 1995).

7 Some political philosophers also debate the heritability of hard work and effort.

8 Ben Jackson and Paul Segal, 'Why inequality matters', *Catalyst*, Oct. 2004.

9 In his famous speech during the 1987 election campaign – 'the first Kinnock in a thousand generations [to go to university]' – collected in Brian McArthur (ed.), *Penguin Book of Twentieth Century Speeches* (Penguin, 1999).

10 Walzer, *Spheres of Justice*.

11 William H. Gates Sr and Chuck Collins, *Wealth and our Commonwealth: Why America should Tax Accumulated Fortunes* (Beacon Press, 2003).

12 See for example, Richard Layard, *Happiness: Has Social Science a Clue?*, Lionel Robbins Lectures (MIT Press, 2003).

13 Michael Sandel, 'What money can't buy: the moral limits of markets', Tanner Lectures, 11–12 May 1998.

14 Albert O. Hirschman, *Exit, Voice and Loyalty* (Harvard University Press, 1970).

15 See, for example, Gordon Brown, 'Equality: then and now' (1997), in Patrick Diamond (ed.), *New Labour's Old Roots* (Imprint Academic, 2004), and Roy Hattersley, 'Why I'm no longer loyal to Labour', *Guardian*, 26 July 1997.
16 Jackson and Segal, 'Why inequality matters'.
17 See e.g. Harry Frankfurt, 'Equality as a moral ideal', *Ethics*, 98 (1987), pp. 21–43.
18 Richard Arneson, 'Why justice requires transfers to offset income and wealth inequalities', *Social Philosophy and Policy*, 19 (2002), pp. 172–200.
19 M. Brewer, A. Goodman, M. Myck, J. Shaw and A. Shephard, 'Poverty and inequality in Britain: 2004', Institute for Fiscal Studies, 2004.
20 Sen, *Inequality Reexamined*.
21 Anthony Crosland, *Socialism Now and Other Essays*, (Jonathan Cape, 1974).

3 Inequality in the new knowledge economy

1 Peter Drucker, *Post-capitalist Society* (Harper Business, 1993), p. 96.
2 David H. Autor, Lawrence F. Katz and Melissa S. Kearney, 'Trends in US wage inequality: re-assessing the revisionists', paper, July 2004, p. 63.
3 'Effective tax rates, 1979–1997', Congressional Budget Office, Oct. 2001.
4 Thomas Piketty and Emmanuel Saez, 'Income inequality in the United States, 1913–1998', *Quarterly Journal of Economics*, 118:1 (Feb. 2003), pp. 1–39.
5 Timothy M. Smeeding and Andrej Grodner, 'Changing income inequality in OECD countries: updated results from the Luxembourg Income Study (LIS)', in Richard Hauser and Irene Becker (eds), *The Personal Distribution of Income in an International Perspective* (Springer-Verlag, 2000), pp. 205–24.
6 Ibid.
7 A. B. Atkinson, 'Income inequality in OECD countries: data and explanations', CESifo Working Paper 881, 2003.
8 Robert H. Frank and Philip J. Cook, *Winner-Take-All Society: How More and More Americans Compete for Ever Fewer and Bigger Prizes, Encouraging Economic Waste, Income Inequality, and an Impoverished Cultural Life* (Free Press, 1995), p. 5.
9 Erik Olin Wright and Rachel E. Dwyer, 'The patterns of job expansions in the USA: a comparison of the 1960s and 1990s', *Socio-economic Review*, no. 1 (2003), p. 291.
10 Maarten Goos and Alan Manning, 'Lovely jobs and lousy jobs: the polarization of work in Britain', Centre for Economic Performance, London School of Economics, Jan. 2004; at http://158.143.98.51/~goos/badjobsJAN04-2.pdf.
11 Autor, Katz and Kearney, 'Trends in US wage inequality', p. 12.

12 Frank Levy, *The New Dollars and Dreams* (Russell Sage Foundation, 1998), p. 73.

13 Autor, Katz and Kearney, 'Trends in US wage inequality', p. 9. It is interesting that the college wage premium in Korea is quite small relative to that of the United States, perhaps reflecting its level of development which is close to where the US was in the 1960s, when the college wage premium was smaller.

14 From Current Population Survey (CPS) data in a presentation by Kevin McCabe, Center for Labor Market Studies, Boston College, to the Computer Systems Policy Project retreat, Hilton Head, South Carolina, 3 June 2004.

15 Autor, Katz and Kearney, 'Trends in US wage inequality'.

16 Robert D. Atkinson, 'The Bush manufacturing crisis', Progressive Policy Institute, Oct. 2003.

17 Robert D. Atkinson, 'Understanding the offshoring challenge', Progressive Policy Institute, 24 May 2003.

18 Wright and Dwyer, 'The patterns of job expansions in the USA'.

19 Ibid.

20 US Bureau of Labor Statistics at www.bls.gov.

21 Wright and Dwyer, 'The patterns of job expansions in the USA'.

22 Alan Manning, 'We can work it out: the impact of technological change on low skill workers', Centre for Economic Performance, London School of Economics, 2004, p. 8.

23 Goos and Manning, 'Lovely jobs and lousy jobs', p. 20.

24 The share of US production subject to foreign competition rose from 19 per cent in 1985 to 28 per cent in 1994.

25 Marina Whitman, *New World, New Rules: The Changing Role of the American Corporation* (Harvard Business School Press, 1999), p. 11.

26 Frank and Cook, *Winner-Take-All Society*.

27 A chief executive appointed after 1985 was three times more likely to be fired than one appointed before that date: R. Khurana, *Searching for a Corporate Savior: The Irrational Quest for Charismatic CEOs* (Princeton University Press, 2002).

28 A recent study of workers in California found that four out of ten workers had been at their jobs less than three years: E. Yelin, *California Work and Health Survey*, (Field Institute, San Francisco, 1999).

29 Frank and Cook, *Winner-Take-All Society*, p. 4.

30 W. Michael Cox with Richard Alm, '*Myths of Rich and Poor: Why We're Better Off than We Think,*' (Basic Books, 1999), p. 72.

31 Ibid., p. 87.

32 Kevin Haslett, 'Rich man, poor man: how to think about income inequality (hint: it's not as bad as you think)', American Enterprise Institute, May 2003; at www.aei.org/news/newsID.17509,filter./news_detail.asp.

33 Ibid.

34 At http://ncrve.berkeley.edu/CW73/Reich.html.

35 Alan Greenspan quoted in Nell Henderson, 'Greenspan says workers' lack of skills lowers wages', *Washington Post*, 22 July 2004, p. A01.
36 Atkinson, 'The Bush manufacturing crisis', and Robert D. Atkinson, 'Meeting the offshoring challenge', Progressive Policy Institute, 20 July 2004.
37 Drucker, *Post-capitalist Society*, p. 96.
38 For example, see Manning, 'We can work it out'.
39 Stephen Herzenberg, John A. Alic and Howard Wial, *New Rules for a New Economy: Employment and Opportunity in Postindustrial America*, (Cornell University Press, 1998).
40 See www.ssda.org.uk/.
41 Robert D. Atkinson, 'Creating a National Skills Corporation', Progressive Policy Institute, 14 June 2002.
42 Remarks by Alan Greenspan, 'The critical role of education in the nation's economy', at the Greater Omaha Chamber of Commerce 2004 Annual Meeting, Omaha, 20 Feb. 2004.
43 This idea is similar to one recently proposed by economist Robert J. Shiller in the *The New Financial Order: Risk in the Twenty-First Century* (Princeton University Press, 2003).

4 Opportunity and life chances

1 Anthony Giddens, *Modernity and Self-Identity* (Polity, 1991); Martin O'Brien and Sue Penna, *Theorising Modernity: Reflexivity, Environment and Identity in Giddens' Social Theory* (Longman, 1998); Ulrich Beck, *Risk Society: Towards a New Modernity* (Sage, 1992).
2 Alissa Goodman and Zoë Oldfield, *Permanent Differences? Income and Expenditure Inequality in the 1990s and 2000s* (Institute for Fiscal Studies, 2004).
3 Michael F. Förster, 'Trends and driving factors in income distribution and poverty in the OECD area', Occasional Papers 42, Labour Market and Social Policy, OECD, Paris, 2000.
4 Goodman and Oldfield, *Permanent Differences?*
5 Förster, 'Trends and driving factors in income distribution and poverty'.
6 Ibid.
7 Stephen P. Jenkins and Philippe Van Kerm, 'Trends in income inequality, pro-poor income growth and poverty', Working Paper 904, Institute for the Study of Labour (Forschungsinstitut zur Zukunft der Arbeit), Bonn, 2003.
8 Förster, 'Trends and driving factors in income distribution and poverty'.
9 Ibid.
10 Robert Walker, Andrew Shaw and Lisa Hull, 'Responding to the risk of unemployment', in ABI (Association of British Insurers) (ed.), *Risk, Insurance and Welfare* (ABI, 1995); Karl Ashworth, Martha Hill and Robert Walker, 'A new approach to poverty dynamics', in David

Rose (ed.), *Researching Social and Economic Change* (Routledge, 2000).

11 John Rigg and Tom Sefton, 'Income dynamics and the life cycle', CASE Paper 81, London School of Economics, 2004.

12 European Commission, *European Social Statistics: Income: Poverty and Social Exclusion*, 2nd report, 2002 Edition Data 1994–1997 (Office of Official Publications of the European Communities, 2002); Didier Fouarge and Richard Layte, 'Duration of poverty spells in Europe', EPAG Working Paper 2003–47, University of Essex, 2003.

13 Robert Walker and Claire Collins, 'Families of the poor', in Jacqueline Scott, Judith Treas and Martin Richards (eds), *Blackwell Companion on the Sociology of the Family* (Blackwell, 2003).

14 Walker, Shaw and Hull, 'Responding to the risk of unemployment'; Stephen P. Jenkins and John A. Rigg, 'The dynamics of poverty in Britain', Working Paper 157, DWP, London, 2001.

15 Rigg and Sefton, 'Income dynamics and the life cycle'.

16 Jenkins and Rigg, 'The dynamics of poverty in Britain'.

17 Elaine Kempson, Alex Bryson and Karen Rowlingson, *Hard Times* (Policy Studies Institute, London, 1994); Kathryn Edin, Lara Lein, Timothy Nelson and Susan Clampet-Lundquest, 'Talking to low-income fathers', Newsletter 4, 2, Joint Center for Poverty Research, University of Chicago, 2000.

18 Ian Dennis, and Anne-Catherine Guio, 'Poverty and social exclusion in the EU after Laeken – part 1', Statistics in Focus, Population and Social Conditions Theme 3, 8/2003, Eurostat, Luxembourg, 2003.

19 Fouarge and Layte, 'Duration of poverty spells in Europe'.

20 Rigg and Sefton, 'Income dynamics and the life cycle'.

21 Andreas Cebulla and Janet Ford, 'Confronting unemployment: families' management of risk in the flexible labour market', *Risk and Human Behaviour, Newsletter of the ESRC research programme on Risk and Human Behaviour*, no. 8 (2000), pp. 2–6; Andreas Cebulla, Hubert Heinelt and Robert Walker, 'Unemployment and the insurance compensation principle in Britain and Germany', Anglo-German Society, London, 2001; Stephen McKay and Elaine Kempson, 'Savings and life events', Research Report 194, DWP, London, 2003.

22 Barbara Dobson, Alan Beardsworth, Teresa Keil and Robert Walker, *Diet, Choice and Poverty* (Family Policy Studies Centre, 1995); Anna Leeming, Judith Unell and Robert Walker, 'Lone mothers: coping with the consequences of separation', DSS Research Report 30, London, 1994.

23 Elaine Kempson, Stephen McKay and Maxine Willitts, 'Characteristics of families in debt and the nature of indebtedness', Research Report 211, DWP, London, 2004.

24 Walker and Collins, 'Families of the poor'.

25 Matt Barnes and Maxine Willitts, 'Families and children in Britain: findings from the 2002 Families and Children Study (FACS)', Research Report 206, DWP, London, 2004.

26 Christopher T. Whelan, Richard Layte and Bertrand Maître, 'Persistent income poverty and deprivation in the European Union: an analysis of the first three waves of the European Community Household Panel', *Journal of Social Policy*, 32: 1 (2003), pp. 1–18.

27 Christopher T. Whelan, Richard Layte and Bertrand Maître, 'Multiple deprivation and persistent poverty in the European Union', *Journal of European Social Policy*, 12: 2 (2002), pp. 9–105.

28 Whelan, Layte and Maître, 'Persistent income poverty and deprivation'.

29 Kempson, McKay and Willitts, 'Characteristics of families in debt'.

30 Bruce Katz, 'Neighbourhoods of choice and connection: evolution of American neighbourhood policy and what it means for the United Kingdom', paper prepared for the Joseph Rowntree Centenary Event, London, 8 July 2004, JRF, York, 2004; Bob Holman (ed.), *Faith in the Poor* (Lion, 1998).

31 Walker and Collins, 'Families of the poor'.

32 Robert Walker and Jennifer Park, 'Unpicking poverty', in Carey Oppenheim (ed.), *An Inclusive Society* (IPPR, 1998).

33 Edin, Lein, Nelson and Clampet-Lundquest, 'Talking to low-income fathers'; Elaine Kempson, *Life on a Low Income* (Joseph Rowntree Foundation, 1996).

34 Sharon Landesman Ramey and Bette Keltner, 'Welfare reform and the vulnerability of mothers with intellectual disabilities (mild mental retardation)', *Focus*, 22: 1 (2002), pp. 82–6; Kempson, *Life on a Low Income*.

35 Jill Vincent, '*Qualitative research on disallowed and sanctioned claimants*', Research Report 86, Department for Education and Employment, London, 1998.

36 Hartley Dean and Margaret Melrose, 'Manageable discord: fraud and resistance in the social security system', *Social Policy and Administration*, 31: 2 (1997), pp. 103–18; F. Haines, 'A few white lies', MA diss., University of York, 1999.

37 D. P. Farrington, 'Early developmental prevention of juvenile delinquency', *Criminal Behaviour and Mental Health*, 4: 3 (1995), pp. 209–17.

38 Marianne Heaster and Nicole Westmorland, 'Tackling street prostitution: towards a holistic approach', Research Study 279, Home Office, London, 2004.

39 C. Lloyd, 'Risk factors for problem drug use: identifying vulnerable groups', *Drugs: Education, Prevention and Policy*, 5: 3 (1998), p. 217.

40 Robin Burrows, 'The social distribution of the experience of homelessness', in Robin Burrows et al. (eds), *Homelessness and Social Policy* (Routledge, 1997).

41 S. Tabberer, C. Hall, S. Prendergast and A. Webster, *Teenage Pregnancy and Choice, Abortion or Motherhood: Influences on the Decision* (JRF, 2000).

42 Jonathan Bradshaw, Peter Kemp, Sally Baldwin and Abigail Rowe, 'The drivers of social exclusion: review of the literature of the Social Exclusion

Unit in the Breaking the Cycle series', Social Exclusion Unit, ODPM, London, 2004.

43 D. R. Fletcher, D. Woodhill and A. Herrington, *Building Bridges into Employment and Training for Ex-Offenders* (JRF, 1998).

44 K. Pickering, S. Fitzpatrick, K. Hinds and P. Lynn, 'Tracking homelessness: a feasibility study', Scottish Executive, Edinburgh, 2003.

45 Jeffrey R. Kling, Jeffrey B. Liebman and Lawrence F. Katz, 'Fear in the ghetto and its ramifications for parents', Policy Brief 3, 10, Joint Center for Poverty Research, University of Chicago, 2000.

46 Kempson, Bryson and Rowlingson, *Hard Times*.

47 Lorenzo Cappellari and Stephen P. Jenkins, 'Modelling low income transitions', Discussion Paper 504, Institute for the Study of Labour (Forschungsinstitut zur Zukunft der Arbeit), Bonn, 2002; Martin Biewen, 'Measuring state dependence in individual poverty status: are there feedback effects to employment decisions and household composition?', Discussion Paper 1138, Institute for the Study of Labour, Bonn, 2004.

48 European Community, *European Social Statistics: Income;* Fouarge and Layte, *'Duration of poverty spells in Europe'.*

49 Cappellari and Jenkins, *'Modelling low income transitions'.*

50 Biewen, 'Measuring state dependence in individual poverty status', p. 20.

51 Walker and Park, 'Unpicking poverty'; J. Gershuny, 'Thinking dynamically: sociology and narrative data', in Lutz Leisering and Robert Walker (eds), *The Dynamics of Modern Society: Poverty, Policy and Welfare* (Policy Press, 1998), pp. 34–48.

52 Paul Johnson and Howard Reed, 'Intergenerational mobility among the rich and poor: results from the National Child Development Survey', *Oxford Review of Economic Policy*, 12: 1 (1996), pp. 127–42; Lorraine Dearden, Stephen Machin and Howard Reed, 'Intergenerational mobility in Britain', *Economic Journal*, 107 (Jan. 1997), pp. 47–64.

53 Paul Gregg, S. Harkness and Stephen Machin, *Child Development and Family Income* (JRF, 1999); John Hobcraft, 'Intergenerational and life-course transmission of social exclusion; influences of childhood poverty, family disruption and contact with the police', CASE paper 15, London School of Economics, 1998.

54 John Hobcraft, 'Intergenerational and life-course transmission of social exclusion: influences of childhood poverty, family disruption, and contact with the police', in 'Persistent poverty and lifetime inequality: the evidence', CASE report 5, proceedings from a workshop held at HM Treasury, 1999, pp. 115–20.

55 J. Ermisch, M. Francesconi and D. Pevalin, *Outcomes for Children of Poverty* (Corporate Documents Series, Leeds, 2001).

56 Jeanne Brooks-Gunn and Greg J. Duncan, 'The effects of poverty on children', *Children and Poverty*, 2: 2 (1997), pp. 55–71.

57 Elizabeth Such and Robert Walker, 'Falling behind? Research on transmitted deprivation', *Benefits*, 10:3 (2002), pp. 185–92; E. T. Gershoff,

J. Lawrence Aber, and C. Cybele Raver, 'Child poverty in the US: an evidence-based conceptual framework for programs and policies', in Richard M. Lerner, Francine Jacobs and Donald Wertlieb (eds), *Promoting Positive Child, Adolescent and Family Development: A Handbook of Program and Policy Innovation* (Sage, 2002).

58 Robert Walker, *Poverty Dynamics: Issues and Examples* (Avebury, 1994).
59 Sue Middleton, Karl Ashworth and Ian Braithwaite, *Small fortunes: Spending on Children, Childhood Poverty and Parental Sacrifice* (JRF, 1997); Julia Loumidis and Sue Middleton, 'A cycle of disadvantage? Financial exclusion in childhood', Consumer Research 4, Financial Services Authority, 2000.
60 Alex Bryson, and Diana Kasparova, 'Profiling benefit claimants in Britain: a feasibility study', Working Paper 196, DWP, London, 2003; Gordon Waddell, A Kim Burton and Chris J. Main, *Screening to Identify People at Risk of Long-Term Incapacity for Work: A Conceptual and Scientific Review* (Royal Society of Medicine Press, 2003).
61 Stephen Morris et al., 'Designing an employment retention and advancement demonstration for Great Britain', Cabinet Office, London, 2003.
62 Cappellari and Jenkins, 'Modelling low income transitions', p. 17.

5 Where are the poor?

1 R. Rogers and A. Power, *Cities for a Small Country* (Faber, 2000).
2 K. Mumford and A. Power, *Boom or Abandonment: Resolving Housing Conflicts in Cities* (Chartered Institute of Housing, 2003).
3 Habitat (United Nations Centre for Human Settlements), *An Urbanising World: Global Report on Human Settlements 1996* (Oxford University Press for the UN Centre for Human Settlements, 1996).
4 Habitat, *The Challenge of Slums: Global Report on Human Settlements 2003* (Earthscan, 2003).
5 UNEP (United Nations Environment Programme), *Global Environmental Outlook 3: Past, Present and Future Perspectives* (Earthscan on behalf of UNEP).
6 UN World Population Office, 'World urbanisation prospects: 2001 revision', 2001.
7 A. Power, *Estates on the Edge* (Macmillan, 1999).
8 P. Rowe, *Civic Realism* (MIT Press, 1999).
9 F. M. L. Thompson (ed.), *Cambridge Social History of Britain 1750–1950.* (Cambridge University Press, 1990).
10 A. Power et al., 'A framework for housing in the London Thames Gateway', CASE, London, 2004.
11 Royal Commission on Environmental Pollution, *Twenty-Second Report: Energy – the Changing Climate* (Stationery Office, 2000).
12 A. Briggs, *A Social History of England* (Penguin, 1983).

13 R. Plunz, *A History of Housing in New York City: Dwelling Type and Social Change in the American Metropolis* (Columbia University Press, 1990).

14 Thompson, *Cambridge Social History of Britain 1750–1950*.

15 A. Tosi and W. van Vliet, *International Handbook of Housing Policies and Practices* (Greenwood Press, 1990).

16 N. Lemann, *The Promised Land: The Great Black Migration and How it Changed America* (Alfred Knopf, 1991).

17 DoE (Department of the Environment), *Inner Areas Studies* (HMSO, 1974–7).

18 W. Rees, 'Achieving sustainability: reform or transformation', in D. Satterthwaite (ed.), *The Earthscan Reader in Sustainable Cities* (Earthscan, 1999).

19 DoE, *Inner Areas Studies*; R. Carson, *Silent Spring* (Fawcett Crest, 1962).

20 E. Economy, *The River Runs Black: The Environmental Challenge to China's Future* (Cornell University Press, 2004).

21 P. Hall, *Cities of Tomorrow: An Intellectual History of Urban Planning and Design in the Twentieth Century* (Blackwell, 2002).

22 D. Drakakis-Smith, *Third World Cities*, 2nd edn (London: Routledge, 2000).

23 Satterthwaite, *Sustainable Cities*.

24 Power, *Estates on the Edge*.

25 A. Giddens, *Runaway World: How Globalisation is Reshaping our Lives.* (Profile, 2002).

26 Chinese Academy of Science, 'Glacier inventory', reported in the *Guardian*, 24 Sept. 2004.

27 Habitat, 'State of the world's cities', Habitat, Nairobi, 2001.

28 P. Dunleavy, *Politics of Mass Housing in Britain, 1945–1975: A Study of Corporate Power and Professional Influence in the Welfare State* (Clarendon Press, 1981).

29 J. Hills, *Inequality and the State* (Oxford University Press, 2004).

30 A. Power, *Hovels to High Rise: State Housing in Europe* (Routledge, 1993).

31 P. Marcuse and R. van Kempen (eds), *Globalizing Cities: A New Spatial Order?* (Blackwell, 2000); F. Wassenberg, *High-Rise Housing in Europe* (Delft University Press, 2004).

32 Thompson, *Cambridge Social History of Britain 1750–1950*.

33 G. Wagner, *The Chocolate Conscience* (Chatto and Windus, 1987).

34 Power, *Hovels to High Rise*.

35 A. Power, *Property before People: The Management of Twentieth-Century Council Housing* (Allen and Unwin, 1987).

36 Rogers and Power, *Cities for a Small Country*.

37 ODPM (Office of the Deputy Prime Minister), *English Housing Condition Survey* (ODPM, 2003).

38 K. Mumford and A. Power, *East Enders: Family and Community in East London* (Policy Press, 2003).

39 Habitat, *Cities in a Globalizing World: Global Report on Human Settlements* (Earthscan, 2001).

40 W. J. Wilson, *The Truly Disadvantaged: The Inner City, the Underclass and Public Policy* (University of Chicago Press, 1987).

41 Audit Commission, 'Improving council house maintenance', 1986; S. Wilcox, *Housing Finance Review* (JRF, 1986).

42 Power, *Hovels to High Rise*.

43 L. Rainwater, *Behind Ghetto Walls: Black Families in a Federal Slum* (Allen Lane, 1971).

44 P. Jargowsky, *Poverty and Place: Ghettos, Barrios, and the American City* (Russell Sage Foundation, 1997).

45 I. Turok and N. Edge, *The Jobs Gap in Britain's Cities: Employment Loss and Labour Market Consequences* (Policy Press and JRF, 1999); K. Mumford and A. Power, *The Slow Death of Great Cities? Urban Abandonment or Urban Renaissance* (JRF, 1999).

46 Wilson, *The Truly Disadvantaged*.

47 A. H. Halsey and J. Webb (eds), *British Social Trends* (Macmillan, 2000).

48 Mumford and Power, *East Enders*.

49 H. Glennerster et al., 'Poverty, social exclusion and neighbourhood: studying the area bases of social exclusion', CASEpaper 22, London School of Economics, 1999.

50 R. Lupton, *Poverty Street: Causes and Consequences of Neighbourhood Decline* (Policy Press, 2003).

51 DETR *Our Towns and Cities: The Future. Delivering an Urban Renaissance*, Urban White Paper (HMSO, 2000).

52 A. Power, 'Empowering residents', London School of Economics, 1992.

53 Power, *Estates on the Edge*.

54 A. Power, 'Neighbourhood management and the future of urban areas', CASEpaper 77, London, 2004; Neighbourhood Renewal Unit, 'Neighbourhood management and wardens evaluation', ODPM, London, 2003; Strategy Unit, 'Review of neighbourhood renewal', Prime Minister's Strategy Unit, London, 2004.

55 D. Massey and N. Denton, *American Apartheid: Segregation and the Making of the Underclass* (Harvard University Press, 1993).

56 Giddens, *Runaway World*.

6 The new egalitarianism

1 Ben Jackson and Paul Segal, *Why Inequality Matters*, (Catalyst Working Paper, 2004).

2 Richard Layard and S. Nickell, 'Issues posed by unemployment in Europe', *American Economic Review, Papers and Proceedings*, 79: 2 (1989), pp. 215–19.

3 C. A. R. Crosland, *The Future of Socialism* (Jonathan Cape, 1956).
4 Gøsta Esping-Andersen, *Social Foundations of Post-Industrial Economies* (Oxford University Press, 1999).
5 European Commission, *The Lisbon Strategy for Economic, Social and Environmental Renewal*, report (2000).
6 IPPR (Institute for Public Policy Research), *State of the Nation* (IPPR, 2004).
7 Wolfgang Merkel, 'How the welfare state can tackle new inequalities', in Patrick Diamond and Matt Browne (eds), *Rethinking Social Democracy* (Policy Network, 2004).
8 Leon Feinstein, 'Inequality in the early cognitive development of British children in the 1970 cohort', *Economica*, 70 (2003), pp. 73–97.
9 Gøsta Esping-Andersen, *Why We Need a New Welfare State* (Oxford University Press, 2002).
10 John Denham, 'Advance to go: why low paid workers need more than tax credits', *Progress Journal*, 2 (2004), pp. 39–40.
11 Strategy Unit, 'Strategic audit', report, Prime Minister's Strategy Unit, London, 2003.
12 Esping-Andersen, *Social Foundations of Post-Industrial Economies*.
13 David Miller, *Principles of Social Justice* (Harvard University Press, 1999).
14 Julian Le Grand, *The Strategy of Equality* (George Allen and Unwin, 1982).
15 Howard Glennester, *United Kingdom Education 1997–2001* (CASE, 2001).
16 C. N. Teulings, 'The contribution of minimum wages to increasing wage inequality', *Economic Journal*, 133 (2003), pp. 801–33.
17 Stuart White, *The Civic Minimum* (Oxford University Press, 2003).
18 Polly Toynbee and David Walker, 'Social policy and inequality', in Anthony Seldon and Kevin Hickson (eds), *New Labour, Old Labour: The Wilson and Callaghan Governments 1974–79* (Routledge, 2004).
19 White, *The Civic Minimum*.
20 Willem Adema, *Social Spending in OECD Countries* (OECD, 1999).

7 Inequality and recognition

1 'For one, the principle of equal respect requires that we treat people in a difference-blind fashion. . . . For the other, we have to recognize and even foster particularity': Charles Taylor, 'The politics of recognition', in Amy Gutmann (ed.), *Multiculturalism and 'The Politics of Recognition'* (Princeton University Press, 1992).
2 Ulrich Beck and Edgar Grande, *Das Kosmopolithiona Europa – Gesellschaft und Politik in der Zweiten Moderne* (Suhrkamp, 2004), trans. as *The Cosmopolitan Europe* (Polity, 2005).

3 G. Falkner, *EU Social Policy in the 1990s: Towards a Corporatist Policy Community* (Routledge, 1998); Ute Hartenberger, Europäischer Sozialer Dialog nach Maastricht: EU-Sozialpartnerverhandlungen auf dem Prüfstand (Nomos, 2001).

4 Giandomenico Majone, *Relating Europe* (Routledge, 1996).

5 Ulrich Beck, *Macht and Gegenmacht im globalen Zeitalter. Neue Weltpolitische Ökonomie* (Suhrkamp, 2002), trans. as *Power in the Global Age* (Polity, 2005).

6 Noel Malcolm, 'The case against "Europe" ', *Foreign Affairs*, 74: 2 (Mar.–Apr. 1995), pp. 52–68.

7 Gerlinde Sinn and Hans-Werner Sinn, *Kaltstart. Volkswirtschaftliche Aspekte der deutschen Vereinigung* (Mohr, 1991).

8 Hanspeter Kriesi, 'Nationaler politischer Wandel in einer sich denational-isierenden Welt', *Blätter für deutsche and internationale Politik*, 2 (2001), pp. 206–13. Hanspeter Kriesi and Edgar Grande, 'Nationaler politischer Wandel in Entgrenzten Räumen', in Ulrich Beck and Christoph Lau (eds), *Entgrenzung and Entscheidung. Was ist neu an der Theorie Reflexiver Modernisierung* (Suhrkamp, 2004).

9 Herbert Kitschelt and Anthony J. McGann, *The Radical Right in Western Europe* (University of Michigan Press, 1995).

10 Seymour M. Lipset and Stein Rokkan, 'Cleavage structures, party systems, and voter alignments: an introduction', in Seymour M. Lipset and Stein Rokkan (eds), *Party Systems and Voter Alignments: Cross-National Perspectives* (Free Press, 1967).

11 Beck, *The Cosmopolitan Outlook*.

12 Nancy Fraser, 'From redistribution to recognition?', in Steve Seidman and Jeffery C. Alexander (eds), *The New Social Theory Reader* (Routledge, 2001), p. 287.

13 Fraser, 'From redistribution to recognition?'.

14 C. Offe, 'The democratic welfare in an integrating Europe', in M. Greven and P. Louis (eds), *Democracy beyond the State? The European Dilemma and the Emerging Modern Order* (Rowman and Littlefield, 2000).

8 New global classes

1 I use the term classes rather loosely here – more a designator than a theoretical construct.

2 Kees Van der Pijl, *Transnational Classes and International Relations* (Routledge, 1998); Leslie Sklair,. *The Transnational Capitalist Class* (Blackwell, 2001).

3 For example, Manfred B. Steger (ed.), *Rethinking Globalism* (Rowman and Littlefield, 2004).

4 Jonathan Rutherford, *A Tale of Two Global Cities: Comparing the Territorialities of Telecommunications Developments in Paris and London* (Ashgate, 2004).

5 Saskia Sassen, *Denationalization: Territory, Authority and Rights in a Global Digital Age* (Princeton University Press, 2005).

6 Anne-Marie Slaughter, *The Real New World Order* (Princeton University Press, 2004).

7 Saskia Sassen, *Losing Control? Sovereignty in an Age of Globalization* (Columbia University Press, 1996), ch. 1; and, generally, Sassen, *Denationalization*.

8 Lourdes Benería and Savitri Bisnath (eds), *Global Tensions: Challenges and Opportunities in the World Economy* (Routledge, 2004); Beverly J. Silver, *Forces of Labor: Workers' Movements and Globalization since 1870* (Cambridge University Press, 2003).

9 For a more detailed analysis see Saskia Sassen, 'Local actors in global politics', *Current Sociology*, 52: 4 (2004), pp. 657–74.

10 For a variety of cases, see e.g. Nora Hamilton and Norma Stoltz Chinchilla, *Seeking Community in a Global City: Guatemalans and Salvadorans in Los Angeles* (Temple University Press, 2001); Maria de los Ángeles Torres, 'Transnational political and cultural identities: crossing theoretical borders', in Frank Bonilla, Edwin Mélendez, Rebecca Morales and Maria de los Ángeles Torres (eds), *Borderless Borders* (Temple University Press, 1998).

11 See e.g. Barbara Ehrenreich and Arlie Hochschild (eds), *Global Woman: The Supply of Maids, Nannies, Nurses and Sexworkers* (Metropolitan Books, 2002).

12 Peter Evans, 'Fighting marginalization with transnational networks: counter hegemonic globalization', *Contemporary Sociology*, 29: 1 (2000), pp. 230–41; Sassen, *Losing control?*

9 Britain's glue

1 About which I wrote an essay, 'Too diverse?', *Prospect* magazine, 95 (Feb. 2004).

2 R. Rorty, *Achieving our Country: Leftist Thought in Twentieth-Century America* (Harvard University Press, 1998).

3 Mori poll for the Commission for Racial Equality (2002).

4 Presentation to Policy Network seminar, Amsterdam, 21 May 2004.

5 A. Alesina et al., 'Why doesn't the United States have a European style welfare state?', *Brookings Papers on Economic Activity*, 2001.

6 S. Soroka et al., 'Immigration and redistribution in a global era', in their *Globalization and the Politics of Redistribution* (Russell Sage Foundation, forthcoming).

7 Ibid.

8 David Miller, 'Immigration, nations and citizenship', paper presented at a conference on Migrants, Nations and Citizenship, 5–6 July 2004, sponsored by the Centre for Research in the Arts, Social Sciences, and Humanities (CRASSH), University of Cambridge, p. 14.

9 Michael Ignatieff, 'Less race, please', *Prospect* magazine, 40 (Apr. 1999).
10 Antonio Vitorino, 'Taking asylum and migration seriously', *Progressive Politics*, 2:1 (Jan. 2003).
11 John Denham, 'The fairness code', *Prospect* magazine, 99 (June 2004).
12 Vitorino, 'Taking asylum and migration seriously'.
13 Eric Kaufmann, *The Rise and Fall of Anglo-America* (Harvard University Press, 2004), p. 7.

10 Why gender equality?

1 European Commission, *Employment in Europe* (2004).
2 Ibid.
3 European Commission, *Employment in Europe* (2003).
4 European Commission, *Employment in Europe* (2002).
5 Joelle Sleebos, 'Low fertility rates in OECD countries: facts and policy responses', OECD Social, Employment and Migration Working Paper 15, 2003.
6 See Inter-parliamentary Union, at www.ipu.org.
7 Julie Ballington and Richard Matland, 'Political parties and special measures: enhancing women's participation in the electoral process', United Nations Office of the Special Advisor on Gender Issues and Advancement of Women and Department of Political Affairs Expert Group Meeting, Glen Cove, New York, Jan. 2004.
8 Ibid.
9 Ibid.
10 European Commission, 'Women and men in decision-making', at www.europa.eu.int/comm/employment_social/women_men_stats.

11 Social corrosion, inequality and health

1 M. Marmot and R. G. Wilkinson, 'Psychological and material pathways in the relation between income and health: a response to Lynch et al.', *British Medical Journal*, 322 (2001), pp. 1233–6.
2 Ibid.
3 C. A. Shively and T. B. Clarkson, 'Social status and coronary artery atherosclerosis in female monkeys', *Arteriosclerosis and Thrombosis*, 14 (1994), pp. 721–6.
4 H. Bosma, R. Peter, J. Siegrist and M. Marmot, 'Two alternative job stress models and the risk of coronary heart disease', *American Journal of Public Health*, 88 (1988), pp. 68–74.
5 L. F. Berkman, 'The role of social relations in health promotion', *Psychosomatic Research*, 57 (1995), pp. 245–54; J. S. House, K. R. Landis and D. Umberson, 'Social relationships and health', *Science*, 241 (1988), pp. 540–5; T. E. Seeman, 'Health promoting effects of friends and

family on health outcomes in older adults', *American Journal of Health Promotion*, 14:6 (2000), pp. 362–70.

6 S. Cohen, W. J. Doyle, D. P. Skoner, B. S. Rabin and J. M. Gwaltney, 'Social ties and susceptibility to the common cold', *Journal of the American Medical Association*, 277 (1997), pp. 1940–4.

7 L. Berkman, 'Social networks and health: the bonds that heal', in A. R. Tarlov and R. F. St Peter (eds), *The Society and Population Health Reader*, vol. 2: *A State Perspective* (New Press, 1999).

8 D. J. P. Barker, *Mothers, Babies and Health in Later Life*, 2nd edn (Churchill Livingstone, 1998).

9 L. A. M. Welberg and J. R. Seckl, 'Prenatal stress, glucocorticoids and the programming of the brain', *Journal of Neuroendocrinology*, 13: 2 (2001), pp. 113–28; H. C. Lou, D. Hansen, M. Nordentoft, O. Pryds, F. Jensen, J. Nim and R. Hemmingsen, 'Prenatal stressors of human life affect fetal brain development', *Developmental Medicine and Child Neurology*, 36 (1994), pp. 826–32; F. Drago, F. DiLeo and L. Giardina, 'Prenatal stress induces body weight deficit and behavioural alterations in rats: the effect of diazepam', *European Neuropsychopharmacology*, 9: 3 (1999), pp. 239–45.

10 V. J. Felitti, R. F. Anda, D. Nordenberg, D. F. Williamson, A. M. Spitz, V. Edwards, M. P. Koss and J. S. Marks, 'Relationship of childhood abuse and household dysfunction to many of the leading causes of death in adults', *American Journal of Preventive Medicine*, 14: 4 (1998), pp. 245–58; J. E. Schwartz, H. S. Friedman, J. S. Tucker, C. Tomlinsonkeasey, D. L. Wingard and M. H. Criqui, 'Sociodemographic and psychosocial factors in childhood as predictors of adult mortality', *American Journal of Public Health*, 85: 9 (1995), pp. 1237–45.

11 D. I. W. Phillips, B. R. Walker, R. M. Reynolds, D. E. H. Flanagan, P. J. Wood, C. Osmond, D. J. P. Barker and C. B. Whorwood, 'Low birth weight predicts elevated plasma cortisol concentrations in adults from three populations', *Hypertension*, 35: 6 (2000), pp. 1301–6.

12 E. Brunner and M. Marmot, 'Social organization, stress, and health', in *The Social Determinants of Health*, ed. M. Marmot and R. G. Wilkinson (Oxford University Press, 1999).

13 N. Ross, D. Dorling, J. R. Dunn, G. Hendricksson, J. Glover and J. Lynch, 'Metropolitan income inequality and working age mortality: a five country analysis using comparable data', *Journal of Urban Health* (in press 2005).

14 R. De Vogli, R. Mistry, R. Gnesotto and G. A. Cornia, 'Income inequality is negatively correlated with life expectancy at birth: evidence from Italy and twenty-one wealthy nations', *Journal of Epidemiology and Community Health*, 59 (2005).

15 M. Marmot and M. Bobak, 'International comparators and poverty and health in Europe', *British Medical Journal*, 321 (2000), pp. 1124–8.

16 P. Walberg, M. McKee, V. Shkolnikov, L. Chenet and D. A. Leon, 'Economic change, crime, and mortality crisis in Russia: regional analysis', *British Medical Journal*, 317 (1998), pp. 312–18.

17 R. G. Wilkinson and K. E. Pickett, 'Income inequality and health: a review and explanation of the evidence', forthcoming.

18 R. G. Wilkinson, 'Health inequalities: relative or absolute material standards?' *British Medical Journal*, 314 (1997), pp. 591–5.

19 C. C. Hsieh and M. D. Pugh, 'Poverty, income inequality, and violent crime: a meta-analysis of recent aggregate data studies', *Criminal Justice Review*, 18 (1993), pp. 182–202.

20 R. D. Putnam, R. Leonardi and R. Y. Nanetti, *Making Democracy Work: Civic Traditions in Modern Italy* (Princeton University Press, 1993).

21 R. D. Putnam, *Bowling Alone: Collapse and Revival of American Community* (Simon and Schuster, 2000), p. 359.

22 Ibid.

23 I. Kawachi, B. P. Kennedy, K. Lochner and D. Prothrow-Stith, 'Social capital, income inequality and mortality', *American Journal of Public Health*, 87 (1997), pp. 1491–8.

24 E. Uslaner, *The Moral Foundations of Trust* (Cambridge University Press, 2002).

25 A. de Tocqueville, *Democracy in America* (Hackett, 2000).

26 M. Sahlins, *Stone Age Economics* (Tavistock, 1974).

27 D. Buss, *Evolutionary Psychology: The New Science of the Mind* (Allyn and Bacon, 1999).

28 A. Smith, *The Theory of the Moral Sentiments* (Liberty Classics, 1982), p. 50.

29 J. Gilligan, *Violence: Our Deadly Epidemic and its Causes*. (G. P. Putnam, 1996), p. 110.

30 F. B. M. de Waal and F. Lanting, *Bonobo: The Forgotten Ape* (University of California Press, 1997), p. 30.

31 E. Brunner, G. D. Smith, M. Marmot, R. Canner, M. Beksinska and J. Obrien, 'Childhood social circumstances and psychosocial and behavioural-factors as determinants of plasma-fibrinogen', *Lancet*, 347 (1996), pp. 1008–13.

32 J. M. Long, J. J. Lynch, N. M. Machiran, S. A. Thomas and K. Malinow, 'The effect of status on blood pressure during verbal communication', *Journal of Behavioral Medicine*, 5 (1982), pp. 165–72.

33 M. J. Conyon and R. B. Freeman, 'Shared modes of compensation and firm performance: UK evidence', NBER Working Paper W8448; see http://papers.nber.org/papers/W8448.

34 Bosma et al., 'Two alternative job stress models'; M. Kivimaki, M. Elovainio, J. Vahtera and J. F. Ferrie, 'Organizational justice and health of employees: a prospective cohort study', *Occupational and Environmental Medicine*, 60 (2003), pp. 27–34.

35 G. Gates, 'Holding your own: the case for employee capitalism', *Demos Quarterly*, 8 (1996), pp. 8–10.

36 Conyon and Freeman, *Shared Modes of Compensation and Firm Performance*.

37 R. Oakshott, *Jobs and Fairness: The Logic and Experience of Employee Ownership* (Michael Russell, 2000).

12 Inequality, choice and public services

1 Speech, St Thomas's Hospital, 23 June 2004.

2 David Blunkett, *Towards a Civil Society* (Institute of Public Policy Research, 2003), p. 9.

3 Roy Hattersley, 'Agitators will inherit the earth', *Guardian*, 17 Nov. 2003.

4 HM Treasury, *Public Services: Meeting the Productivity Challenge* (The Stationery Office, 2003).

5 See, for instance, A. Lent and H. Arend, *Making Choices: How Can Choice Improve Local Public Services?* (New Local Government Network, 2004).

6 For instance, John Appleby, Anthony Harrison and Nancy Devlin, *What is the Real Cost of More Patient Choice?* (Kings Fund, 2003).

7 Julian Le Grand, *Motivation, Agency and Public Policy; Of Knights and Knaves, Pawns and Queens* (Oxford University Press, 2003).

8 Ibid., ch. 2.

9 Anna Dixon, Julian Le Grand, John Hendersen, Richard Murray and Emmi Poliakoff, 'Is the NHS equitable?', LSE Health and Social Care Discussion Paper 11, London School of Economics, 2003.

10 Indeed sometimes by anecdotes that make precisely the opposite point from the one intended. For instance, in the *Guardian* article by Roy Hattersley cited above, he gives an example of how he was able to get preferential treatment from his GP through the agitation and pressure he was able to bring to bear on the practice staff at the surgery: a classic illustration of the power of middle class *voice*, not of choice as Hattersley claims.

11 Katherine M. Harris, 'How do patients choose physicians? Evidence from a national survey of enrollees in employment-related health plans', *Health Services Research*, 38: 2 (April 2003), pp. 711–32.

12 Speech, South Camden Community College, 23 Jan. 2003.

13 Le Grand, *Motivation, Agency and Public Policy.*

14 See, for instance, Tessa Crilly and Julian Le Grand, 'The motivation and behaviour of hospital trusts', *Social Science and Medicine*, 58: 10 (May 2004).

15 For an extensive review of the relevant studies see Cavendish Brant and Julian Le Grand, 'School choice, quality and equity', MS, 2004.

16 N. Le Maistre, R. Reeves and A. Coulter, *Patient Evaluation of CHD Choice Scheme* (Picker Institute, Oxford, 2003).

17 Phil Collins, 'Education out of a hat', *New Statesman*, 5 July 2004.

Index